The Temperaments and the Adult – Child Relationship

By Kristie Karima Burns, MH, ND

Dedicated to Sofi, Sunii and Mosi -
Together we cover all the temperaments!
Love, Mama

ISBN 978-0-557-45127-2
Text Copyright © 2010 by Kristie Karima Burns, MH, ND
All rights reserved. Published by Bearth Publishing

Library of Congress Cataloging-in-Publication Data available.

Printed in the U.S.A

Second Edition, May 2010

Index

Preface

My intention for this book is to help the reader in typing himself, family members, students, and friends and to delve into the mysteries of how the different temperaments interact with each other. Because these interactions are unique, depending on the age and relationship of the people, this book focuses only on the adult-child relationship which can differ greatly from the adult-adult relationship or the child-child relationship. Furthermore, this book focuses even more specifically on the relationship between the parent or teacher and the child. Because of this I may use the words parent or teacher now and then but have chosen to use the word "adult" for most of the book to keep the interpretation more flexible as this information can also be extended to any caregiver and child relationship. While this book does focus on the relationships between adults and children, one can also benefit from reading the different sections and applying some of the wisdom to his own relationships with other adults or by extrapolating ideas from the sections to help siblings get along better.

Also note that I have alternated the use of the words "he" and "she" in the different chapters of the book. In discussing the matter with my editors we decided that using the colloquial and somewhat renegade "them" was not suitable for a book directed at all the different temperaments, the use of just the pronoun, "he" would not include the feminine, and the use of "he/she" simply made the document difficult to read. Thus, you will notice that one chapter will read "she" for the entire chapter and the next chapter will read "he" for the entire chapter.

Although this book focuses on the various differences and conflicts between the temperaments, it is not intended to be a negative portrayal of the relationships between them. Rather than creating discord, by bringing awareness to these differences I hope to encourage harmony through greater understanding and respect of the different ways people have of viewing the world and functioning within it. The vignettes in this introduction are not intended to be complete temperament profiles but were created specifically to help the reader to type himself and his child before reading the different sections on interactions.

One must keep in mind that the dynamic between an adult and child is different from that of the dynamic between two children or two adults. It is my assumption that the adult will be the one doing the inner work to understand the child more clearly. The task of the child will not be to read the book and adapt to the adult. Rather, the adult will use some of the creative methods in this book to lead the child to a better understanding of himself and the temperaments. Because the child is still maturing and learning, the burden of adapting to the adult's temperament is not theirs but will be something that they can slowly develop. Adults reading this book should keep in mind that this is a guide to understand himself better, understand his child better, and to instill in the child the same understanding through actions, examples, stories, and loving guidance. This book is not intended to be read to children and children should not be expected to be able to grasp the concepts as they are put forth in this book until after the ages of fifteen or sixteen.

Because the length of this book has already extended beyond 250 pages, specific lessons, games, exercises, herbal therapies, and additional specific work to be done with the child will be included in the second book of this series, "A Temperament *Workbook* for the Adult-Child Relationship". While this book is intended to be a guide, rather than a workbook, each section does include one or more stories, personal examples, and at least one exercise that the parent and child can do together.

In each chapter, the section that says "Helping the (temperament) Child Understand the (temperament) Adult" is the part where the reader can preview a bit of the upcoming workbook. However, one does not need to wait for the workbook to start using this information now:

1. If another parent, teenage child or other person that lives with the child reads this section he can use these wisdoms to help the child understand the adult when the child comes asking questions. For example, a child may often come to the mother or father asking, "Why is daddy/mommy mad at me?" The other parent now has a better explanation that will offer the child more insight instead of the old standby "He's not mad at you honey. He's just in a bad mood."

2. Each of these sections does contain at least one exercise or story. The reader can use these games and stories as a guide in seeking out additional stories and games.

3. The adult can use this section to further his own understanding of the relationship and can make more of an effort to present himself to the child in a clearer way or can offer the child more effective tips on what to do in certain situations. Adults don't always know what to tell a child when they are angry or upset or feeling unwell. Knowing how to help a child better understand the adult can help him provide the child with more useful statements when needed. For example, when a parent is angry they may say to their child "Leave me alone I am in a bad mood." After reading the section on the sanguine parent and choleric child, however, they may learn to say, "Let's talk in a half hour (giving the child a hug)."

As I wrote the book I was amazed at how different each section was. I feared that through repeating the section "Helping the Adult Understand the Melancholic Child" four times that the sections would start to sound the same. However, by focusing on helping the diverse temperaments get to know the melancholic temperament, the different aspects of the melancholic emerged differently in each section. Each section is very different from the next - even though they cover a similar topic. This means, that if a person has a child of a certain temperament he could benefit from reading every section that includes that child's temperament.

What are the Temperaments?

"If then, on the one hand, it is unquestioned that man's greatest riddle is man himself, we may say that in relation to life this expression may have a still deeper significance in that it is necessary on the other hand to emphasize what each of us feels upon meeting another person-namely, that fundamentally each single person is in turn an enigma for others and for himself because of his special nature and being." – Rudolph Steiner, winter 1908-09

The study of the temperaments is one method of studying this enigma of man. The studies of the temperaments have been used even before Greek thinkers and physicians starting around 400 BC kept written records. And can also be traced back thousands of years to before the time of the Ancient Egyptians. Since 400 BC, hundreds of temperament and typing systems have emerged from the original systems that were distinguished by four temperaments: phlegmatic, melancholic, sanguine, and choleric. Today, most people have been exposed to at least one of these systems and many companies use the theory of temperaments to evaluate potential employees or to improve performance and employee relations.

There are four temperaments in the Waldorf system of education. These correspond with the four temperaments as studied by Greek healers as well as healers and scholars in the Middle East. The sanguine is restless like the butterfly and adaptive like the seasons. The choleric is vibrant like the fire. The melancholic is solid and steady like the earth. The phlegmatic is like a river, both peaceful and mysterious, and can look flowing and simple on the outside but have a rich inner world. If a person considers each of these natural phenomena it cannot be said that one is more important than the other or that one is better than the other. A flowing river is just as beautiful and important as a colorful fluttering butterfly. The earth and the fire are equally important elements, each with their own beauty, power, and value. However, when people consider each other they often have difficulty feeling this way about their fellow man.

Thus, by studying the temperaments one can become more accepting of the differences between people and more appreciative of the beauty within each individual. Knowledge of the temperaments teaches tolerance, improves relationships, heals the individual, speeds up personal growth, and helps people reach their full potential with greater ease.

The source of each person's temperament has been defined in many varied ways. The Ancient Greek Physician, Galen, felt that the four humors were naturally formed in the body itself, while other writers attributed them to divine designation or a product of environment and nurturing. Rudolph Steiner, the originator of the Waldorf method of education, believed that the temperaments were a combination of all of these factors. Steiner felt that temperament was a product of the two "streams" of heredity and individual divine experience. The first "stream" is what a person inherits from their ancestors through genetics and nature. The second "stream" is what a person is given from their individual nature or spirit. Steiner attributed this to past life experiences, however it could also be attributed to divine designation. Steiner visualized the temperament of a person as the place where the two streams meet and imagined that if one stream was blue and the other yellow, that the resulting stream or temperament would be green. Environment and nurturing of the individual can help shape the temperament; however, it cannot truly alter the core temperament of the individual.

There are five main factors which can make a person's temperament appear to change:
1. If a child was under seven when he was typed, he could change after age seven because he was typed incorrectly to begin with.
2. If a child was traumatized, he can develop a "mask temperament".
3. If a child feels stress in his life, he can develop an adaptive type.
4. If a child was raised in a home with many people of one type, he can take on those traits temporarily.
5. As a person ages they become more balanced and if he works on personal growth he can actually become so balanced it is hard to tell which type he is.

Ultimately, although each person has one or two temperaments that rule them, all four temperaments exist to some degree. This makes it difficult to type people because one often notices only similarities, and thus think others are the same type, or one sees only differences and assumes others are a different type. Furthermore, it can be difficult to type people of the same temperament because it is hard to admit ownership of those irritating traits that are obvious in others.

As with any system, pure typology does have its limitations. Some people imagine that typology helps create prejudices and stereo-types, however, it is actually stereotypes that already exist that can influence temperament. For example, in some traditional societies men are "supposed to be" melancholic or choleric and women are "supposed to be" phlegmatic or sanguine. Children in many societies are often stereotyped as sanguine and if a child does not act sanguine it is perceived that something is wrong with them. When people are aware of these expectations and influenced strongly by them, their efforts to fit into society's mold can often temporarily alter the way their temperament presents itself. Additionally, gender and social norms can combine to result in the melancholic temperament revealing itself in a slightly different way in females and males. In spite of these influences, the radiance of a person's temperament still shines through.

The final part of knowing about one's temperament is seeking balance. If a person knows which temperament he is, then the person can seek to balance that. The ultimate goal is for each person to learn how to be the best he can be within his own temperament and to balance oneself in all the temperaments to the extent that it might be difficult for someone to tell quickly which temperament the person is. In balancing ones temperament there are numerous options. One method is to provide the temperaments with the physical substance that will balance them. For example, the choleric, being hot and dry would benefit from fruits which are cold and/or wet. Another example would be using swimming as a way to balance the hot and dry choleric temperament. In many circumstances the appropriate thing to do or the easiest way to balance would be to provide the opposite element. This method is very similar to how herbs were prescribed in traditional herbology.

A second method of balancing one's temperament is to provide each person with support for his temperament. This can be viewed as more of a homeopathic technique rather than an herbal method. By giving a person small doses of his own temperament this accomplishes two things. The first is by allowing the person to experience the support he needs so he does not rebel and find, perhaps, more destructive ways to fulfill those needs. For example, a phlegmatic who likes to be in their comfort zone is often seeking to "stay at home" or "be alone". If this person is not allowed doses of that then he will seek out needs in alternate ways. A person may pretend to be sick to stay home or he may get angry and slam the door to be alone or withdraw in other ways.

The second benefit of giving "homeopathic doses" of a person's own temperament is that when these doses come from the outside it can be an effective catalyst for change or balance. Such as, if a choleric is pushing and nagging for something they want and won't stop asking, sometimes it is as effective to answer them with the same answer "over and over". So, for example, they may be repeating, "I want chocolate NOW!" But if the other person, in turn, answers over and over the same thing, "You may have chocolate after you finish your dinner, my love." then the choleric person has a chance to experience a small dose of his own temperament. Thus, by experiencing this small dose of his temperament "over and over" there is something intuitive in the person that says "this is not working" and he is able to balance more effectively.

- ## An Important Typing Tip

When reading through the next four sections that describe each temperament in detail one must be sure to explore all aspects of the person – physical, emotional, and psychological. Each type is so unique in the way they eat, how they paint, how they walk, how they sleep. All of these will give you clues. It is not always the big picture - sometimes it is the details.

The
Temperaments

The Melancholic Temperament

"In a melancholic we have seen that the physical body, that is, the densest member of the human being, rules the others. A man must be master of his physical body, as he must be master of a machine if he wishes to use it. But when this densest part rules, the person always feels that he is not master of it, that he cannot manage it. For the physical body is the instrument that he should rule completely through his higher members. Now, however, this physical body has dominion and sets up opposition to the others. In this case the person is not able to use his instrument perfectly, so that the other principles experience repression because of it and disharmony exists between the physical body and the other members. This is the way the hardened physical system appears when it is in excess. The person is not able to bring about flexibility where it should exist. The inner man has no power over his physical system; he feels inner obstacles."– Rudolf Steiner, 1908-09

The melancholic person is ruled by the physical body and thus has a deep connection with the earth. Like the earth the melancholic can be solid and obstinate but can also be dependable and comforting. Like the earth the melancholic functions within an intricate order that follows certain intrinsic rules and links resulting in a harmonious structured system.

The Physical Traits of the Melancholic

The melancholic may exhibit some or few of the following physical traits. A Melancholic often has rough, dry or cold skin, dark brown or black hair, and a medium build or slim body build. Because a melancholic is ruled by the physical body she may have a large appetite, slow digestion and thick, pale urine. Because a melancholic person is so physically aware, she may also appear to be uncomfortable in her body in some way. When eating, a melancholic can be very picky. Because a melancholic is particular and discerning in taste it may take her some time to decide what to eat. However, once the melancholic person decides what to eat, she will eat in a deliberate and organized manner, often not allowing the food on their plates to touch.

The Melancholic in Social Situations

The melancholic can become so caught up in the intricate order of her carefully constructed and harmonious environment that it can become painful or unattractive to invite other people into her realm. When other people are introduced into the carefully balanced system there is too much potential for disharmony so the melancholic may avoid such situations. Because of this melancholics prefer to spend time alone and are not usually comfortable in crowded situations for long periods of time. Because it is a complex and often confusing process to figure out where new people fit into the melancholic's personal biosphere the melancholic may find it difficult to make new acquaintances and usually only shares inner thoughts with people who are already trusted members of her inner circle. Despite the closed facade of the melancholic, she really does desire to express thoughts and connect with others. However, because it requires so much effort on her part and because lack of practice has made her awkward, the melancholic may avoid making those connections that she so badly needs and wants.

Because the melancholic often dwells on the past, worries about the future or reflects inwardly, she may feel much burden and may long to share this load with another. When the melancholic bears the weight too long a feeling of sorrow may rise to the surface and she may express herself by sharing grief or complaints. If these thoughts are shared suddenly or in inappropriate situations the melancholic may appear to be pessimistic and off-putting. When shared too frequently the melancholic may appear to be depressed.

The melancholic may often blame others for her troubles. This has less to do with any fault of the other person and more to do with the unease the melancholic person has with other people's methods of living and her belief that the melancholic outlook on life is the superior one. The more the melancholic person can grasp the benefit of the other temperaments, the less this trait will display itself.

The melancholic person appreciates order in general and thus in relationships as well. In relationships the melancholic person will feel most comfortable when people fall into defined roles. Because of this a melancholic is most comfortable in traditional societies where cultural roles are defined for the individual, in jobs where the hierarchy of the workplace is clear and in a classroom where rules and guidelines are apparent. A part of these clear regulations in life have to do with moral principles and standards of behavior.

A melancholic will often donate money or time to family members or people in need as this is part of their belief system. Because a melancholic is very serious about her own standards and principles and expects others to feel the same. Furthermore, the melancholic type often judges right and wrong, success or failure according to how closely the actions of others match the melancholic's principles. However, in some cases, if the other person has a very clearly defined moral compass the melancholic will respect that and will judge the person by how closely she follows her own system. In the end, however, the ultimate goal for the melancholic is to observe everyone following the system she claims to be part of. Melancholics have little tolerance for hypocrisy.

The melancholic may often display emotions that do not seem to match the situation she is in. This is because the melancholic has trouble dealing with emotions that do not fit into the ideal structure she envisions for life. Thus, when a melancholic feels fear she may have trouble understanding or admitting that fear and may instead exhibit agitation at another person. When a melancholic feels discomfort this emotion may display itself as anger and so on.

A melancholic person often has a sizeable sense of humor which she has developed over time in efforts to harmonize imbalanced social skills or emotions. This sense of humor can often be and entertaining and healthy way to deal with problems. At other times is can become hurtful to others who may not understand the source of it.

One situation in which the melancholic person feels uncomfortable is in crowds. At airports, malls, parties or other places where there are crowds, the melancholic person may feel overwhelmed trying to process the amount of social data that she feels the need to organize. During the outing the melancholic person may become agitated or have trouble interacting with people or may become rigid in her interactions, insisting that strict social rules be followed. After such an outing the melancholic person may need to sleep for a period of time to recover.

The melancholic person is happy with a few close relationships and tends to maintain friendships for a long period of time and enjoy spending time with family and extended family. Although the melancholic can be judgmental once she establishes a long-term relationship with another person the level of comfort she feels overrides the desire to mend people. This can create a feeling of confusion as some new relationships can question why the melancholic accepts behavior from old friends or family members that she does not accept with the new friend. This can also be a source of stress in the melancholic person's life as they struggle to maintain challenging relationships for the sake of security and familiarity. However, this also means that the melancholic person is a loyal and true friend for life once a person enters her circle of trust.

Although the melancholic keeps some emotional distance from their family and friends, everyone always knows exactly where he or she stands with the melancholic type. Instead of running relationships on the basis of emotional intimacy, the melancholic feels that the best relationships are run on a principle of fairness This means that the melancholic may focus on spending equal time with each person rather than perceiving how much time each one actually needs or may focus on fulfilling what they feel are a person's basic life needs, rather than those needs the person has defined for herself.

This strict adherence to regulation is felt quite differently by the melancholic than by other people. Friends and family can feel they are being railroaded into acting or responding in set manners. However, when these set manners are not followed, the melancholic can feel as if her train as derailed.

The Inner Life of the Melancholic

The melancholic is like the alchemist - always seeking perfection of form, the perfect formula and always seeking to distill the pure from the primitive. The melancholic thus sees herself as the keeper of standards and a guardian of all things virtuous and sublime. Because of this the melancholic excels at all things involving ritual and ceremony. It is often said that if there were no melancholics on earth there would be no calendars, no datebooks and no train schedules. If there were no people of the melancholic temperament there would be buildings, no roads and no businesses – for where would all of these things be without the careful planning and organization that goes into such endeavors?

Although the melancholic's strict system of rules and standards may seem confusing or difficult to maintain for someone of another temperament the melancholic has a number of skills and traits that make it easy for her and even pleasurable. Many people make the mistake of feeling pity for a melancholic who works too much, who seems stuck in a repetitive job or who appears to be a prisoner of her standards. However, the melancholic is actually very content with this lifestyle as it suits her needs and uses the skills she naturally has.

The melancholic is often reflective. In attempting to maintain equilibrium in her life the melancholic seeks to bring the future and past into balance with the intensity of the present moment. It is often more pleasurable for the melancholic to dwell upon the past than to live through the passion of the present. The melancholic also uses the world of the past and the future as ways to create a better present. The melancholic can often be visionary in this way as she seeks correlations between events. When the melancholic makes a decision it is based on an evaluation of past, present, and current events distilled into what she feels is the ideal choice. In many cases this method of decision making can result in well thought out, accurate and important decisions as the melancholic can see the wide-reaching effects of each decision that is made within the time frame of history and progress. In other cases, however, this can restrict possibilities and can appear to be short-sighted to those of other temperaments who think outside of set parameters and experiences and take endless possibilities into consideration. A good decision making team would include at least one melancholic, but not only a melancholic person.

The melancholic has a rich but struggling spiritual life. She enjoys meditation and prayer but often feels inadequate and discouraged in her spiritual pursuits. Because of this struggle and constant pursuit of perfection, the melancholic may have a very intense spiritual practice but still feel very unsure and anxious about the spiritual realm.

Spiritual Practices for the Melancholic

Spiritual Support
The melancholic person will benefit from attending regular prayer groups, religious gatherings or spiritual assemblies. If this is not possible or part of their culture, then the melancholic must find time each day to focus on inner work, meditation and or private prayer - these things act as a balm to sooth the melancholic's insecurities and gives her courage and peace. A melancholic would also benefit from having an inspirational book nearby their bed to read from each evening – anything from *"The Power of Now"* by Eckhart Tolle, to the poetry of Rumi, to the Bible.

Clarity of Communication

The melancholic person must make a daily practice of verbal communication in a clear way to the people at work and at home. However, because these sessions may seem intense for workmates and family members the melancholic must be careful to admit that these efforts at communication are for the benefit of the listener and not for the melancholic. If this is not expressed then people around her may simply feel ordered around. On the contrary, if this exercise is done with care, it can nurture more confidence in the melancholic and create stronger bonds between her and her colleagues, classmates, friends and family. This daily practice could take one of many forms and should be performed in every aspect of the melancholic's life on a daily basis, or, at the very least, on a weekly basis. This daily practice could take place as a family meeting, a daily journal entry shared with the family, business meetings, lists of needs shared with other people or lists posted to a blackboard or public calendar on a daily basis. The goal of this practice is to ensure that the needs and desires of the melancholic are being communicated clearly and regularly to those around her. One of the main difficulties the melancholic will encounter with other people stem from misunderstandings in this area. A child who is taught this practice from an early age will be able to continue it as an adult. For an adult who is just starting this practice may be difficult at first but she needs to be patient and preserve.

Respect for Other Temperaments

One must always encourage the melancholic to see the beauty in other temperaments and other points of view. With children this can be done through storytelling, focusing on stories that shed a favorable or heroic light on those people of other temperaments or fables that teach lessons to the melancholic person. Fables and fairytales that include morals like "consider the wisdom of others", "don't put blinders on", "be careful not to get stuck in a rut" or "don't get trapped in the past or future" are perfect for the child of the melancholic temperament. A few of these stories are included throughout this book and can also be found readily in fairytale anthologies. William Bennett's "Book of Virtues" is a useful book to invest in as the traditional stories in the book are categorized by life lessons that can be learned. One can also do Internet searches for types of fairytales and stories. One can search within categories such as "tales of type 1430: Daydreams of Wealth and Fame" and hundreds of other categories. Within each category one will find numerous examples of such stories.

A useful resource for finding stories by folktale type can be found online at: http://www.pitt.edu/~dash/folktexts.html. As an adult the melancholic will benefit from reading books that talk about different types of people. Such books can include books about blood types, archetypes, temperament or other topics.

Asking for Help

The melancholic must make it a daily practice to ask for help. In the classroom it is useful for her to work with a partner that has skills she can learn from as well as work with people whom she can help. Because the melancholic is so able she may often be the student that others rely on for assistance. However, it is important that the melancholic have someone she can rely on as well. It is even more important that this person be near the same age or status in life. Without this key element the melancholic will learn over time that she can only learn from people who are far superior in power, education, age or status. This attitude makes it increasingly difficult for her to respect the opinions and thoughts of family, friends and colleagues at work or school.

Practice Visualizing Mistakes and Solutions

The melancholic will benefit from the process of visualizing problems and solutions so she can learn that this process is not painful and to be avoided. This can be done in many ways. In school, solving story problems, mysteries and puzzles are a healthy practice for the melancholic. Scientific experiments that are designed to create order out of chaos are also beneficial to the melancholic. Knitting is also a beneficial practice as the melancholic can learn to solve problems on a basic level such as what to do when a stitch is slipped or how to repair a hole in knitting. A melancholic may migrate towards more logical and straightforward tasks in life and may resist suggestions that she does something involving the easy possibility of error. However, it is important that the melancholic has a daily dose of such practices so she may become more comfortable with the problem solving process. It is important that these problems come from an external source as this is the source that the melancholic has the most difficulty in managing. If the melancholic is allowed to choose her own puzzles, and levels of challenge or is always lead into expecting when the chaos will occur, the learning experience will not be the same.

Finding Beauty in Chaos

The melancholic will benefit from practices that allow her to explore beauty in chaos. Studies of modern art or other forms of art based on this theme should be an essential experience in the melancholic's education. Upon first experiencing such chaos in art the melancholic may initially balk and exclaim that the art is worthless and unattractive. However, further exposure with help her develop at least a familiarity with the feelings such art evokes, even if she does not come to prefer or enjoy that style of expression. Music or verse that follows unusual rhythms or verses that speed up or slow down are beneficial to the melancholic's experience with music. Studies of scientific phenomenon that involve chaos are also beneficial to the melancholic.

Nurturing the Melancholic

Although the melancholic seems confident and secure one must always encourage her. The melancholic usually feels at ease only when certain criteria are met and has become accustomed to pretending she is at ease otherwise. Adults, family members and friends can help the melancholic become less fearful of failure and life outside her comfort zone by offering frequent encouragement in the form of short but sincere compliments, or simply acknowledgements of her successes – however large or small.

If the melancholic is yelled at, reproached, or treated harshly in any way she can become paralyzed in efforts to move forward or relate to people. When the melancholic exhibits such forms of speech it actually represents a level of discomfort and should not be mistaken as something she can cope with when returned back. A melancholic will be most grateful to someone who offers friendly advice with patience, kindness and understanding.

A melancholic needs gentle reminders as she does not like to be exposed or told she is wrong. It can even be effective to be subtle with the melancholic and deflect blame or direct criticism away from them. For example, when asking a melancholic to complete a chore around the house that she has forgotten to do, it may be better received if they are told, "I walked by the kitchen and heard all the dishes screaming, 'help me help me'! (wink and smile)" instead of "You forgot to unload the dishwasher again."

Educating the Melancholic

The melancholic child works best in situations where goals and expectations are well established and clearly expressed. It is important for the adult to not only have a clear system in place, but also to make sure the melancholic child understands that system. When encouraging the melancholic child in her studies it is best to compliment her for skill and expertise rather than personality, emotional enthusiasm or creativity with a lesson. A melancholic child will not consider the compliment valid unless it aims at recognizing them and evaluating them according to objective criteria rather than personal opinion or intuition. This is important to know because an adult could think they are doing a wonderful job of complimenting and encouraging the melancholic but remain frustrated at the child's lack of confidence and enthusiasm if this concept of valid praise is not understood.

The melancholic is methodical and systematic in her work, often checking and rechecking or changing it until it reaches perfection. In this process the melancholic may tear up pictures, crumple up writing, and erase complete paragraphs that may appear attractive to the adult or other students. This usually creates the need in other people to reassure the melancholic and to encourage her to be more accepting of her work. This encouragement does have a place for the melancholic, however, she should instead be asked to save the rejected work and allowed to finish her work process before advice and encouragement are given. It is very important that the melancholic person be allowed to go through her own creative process, no matter how painful this process may appear to the outside observer. Once the process is complete the adult can go over some of the past efforts with the melancholic, ask her what she did not like about the work and then point out some aspects of the work that were successful. The concept of mastery is very important to the melancholic and this can only be achieved through the constant individual process of redoing projects and lessons.

The melancholic learns and experiences life through touch. However, this does not necessarily mean that a melancholic needs to be touched to learn, this actually means that most melancholics are very sensitive to touch because they feel it so deeply and intensely. This means that hands-on activities are a very effective educational tool for melancholics. However, hands on activities that involve a lot of repetition may not be as suitable. For example, the process of building a model of an atom to understand what an atom is would be useful to a melancholic. However, the process of sorting manipulatives over and over to create sets of math concepts may be tiresome and frustrating to the melancholic child. Some repetitive actions may be comforting and appeal to the melancholic's sense of order. However, the adult must always be diligent in observing which repetitive tasks are useful to the melancholic and which are frustrating so she can adapt the lessons accordingly.

Another reason an adult must be diligent in observing the melancholic's relationship with repetitive activities is because the melancholic may often use such actions as a soothing or comforting mechanism. When the melancholic feels insecure or frightened she may perform actions over and over in attempts to find comfort in some order of the universe. If a melancholic is focusing on a subject intensely for the purposes of building towards a goal such as is described in their method of seeking perfection, this is healthy. If, however, the melancholic is focusing on a goal in a repetitive manner without making progress this may indicate that she is feeling imbalanced, upset, or anxious in some way. The melancholic can be allowed to continue her repetitive soothing behavior. However, the source of the problem should be explored if it is a frequent occurrence at home or school.

In an educational environment the melancholic is most confident when she feels that everyone is "on the same page". If there is disharmony in the classroom the melancholic may feel unable to perform to her best abilities so the balance of the classroom is very important to the melancholic. A classroom that is often chaotic may reduce the melancholic's abilities to learn.

A melancholic enjoys logical tasks and may most enjoy grammar, math and science projects however, they will benefit from all aspects of the educational environment.

When being asked to participate in class or produce a result the melancholic may be reluctant or nervous if she feels there is too much pressure or attention on her. The melancholic may become clumsy in such a situation and forget words, make mistakes and stumble over concepts that are easy. It is better to allow the melancholic time and space in which to complete projects and to allow them to display such projects in a public manner when she feels it is the appropriate time. Other more comfortable methods of class participation for the melancholic would be to present in a group, to answer questions as part of a small group, to have work displayed on the classroom wall or to give a report based on clear questions and guidelines she can fill in the blanks to. As the child becomes more comfortable with these methods of class participation and more familiar with her environment she will naturally ease into more aspects of class participation. However, if forced into public display too soon or too often the melancholic may retreat or become reluctant to participate in any manner. Once the damage is done it takes time and patience to repair.

In the classroom or in school the melancholic is happiest when being kept busy. Because comfort and joy exist in the process of organization and tasks being completed, the melancholic is not as happy if left to her own devices for hours at a time in wandering thoughts.

Relating to the Melancholic

The melancholic is most content when putting order before pleasure or fulfillment. Whereas the sanguine or choleric temperament could not imagine a life where desire and sensual experience do not take center stage, the melancholic cannot imagine a life where they do. A melancholic person actually experiences a greater pleasure in order than she would in the realm of the sensual. Because the sensual world seems all pervasive to the melancholic she is more comfortable when escaping this sensation and experiencing a greater balance. People who relate to the melancholic temperament may think that the melancholic is tough and unfeeling because of this trait. However, it is actually the opposite that is true. Because the melancholic experiences her senses so intensely she feels most comfortable when escaping from them or balancing them rather than indulging in them.

The melancholic is very proud but can appear to be humble and shy because of her fear of being exposed in public. A melancholic would rather forgo public praise than risk being humiliated in any way. However, because of this the melancholic person is quite attached to the private praises that friends and family may bestow upon them.

When a person is relating to a melancholic type one needs to remember the things that are inherent to the type and not take anything too personally. A melancholic appreciates things to be in their proper order so it can help communication and understanding if friends and family make an effort to find out what this "means". The ease in the melancholic type is in how steady and regular the demands can be. She may be very demanding in the few things they do expect, but once a friend or family member figures these things out, it is usually easy to keep a melancholic person calm and happy. Ironically, although these needs and wants are usually predictable, the melancholic person will not usually be skilled at communicating these requirements so it is usually upon the other person to discern them through observation and careful questioning. Part of the spiritual practice of the melancholic should be to practice communicating these needs more often. However, progress in this area may be slow and the people who love the melancholic may need to be patient.

A melancholic person may often give clues as to her needs wants but these clues may be missed if people take them too personally. For example, a melancholic person may say, "Did you remember where the laundry room is?" in a sarcastic attempt to display frustration at the constant disorganization of the laundry in the house. This statement, taken personally, can be the start of an argument or bad feelings between the melancholic and other person. However, if the friend or family member can instead, translate this into, "I feel very uncomfortable when dirty clothing is all over the floor on a consistent basis" then this friend or family member has been able to add one more item to the list of needs of the melancholic.

These clues may also be missed if the person does not understand the intention. If a melancholic person wants to have eggs for breakfast she may ask "Do we have any eggs?" The adult or spouse may answer with a simple "yes" or "no", not realizing that the melancholic is actually asking, "Could you please fix eggs for breakfast?"

Because of the melancholic's behavior people close to her may interpret them as not requiring human companionship. Spouses, children and friends may feel they can depend on the melancholic but may feel that the melancholic person does not really "need" them. However, this is not accurate. The melancholic type needs people very deeply, she just does not show it in the way that others are used to or in the way that is portrayed in the movies. One should not be fooled by the melancholic's cool or aloof demeanor.

If friends and family can make themselves available for the melancholic on a regular basis the melancholic will reach out to them. A friend or family member may want to plan on making herself available to this person every day at a certain time. Even if one just sits in silence with the melancholic for an hour, the melancholic will find comfort in knowing the person is there for that predictable time every day and when she does need someone she will reach out for that person during that time.

One should not strive to meet all of a melancholic person's demands, nor should one completely disregard them because they are so demanding. One should instead strive to meet the melancholic's most important requests on a regular basis.

Affirmations & Cautions for the Melancholic

A melancholic must get to know herself and appreciate and love those traits which are positive and constructive within herself. These include:

The ability to focus on goals and reach those goals
Patience
Compassion for those in need
Clear headedness
High standards of personal conduct

The facility to see long term solutions
The ability to plan for the future
The capability to learn from the past
The skill to see how events connect in time
The talent of creating order and beauty from chaos
Attention to detail and quality control

A melancholic must be cautious of the following traits and work to balance these:

The tendency to become restrictive
Preoccupation with rituals
Apt to become compulsive or obsessive
Desire to control people and situations
Fear of crowds and social gatherings
The inability to be spontaneous
The propensity to be overly judgmental
Easily falling into a negative attitude

In a situation where the melancholic type becomes exaggerated, this exaggeration will completely suppress the other temperament balances. A melancholic can repeat the following affirmation daily and add to it as she thinks of things. This will strengthen the good qualities in the melancholic that she already has. Once the melancholic allows these good qualities to shine and appreciate them in herself, others will too. Some of these qualities may be weak now or yet undiscovered, but they are all there in potential.

Affirmation for the Melancholic

I am like the earth – a harmonious ecosystem
Each aspect working in agreement with another
Each part dependant on the other
Each task and event beautiful and useful to the system
I will breathe deep
Let settle into order that which contributes
Take energy into my lungs
And breathe out all that is unnecessary.
I will feel deep
Taking into my pores the seeds that will grow
Into strong trees
Eliminating those which poison me
Taking in the common elements and
Shaping diamonds and Jade
Through time and careful pressure

Like falling leaves - on the tree
Letting go and releasing the past
Awaiting a new season
Channeling my energy into that which I have been given
To mulch into the ground
To provide cover for a shelter
To grow from the branches
Or to float from the tops of the trees.

Physical Ailments of the Melancholic

Because the melancholic tends to hold things inside, they have a predisposition for ailments that display improper elimination in the body such as constipation, kidney stones, and growths such as moles or tumors. Because the melancholic element in the body is cool, thick and earthy the melancholic person is also prone to coagulation of the fluids in the body and can exhibit itself as lung congestion, liver toxicity, poor circulation or lymphatic congestion. When the melancholic does not release emotions these emotions will often come out in the form of nightmares or the inability to sleep because of frightful dreams that she cannot recall.

Because a melancholic feels everything so deeply in the physical world she is in danger of weakening the nervous system or suffering from repetitive stress injuries, especially involving the joints. The melancholic usually has a strong constitution but once there is injury to the system it takes her a long time to recover. She will need to focus intensely on recovery without distractions to speed the process along.

Because a melancholic is so focused on creating the perfect rhythm, she may ignore the natural rhythms of life and her body. This can result in many disruptions to the rhythmic activities of the body and can exhibit as heart problem, asthma, or other lung problems.

The Melancholic Diet

The most effective therapies for the melancholic involve purging or fasting through use of cleansing fasts or herbs such as senna with cinnamon or cumin. The melancholic needs warming foods, activities and herbs.

The melancholic should avoid sweet, dry, sticky, overly spicy and cold foods such as raw salads and vegetables, ice cream, cayenne pepper, vinegar, or dried foods. If such foods are eaten they should only be consumed infrequently and usually balanced with a food or herb of the opposite quality. The melancholic needs a lot of fiber in her diet in the form of oatmeal, brown rice, and lightly cooked vegetables.

Symbols of the Melancholic

Each temperament relates to a different season of the year, time of day, animal, color and many other things. When an adult is looking for ideas on how to relate better to her melancholic child it often helps to do exercises using these symbols. One can do an exercise with the child by choosing one of the items listed below and comparing it to one of the items listed under her own temperament. During this exercise one can mix shapes with animals or seasons with times of day. There are hundreds of combinations one can try and each one will reveal more depth in the relationship between the adult and child. One can also ask the child to participate in these exercises by drawing pictures, telling stories or acting out different scenarios.

For example, if a person is of the melancholic type, which corresponds to a square and the child is of the sanguine type, corresponding to a squiggle the child and adult could spend some time drawing these two geometric shapes on a paper and observe how they interact.

The symbols of the melancholic one can use in these exercises are:

Dusk
West
Metal
Green
Earth
Square
Owl

The Phlegmatic Temperament

"When there is a strong predominance in an individual of the etheric or life-body which inwardly regulates the processes of man's life and growth, and the expression of this etheric body, the system that brings about the feeling of inner well-being or of discomfort, then such a person will be tempted to wish to remain in this feeling of inner comfort. The etheric body is a body that leads a sort of inner life... It may occur (then) that an individual lives chiefly in this feeling of inner comfort, that he has such a feeling of well-being when everything in his organism is in order that he feels little urgency to direct his inner being toward the outer world, is little inclined to develop a strong will. The more inwardly comfortable he feels, the more harmony will he create between the inner and outer. When this is the case, when it is even carried to excess, we have to do with a phlegmatic person." – Rudolf Steiner, 1908-09

The phlegmatic person can be typed by his rich inner existence which is largely misunderstood by the outside world. Phlegmatic people have often been labeled with negative terms such as stubborn, shy, insecure, selfish, cold, or slow. However, when one understands the peaceful inner life they occupy then it becomes clear that better words to describe them would be willful, introverted, inwardly reflective, serene, and flowing.

The Physical Traits of the Phlegmatic

The phlegmatic person may exhibit all or only some of the physical traits of the classic phlegmatic. People of the phlegmatic temperament may tend to have pale, soft and smooth skin. Their skin may tend to be cold and moist so their hands or feet may be cold to the touch and they may sweat readily or get hot easily.

Because of this the phlegmatic person may prefer winter and cold weather over summer and may have a difficult time attending summer festivals and events while the weather is hot or especially hot and humid. He may become irritated easily when he does not feel his body is at a comfortable temperature.

A person of the phlegmatic type may have dark blond, or blond hair, hairless bodies (or for men, less hair than a man might usually have). Phlegmatic types also tend towards a fat or flabby body build so he can easily become overweight if not participating in a regular exercise program. Many people of the phlegmatic temperament are actually quite fit because they enjoy being comfortable and have discovered that regular exercise is the only way to achieve that. A phlegmatic who is in touch with his physical needs can actually feel ill or imbalanced if he doesn't perform an exercise routine on a daily basis. This routine can include biking to work, a daily walk, a regular swim or any other form of physical exercise. Phlegmatic people prefer to exercise outdoors, however, they may change to indoor exercise if the weather becomes uncomfortable. A person of the phlegmatic temperament can get agitated in a short period of time if they miss a day of physical activity.

When it is time to eat a person of the phlegmatic temperament is the most deliberate and careful eater. The phlegmatic is usually the last one to finish a meal. Thus, if a phlegmatic person follows a vegetarian diet or healthy diet, they will enjoy the benefits of a fit digestive system that come with regular exercise and the thorough chewing of one's food. However, if the phlegmatic has an unwholesome diet or one that is filled with excess fats and proteins, he will easily gain weight. Because of their unique digestive systems and physiology, phlegmatics who maintain a healthy weight may actually appear to be underfed.

The Phlegmatic in Social Situations

The phlegmatic person prefers to be on the periphery of social events and enjoys the company of others as long as he is not in the spotlight or forced to interact with the people around him. For this reason the phlegmatic person may prefer to attend functions where there are many people so they can remain anonymous or the phlegmatic may prefer to attend functions with a close friend who will hold up the social end of the conversations. In personal relationships the phlegmatic enjoys having many friends so that he remains safe from revealing himself too deeply to any one person. A person of the phlegmatic type may migrate towards close friendships from time to time however, these will usually be with people of the phlegmatic temperament whom they have known for an extended period of time. When the phlegmatic person grows close to a person that is not of his temperament this is usually done because he feels comfort in the fact that another person will maintain the social aspects of his life. However, he may find it uncomfortable as the relationship progresses, as he is not accustomed to sharing himself so deeply, and he may soon end the relationship and retreat back to his comfort zone of family, childhood friends, many friendships and large gatherings.

Despite his desire to spend time alone, the phlegmatic person is actually one of the best friends a person could have. People of the phlegmatic type are not confrontational, are peaceful, are loyal, and are remarkable listeners. As long as the phlegmatic person does not feel threatened or judged in any way he enjoys listening to other people speak and is genuinely interested in what they have to say.

A person of the phlegmatic temperament enjoys frequent periods of seclusion and introspection. Of all the temperaments the phlegmatic is the most comfortable being alone. Because of this trait the phlegmatic may think he is shy or may appear shy to other people. However, it is more accurate to say that he is simply very comfortable within his own inner world.

A phlegmatic person does not necessarily have a fear of social situations or insecurity about being in them. It is more common for the phlegmatic person to feel that these social situations are stressful and unnecessary in many ways. Because the phlegmatic is very confident and comfortable in his rich inner life, he may have little motivation to leave that world and step out of his comfort zone. A well balanced phlegmatic has learned over time to maintain equilibrium between his inner life and his social exposure by attending frequent social events and maintaining a regular group of friends. He also works in the same place for an extended period of time, or maintains a regular group of acquaintances he may encounter frequently at regular gatherings of clubs, organizations, or church groups. An imbalanced phlegmatic may have spent so much time in his inner world as a child and/or young adult that he has lost confidence in his ability to interact with other people and may even feel that his social skills are lacking. Over time the phlegmatic may come under the impression that this lack of social skills is something that was born into him. However, it is actually only a result of lack of practice and can be easily regained. The phlegmatic is a sensitive and intelligent person with a great respect for tradition who should have no trouble learning and following social customs.

Despite the phlegmatic person's potential to have a balanced social life he may actually avoid pursuing one because of his conflict with trust and honesty. Integrity is such an important attribute for the phlegmatic person that they will often be so frank that it comes across as blunt, lacking tact, and not very diplomatic. Some of his statements may even border on the politically incorrect. A phlegmatic person eventually becomes aware that belonging to a social group means that he will need to temper his candor and this may be a difficult task to accomplish or a distasteful one if he has not been taught more appropriate ways of expressing himself as a child or young adult. The phlegmatic person may not realize that there are more socially acceptable ways to express oneself and still maintain integrity. Without this knowledge the phlegmatic may tend to withdraw from society and from the people who try to become close to him.

Because of this close attachment with the facts, a person of the phlegmatic temperament will become increasingly judgmental towards friends and family members if he withdraws too much from social interactions. The more frequently the phlegmatic lives in his own inner world and the less he interacts with others outside that world, the more convinced the phlegmatic person will become that his world is the correct, right and superior one. Because the phlegmatic person also tends to be a stubborn defender of the truth, this attitude can make him appear confrontational, critical, and abrasive.

In social situations a person of the phlegmatic temperament can often seem uncommunicative. However, he simply enjoys keeping thoughts and opinions to himself. The phlegmatic does not feel it is necessary to share thoughts and feelings without a deliberate reason or goal in mind. Whereas some temperaments enjoy sharing feelings, thoughts and emotions as entertainment or ways to connect and learn about each other, the phlegmatic does not have this need or desire to share his innermost thoughts. If a friend or family member shares feelings or emotions and the phlegmatic person cannot understand the reason for this, he may become overwhelmed and look for ways to end the conversation. The phlegmatic is so completely in tune with the flow of the connection between all living beings that he feels these emotions without needing to express them. Whereas the sanguine intuits the needs of others and enjoys learning through conversation and exploration, the phlegmatic lives in the one ocean of feelings and emotions all people share and does not always need to be told what another is thinking or feeling.

This skill can be good and bad for the phlegmatic person. On the positive side, it can result in a very understanding and compassionate phlegmatic person. On the negative side, it can result in a confused and fearful phlegmatic person who cannot tell the difference between the emotions that belong to him and the emotions that belong to others. A phlegmatic person who has learned to combine his unique emotional attunement with some basic communication skills will live a content, peaceful, and harmonious existence.

The Inner Life of the Phlegmatic

A person of the phlegmatic temperament is thoughtful, deliberate, cautious, and sensible in making decisions. The phlegmatic person may spend weeks researching the perfect car online, in magazine articles, and by interviewing friends before he makes a purchase. The phlegmatic child will spend weeks observing a person before deciding to be his friend. A phlegmatic child may even spend days smelling or scrutinizing a certain food before trying it. Because of this caution, mistakes may be especially traumatic for the adult or child of the phlegmatic temperament. Because he is careful not to make too many mistakes he does not have a lot of practice in how to deal with mistakes and does not necessarily recognize that mistakes are an important part of the learning process. Rather, a mistake, to a phlegmatic, is a moment in which he is exposed for the world to see in a negative light. However, a positive attribute of this caution is that a phlegmatic person is very careful and can be trusted with projects that require quality control or careful considerations. Additionally, because a phlegmatic person is accustomed to following a slow and steady decision making process, he is usually very persistent and does not easily give up on tasks.

A phlegmatic person is at peace with how things are in the universe and within himself as long as these things are not questioned directly. The person of the phlegmatic temperament is not motivated by ambition or lofty goals or a view of the world that is limitless. Rather, the phlegmatic is motivated by his desire to keep life exactly as it naturally occurs, which suits him just fine. A balanced phlegmatic person, left to his own devices will live at peace and be able to convey that peace to those around him and provide comfort and security to friends and family in times of chaos. However, a phlegmatic that is pushed to ambition or constant action will withdraw into his inner world and will convey an aura of petulance Rather than peace.

A phlegmatic who is allowed time to explore his inner world can often gain insight into problems or issues that the other temperaments cannot see as deeply. Although the phlegmatic is not motivated by ambition he can actually be very creative and has many thoughts and ideas that could become successful if he had the ambition to follow them through into action. Although one will usually find phlegmatic people working regular and steady jobs with little glitz or glamour, one can find phlegmatics in successful and/or powerful careers if he has an agent, secretary, wife, or other helper that can bring his unique inventions, ideas, art and thoughts to life or at least into the public eye.

The phlegmatic is often engaged in intellectual pursuits. Because he finds the life of the mind so enjoyable but does not feel that emotional exploration is an ongoing requirement, the phlegmatic has a great need and desire to fill his mind with intellectual thoughts and information. The phlegmatic person experiences information in a very sensual way, in the same way a choleric would experience a hug or a sanguine would experience a delightful taste. Education, knowledge, and information are food for the phlegmatic's eager mind. Libraries, the internet, television, newspapers and other forms of informational technology or tools are the phlegmatic's dream buffet. However, the phlegmatic person does not gain knowledge towards a particular goal or to become known as an expert in a field or even for the purposes of earning a degree. The phlegmatic acquires knowledge for the same reason other people eat – because he needs to and finds it enjoyable. As in his or his food preferences, the phlegmatic may have preferences for some kinds of information over others, but in general is accepting of all forms of education and knowledge. Additionally, just as the phlegmatic eats a meal very slowly he will also consume and digest information very slowly and may enjoy reading books more than once or attending a variety of lectures on the same topic.

Spiritual Practices for the Phlegmatic

Self Expression
Although the phlegmatic enjoys his inner world there are many dangers to inhabiting that world too frequently and without balance from the outside stimulation. The mind and body are intimately connected so any imbalance in the emotional or spiritual realm will be felt in the body of the phlegmatic. However, the only way for the phlegmatic person to comfortably inhabit the outside world is to learn to express himself to other people. Without this skill of self expression other people may reject the phlegmatic, may not understand his needs or may remain aloof. To attain a healthy dose of daily self expression the phlegmatic person should draw, paint, write, sing, play an instrument, garden, or perform other tasks that allow him to express himself in a visual or auditory manner to which others can relate.

Venturing Out of the Comfort Zone
The phlegmatic person suffers the most from what can become the prison of his comfort zone. The phlegmatic is often not aware of this comfort zone and may even deny it exists. However, in general, the phlegmatic does tend towards habits, patterns, and boundaries. Although this state of being can feel very comfortable for short or long periods of time and a phlegmatic person can even become accustomed to the down-sides of such an existence, this confinement can result in emotional, spiritual and even physical demise. A phlegmatic person must make it a daily practice to venture out of the comfort zone he have created and do one new thing each day, or at least each week. This new thing could be as simple as trying a new food or walking a new way to work. However, each day the phlegmatic can benefit from pushing himself a tiny bit outside the world he has created. This process will widen the circle the phlegmatic has drawn around himself and will enrich his emotional, spiritual, and physical health.

Expressing Needs

The phlegmatic person prefers to keep peace Rather than express his needs. A phlegmatic child or adult may avoid asking for what he wants because the prospect of the other person saying "no" feels too much like disharmony and the phlegmatic finds disharmony painful. This inclination to seek peace Rather than confrontation can lead to many relationship difficulties at home, work, and among friends. To be able to reach his full potential and maintain a balanced life the phlegmatic needs to learn to express his needs to those around him. The phlegmatic needs to understand that it is not by avoiding those expressions that life will remain harmonious. For when conflict is avoided relationships become stagnant and confusing like a river that is blocked by rubbish and quits flowing. To keep the rivers of health and relationships flowing, the phlegmatic person needs to accept that it is sometimes only through conflict and expression of his needs that growth can take place. Nature provides some wisdom on this topic. Scientists have found that plants that are treated with pesticides and bred to produce in ideal ways and avoid problems develop into food sources that lack the proper amounts of essential nutrients. On the other hand, plants that are left to fight in their environment and grow stronger and learn from this process develop into food sources that excel in their ability to provide nutrients. In the field of herbal healing, herbs that are wild-crafted in nature are valued for their superior healing ability.

The phlegmatic must make a deliberate effort once a day or at least once a week to make a request from someone at work, in his family, or among friends or even a stranger. These requests can be as simple as asking to borrow a book, seeking a hug, asking for the heat to be turned down in the office, or requesting an extra pillow with which to sleep. As a spiritual practice only deliberate acts count for this exercise as each time an act of asking is performed, the phlegmatic person must consider that his request may be denied and should prepare himself for that possible outcome.

Completing Projects

A phlegmatic person will always have more ideas than come to fruition because of his lively and creative inner life. However, the phlegmatic must be careful not to become lethargic with the weight of so many un-nurtured thoughts in his mind. These thoughts are like little seeds and each one could grow into an amazing plant. Imagine what would happen to a garden if seeds were planted year after year but were not nurtured with sun, rain, and food and never allowed to grow into trees, vegetables, herbs, or flowers. The garden would eventually become overburdened and lifeless and would be increasingly difficult to cultivate. This toxic stagnation of the garden of the mind can reflect itself in toxins being held in the physical body and can harm the phlegmatic person on a physical level as well as an emotional level. A phlegmatic person with a stagnant garden may even appear to be unkempt in his appearance. To keep the garden of the mind cleansed and the spiritual, emotional, and physical body cleansed as well the phlegmatic must keep a daily practice of completing projects, even if these projects are small. Some ideas for daily practice include putting together a puzzle, assembling a model, completing a story or picture, repairing something around the house, cleaning a room, finishing an assignment or finishing a book.

Learning to Feel Comfortable with Intuition

The phlegmatic person relies so much on his carefully thought out plans that this insistence on being so careful and cautious can prevent him from accomplishing the dreams he wants to experience. The phlegmatic person needs to keep a daily practice of using his intuition so he becomes comfortable with other methods of decision making that could result in more of his dreams being realized.

One way to practice intuition is to play a simple game of "What am I thinking?" In this game a family member or friend will think of a person, place, thing or number and the phlegmatic person must try to intuit what he are thinking. Another good practice to develop the intuition is to keep an intuition notebook. Whenever an intuitive thought turns out to be correct the phlegmatic person should make a note of it in the intuition notebook. Recognition of the success and ability to intuit accurately is the most effective way of developing the intuition in any temperament.

Nurturing the Phlegmatic

The phlegmatic person is nurtured by reassurance, space to be alone, acceptance, respect, honesty, kindness, home-cooked meals, good food, interesting conversation, books, intellectual opportunities, hugs, gentle touches, and physical exercise. One must be careful of being too critical of the phlegmatic as this will damage his confidence and inner balance and it will take him much longer to recover this confidence than it would for people of the other temperaments.

A phlegmatic person can be harmed by yelling, shouting, intense discussion, canned foods or junk foods, milk products, sitting for long periods of time, constant noise or activity in the environment, loud music, or anything sudden or unexpected. It is also important to note that any harm that comes to the phlegmatic takes a long time to heal without outside assistance so people of the phlegmatic type will benefit greatly by using herbal therapies, aromatherapy and Bach flower remedies, and having a strong emotional support system in the form of good and steady friends and/or dependable family members.

Educating the Phlegmatic

The phlegmatic does not have inner ambition towards being knowledgeable but rather an inner desire to collect knowledge. For this reason he is often interested in educational pursuits but does not feel the need to quickly finish educational tasks or pursue many of them in greater depth. For the phlegmatic it is the process that is the reason for knowledge and not the product. This gem of wisdom could benefit many of the other temperaments if they have the inclination to learn from the example of the phlegmatic. However, this aspect of the phlegmatic's temperament can also prevent him from learning the things he needs to learn.

A phlegmatic will be a content student, but only if he is motivated by outside sources. When teaching the phlegmatic child one must be sure to provide constant outer motivation to the child in the form of games, cooperative competitions, challenges, assignments, deadlines and other methods. An adult must also allow the phlegmatic time to absorb and explore concepts. This ability to reflect on a topic is a skill that should not be stifled in exchange for the ability to finish an assignment or a test quickly and without understanding. One must realize that the phlegmatic learns by example and observation more than anything and may often appear detached or confused when he is actually in the process of absorbing information. The final puzzle piece of understanding may fall into place after days or weeks of observation and repetition so a phlegmatic can appear to not understand and then, within one day, appear to completely grasp the concept. The best adult for the phlegmatic is one who has confidence in the phlegmatic's ability to observe, follow examples, and use the tool of time.

Relating to the Phlegmatic

The phlegmatic person has a quiet will of iron and will turn into a wall when pushed against his will. The phlegmatic may resist change and seem lazy at times and may not be the most exciting person but he is most often kind, takes time with friends and family, is easy to get along with, is inoffensive, is a good listener, compassionate, and patient. Keep in mind that the life of the phlegmatic is to be appreciated for its steadiness Rather than its excitement or romantic nature. This type is often unappreciated since he does not provide the "glitter" and "glamour" that attracts a lot of people, but he is usually appreciated by his friends and family who know they can always depend on him.

Affirmations & Cautions for the Phlegmatic

A phlegmatic must get to know himself and appreciate and love those traits which are positive and constructive within himself. These include:

Perseverance
Patience
Skilled at listening
Skilled at uniting people
Compassion
Peacefulness

A phlegmatic must be cautious of the following traits and work to balance these:

Negativity
Fear
Guarded
Critical
Closed
Solitary

In a situation where the phlegmatic becomes exaggerated this exaggeration will completely suppress the other temperament balances. A phlegmatic should repeat the following affirmation daily and add to it as he thinks of new things. This will strengthen the good qualities already in the phlegmatic. Once the phlegmatic is able to let these good qualities shine and appreciate them within himself, others will appreciate them too. Some of these qualities may be weak or yet undiscovered, but they are all there in potential.

Affirmation for the Phlegmatic

I am like the river flowing, steady
Rich life beneath my surface
Diving under to bring forth
shells, fish, and sparkling river stones
Merging into the ocean of mankind
Embracing rocks, trees, and plants
My reservoirs are deep and run through
The streams of my soul.

I am like the river staying the course
Patient, enduring, accepting and meditative.
I remain peaceful while chaos erupts around me.
I nurture animals and plant life
I carry friends and family safely across to the other shore.
My friends float in my calm ripples
My friends dive into the depths, searching for pearls
And I embrace them.

Physical Ailments of the Phlegmatic

Phlegmatic types often complain of soreness and pain in the lumbar region, unhealthy teeth, arthritis, joint pain, thinning or balding hair, pain in the knees, hips, ankles or feet or weakness in hearing or vision. Phlegmatic types may have trouble with fertility or maintaining a pregnancy. Phlegmatic types may also tend towards disorders of the nervous system. A phlegmatic type will be likely to have an excess of phlegm when he becomes ill which can accumulate in the lungs, throat, nose or lymphatic system. A healthy phlegmatic person will enjoy the benefits of the balanced phlegmatic humor in his body which has a beneficial cooling and moistening effect on the heart and strengthens the function of the lower brain and the emotions. Phlegm also maintains proper fat metabolism and the balance of body fluids, electrolytes, and hormones through the circulation of lymph and moisture in the same way the sanguine or blood provides nutrition through the circulation system.

The Phlegmatic Diet

Phlegmatics can be balanced in general by keeping away from phlegm inducing foods such as milk, wheat and sweets, eating more heating foods and engaging in more heating activities such as running, walking, swimming, or other sports. Slow physical activity such as yoga or tai chi may not be as beneficial to the phlegmatic person unless it is designed for his temperament. Many general yoga and tai chi programs are not designed with a certain temperament in mind. People of the phlegmatic type are benefitted by the herbs anise, cinnamon, valerian root, fenugreek, cardamom, garlic, and ginger. The phlegmatic person should avoid cold, damp, sweet, raw foods, salty foods, and juicy fruits when he can and should focus on eating seafood, legumes, nuts, seeds and grains. Root foods such as potatoes and raw vegetables are not as beneficial for the phlegmatic as cooked vegetables and leafy greens.

Symbols of the Phlegmatic

Each temperament relates to a different season of the year, time of day, animal, color, and many other things. When an adult or adult is looking for ideas on how to relate better to the phlegmatic child, it often helps to do exercises using these symbols. To do an exercise one should choose an item listed below and compare it to one of the items listed under the adult's temperament. One can mix shapes with animals or seasons with times of day. There are hundreds of combinations that can be tried in this exercise and each one will reveal more depth in the relationship. The adult can also ask the child to participate in these exercises by drawing pictures, telling stories, or acting out different scenarios.

For example, if someone of the melancholic type, which corresponds to a square, were to work with a child of the sanguine type, corresponding to a squiggle, the two could spend some time drawing these two geometric shapes on a paper and observe how they interact.

The symbols of the phlegmatic one can use in exercises are:

Water
Winter
Midnight
Fear
Maturity (old age)
Cold
The kidney
A circle
A dolphin
The number one

The Sanguine Temperament

"When the astral body predominates in an individual, the physical expression will lie in the functions of the nervous system, that instrument of the rising and falling waves of sensation, and what the astral body accomplishes is the life of thoughts, of images, so that the person who is gifted with the sanguine temperament will have the predisposition to live in the surging sensations and feelings and in the images of his life of ideas." – Rudolf Steiner, 1908-09

Coming from this astral realm of experience the sanguine is, as its corresponding element "air" suggests, much like a zephyr. The sanguine person is ruled by her nervous system and responds to sensations around her. Because of this, an ungrounded sanguine may flit from one impression to another or one experience to another like a butterfly seeking the most delicious nectar from a flower. However, a grounded sanguine has the ability to respond to the rhythms of her environment in an amazingly intuitive way and can create her rhythm of syncopation within what may seem to others a series of haphazard actions. This unique rhythm can be described more accurately in terms of a person who "has seasons", rather than a person who "lives in surging sensations and feelings." However, grounded or ungrounded, the sanguine does have some physical traits and psychological habits that define her. A sanguine person may not have all of the traits in her physiology as every person is actually a unique mix of all the temperaments. However, with a person who is ruled predominately by the sanguine temperament, one will find that she possesses many of the traits listed below.

The sanguine type can be like a butterfly, a zephyr or the seasons, but perhaps the easiest metaphor to understand is the sanguine as a plant in a vegetable garden. The spring comes and the plant grows larger and larger and stronger and stronger until one day it blossoms. How well the plant does is directly related to the soil it grows in and the gardener who tends it. In the summer its blossoms become fruit and it offers this fruit to those around it. When fall comes, the fruit diminishes, the richness of the green plant fades, and it begins a cycle of decline. The leaves change color, the fruit fades away, the plant wilts and mulches itself into the soil around it and decomposes. The inevitable winter follows. The plant is completely mulched into the ground and "dies." But then the spring comes again and the plant once again starts to blossom. And this time it blossoms more splendidly because the mulch from the previous year has enriched its soil even more. It does not matter what the soil was to begin with, the next year is always better for the plant as each year its mulch enriches the soil around it.

Because of this, the sanguine person is very affected by the people around her, the place she lives in, the weather, and all other external stimuli, including books and movies. The sanguine person is also very affected by the "gardener." This usually is the spouse, mother, father, friend, or doctor. The key element to watch for in a sanguine is overstimulation (over-watering the garden) which creates a selfish and dissatisfied attitude, or under-stimulation which creates an angry and dissatisfied individual. The sanguine type also needs to realize what stage she is in. She will be either under- or over-stimulated most of the time so she needs to seek balance. When she is not balanced, she needs to hold her tongue about temporary dissatisfactions and instead administer the cure, which would be either to cut down or increase activity, nurturing and/or nutrition.

The Physical Traits of the Sanguine

A person of the sanguine temperament may have larger veins than most, more visible veins or veins that appear more "full." Her skin may be red or flushed or may flush easily when she is embarrassed or when she engages in intense physical activity. The sanguine person may experience shortness of breath due to anxiety, exertion, allergies or other reasons. She also tends to have darker urine than the other temperaments. This can be partially attributed to the fact that the sanguine person does not often feel thirsty. As the sanguine person lives so firmly in the astral body, she may become unaware of the physical body and forget to eat, forget to drink and even forget to go to the bathroom or sleep. She simply does not feel the need for sleep, as the other temperaments do. A sanguine may become so accustomed to ignoring the sensation of thirst or hunger that she may eventually lose the ability to feel the initial sensations and will only be alerted of hunger or thirst when she is feeling faint.

Despite a poor relationship with the messages the body sends her, a sanguine loves food and has a quick and easy digestion. She often has regular bowel elimination and rarely suffers from constipation. A sanguine would typically "eat everything in sight" and loves the experience of food. However, she can easily become distracted with all the noise, choices and sensations at a restaurant and may have a hard time focusing or making a choice from the menu. After a time, an adult sanguine may make the decision to simply eat the same thing every time she visits the restaurant simply to avoid this challenge. However, it is not characteristic of the sanguine to always eat the same thing; she loves variety and the sensations she gets from the textures, temperatures, and tastes of foods. Food is an adventure, like everything else in life.

A sanguine person may also possess some of the following physical characteristics: ruddy complexion, smooth skin, firm skin, moist and warm skin, dark brown or fair hair, a hairy body, medium stature and a muscular body build, or a tall stature with medium body build. A sanguine often has an expressive face and eyes that "sparkle." She may have curly or wavy hair rather than straight hair. She may walk with a little "bounce" and is usually light-footed and graceful, but can sometimes appear clumsy when out of balance or upset.

The Sanguine in Social Situations

The sanguine is usually self-composed and can even appear bold or forward in mannerism. She enjoys expressing herself before a group and likes to be heard. A sanguine may migrate to any form of public expression including public speaking, journalism, online social networks, or blogs.

The sanguine loves to be in group activities, but she usually wants to lead that group. She finds other people inspiring; however, she sometimes finds social situations over-stimulating and confusing so she also needs time to retreat or be alone. For this reason, she prefers to be the leader of the activities so she can maintain more control of when and where the activities happen. However, despite the fact that she enjoys leading and being in control, the sanguine is actually the most adaptive of the four temperaments and can sometimes have chameleon-like traits. Because of this, if one meets a sanguine and does not know them well, one could be fooled into thinking she is a melancholic, phlegmatic, or choleric person. Depending on what season the sanguine is in that day, depending on with whom she is speaking and depending on the environment, she could exhibit traits from any one of the four temperaments. However, this also makes the sanguine, in general, very agreeable! She is not insistent upon her ideas or plans and may readily agree with another's wishes. This may not appear obvious as she is very articulate and can appear to be firm and determined in her path. However, when one gets to know a sanguine, one will realize that she is actually very agreeable, yielding and sometimes very compliant.

The sanguine makes friends easily, but may find it challenging to juggle more than a few close friendships and will tend towards having many casual friends and/or only a few close friends. A sanguine will usually not be comfortable being part of a large group or an extended family where there are many relationships to juggle on a consistent basis.

The sanguine is very helpful to neighbors and friends and is always willing to lend a hand. However, because overall personality can seem frivolous, people may not take such generosity seriously and make think it is just "for show." On the contrary, the sanguine is one of the most giving temperaments of all. Because she does not feel a strong attachment to the physical realm, including her own body, she often finds it very easy to give of self, money and possessions. When told she is being generous or helpful, she may be sincerely confused.

Those who have a sanguine adult, spouse or child will notice that she may get mad easily, but just as easily forgets she was mad and usually bears no grudge. This can be very confusing for the sanguine interacting with other temperaments as she can assume that everyone else is as adaptable. A sanguine could have an argument in the morning and then be confused when the person she argued with is still angry with her in the evening. She may not even remember having had an argument by then.

The Personal Life of the Sanguine

The sanguine is keenly aware of her environment. To the outside observer she may seem very carefree and ever-changing. However, in reality, she can be almost perfectly in sync with the seasons, environment, and culture around her. A sanguine has the ability to blend into any culture or situation if so desired – and often does. A sanguine has an appetite and curiosity for all things in life and enjoys learning about other cultures, people, and places. Because she is so in tune with her environment, she usually makes transitions easily. However, an older sanguine can wear out after years of changes and transitions and can eventually resist them and have less desire to adapt. She never loses the ability to adapt, but can lose the desire and, for a sanguine, desire is fuel.

A sanguine is usually quick and decisive in movement and often exudes a strong energy and vibrancy. An imbalanced sanguine may turn from one activity to the next in rapid succession and have little perseverance. She may also experience frequent fluctuations in mood between elation and depression. A person of the extreme sanguine temperament, especially a child who is in the sanguine age of life, may appear superficial and unable or unwilling to penetrate to the depth of concepts, social situations and problems.

Because of this tendency to skim the surface of many things, the sanguine has the ability to see similarities and correspondences between systems and can often see things that others cannot. A sanguine has the ability to bring together people and concepts in unique ways that would not be possible if she spent too much time thinking about the depth of them. Although others may experience her as merely skimming the surface, she experiences a bird's-eye view of many situations.

The sanguine is an optimist and looks at most things from the brighter side. The glass is always half full for the sanguine. Because of this, a sanguine can be very confident and assume that what she imagines and desires will always come to be. She can be disappointed when this does not happen. At such times the sanguine, while preferring otherwise, will be forced to reflect on her inner life. To reflect inwardly feels very lonely for the sanguine as she thrives on her connection to other people, animals and things in life. When a sanguine feels connected she is alive and vibrant. When she disconnects, she may feel suddenly insecure, lonely and fearful. Because of this the sanguine may prefer to meditate in groups or while engaging in movement of some kind such as walking or driving. If her eyes suddenly glaze over, then it may be assumed that she has actually gone to another place in her mind. A sanguine who is meditating in public may not be aware she has gone into this state and may not have even done it on purpose but will be unable to hear anything said to them, completely unaware of the surrounding environment.

The Spiritual Practices for the Sanguine

To make the best of who she is, the sanguine person must allow herself time to reflect and time to re-connect with the physical world. A sanguine person must learn to identify her rhythms and work with them instead of against them. However, she must also learn the skill of working through them when needed.

Time Outs
There are some who say "time outs" were created for adults - not children. This is especially true with the sanguine. When the sanguine feels her anger or anxiety levels rising, she should take a break. For an adult this could simply be excusing oneself to go to the bathroom or get a drink of water. With a child, she could explain to them that she is taking a "time-out." With a store keeper she could simply say, "I'll think about it and come back later" and then leave right away.

Practice Waiting for Things
When the sanguine wants to buy something or participate in the conversation, she should practice waiting. If she wants to buy a shirt, she should wait a couple days first. If the sanguine person wants to talk, she should let the person finish first.

Exercise
The sanguine type has a lot of excess energy that can seem endless when spent on herself and those around her. A sanguine needs to exercise to keep her energy levels flowing evenly and to keep organs in balance.

Recite Affirmations
A sanguine needs to constantly remind herself of all the positive traits she has by reciting affirmations on a daily basis.

Daily Prayer or Meditation
The sanguine type needs to connect with a central power on a regular basis to remain steady and feel she has a place of safety, privacy, and protection.

Have a Hobby
The sanguine type has a great need for personal growth and is very intense. A sanguine needs a place to put this energy and intensity other than her friends and family.

Be Touched
A sanguine needs regular touch in the form of massage, reflexology, facials, and even hugs. This is to soften the natural tension that is in her muscles and system get her used to the feeling of relaxation. Part of the reason a sanguine cannot relax is because she is not used to feeling that way. When a sanguine creates a regular schedule of relaxation, her body will slowly realize that relaxation can be a "normal" state.

Nurturing the Sanguine

Using the analogy of the plant as a guide to the sanguine, one can easily think about the ways in which she can best be nurtured. What does a plant need to grow? What will kill a plant and what will hurt its growth? What will cause it to blossom and bear fruit and what causes undeveloped buds? There are many analogies that can be drawn. Experiences like moving can be harmful to the sanguine as she is then forced to put roots down in new soil. This will slow the development of a sanguine person, although in some cases it can also strengthen the person and cause a new, stronger breed to grow.

Another thing that is harmful to a sanguine is being enclosed. A sanguine person, in spring and summer, hates being shut in. She needs to feel that her roots have space to grow down, and that her leaves and branches have space to grow up. Periods of "drought" (being neglected as a child or being neglected by a spouse) or periods of "flooding" (being spoiled as a child or being constantly given what they want as an adult) can be equally damaging to a sanguine person. The happiest plant is one where everything in its life is regular and consistent. The happy sanguine likes to be watered at the same time every day and to have all the sun, water, food and nurture come to it in regular, steady intervals.

Educating the Sanguine

A sanguine is usually viewed as gifted in some way as they are the only type that produces fruit effortlessly. She naturally does so many things well. For this reason she is often envied by peers. She may also feel guilty and self-conscious for being so skilled without having to work at it. A sanguine person does not usually have to attend college or school to learn to read or write or to learn anything at all. A sanguine person learns naturally from books and the world around her. However, school should be taken advantage of as a grounding experience and an opportunity to practice balance and social skills. The best school for a sanguine person would be one that embraces all angles of education (handiwork, music, spiritual, mental and social) and not just the academic aspects of education. To emphasize only academics creates imbalance within the sanguine. This will be evidenced by mood swings, depressions or social problems.

Relating to the Sanguine

A sanguine person hates direction and correction, viewing it as an invasion of privacy. Telling a sanguine what to do without an invitation, is like knocking on the door to someone's house at five in the morning. To tell a sanguine something, write it down or mention it casually and don't try to get an immediate response. She will register what has been said, file it away, and when ready she will "listen" later.

There is much variance within the sanguine all the way from "psychotic" to psychic. This depends on the level of self-awareness and nurturing the person has. These two things are critical for the sanguine. If a sanguine person is not aware of whom she is and thinks she is "broken" because she is not like everyone else (or if others communicate this belief) and if there is a lack of nurturing foods, people and places, the sanguine can enter states that can mimic clinical depression, manic depressive syndrome and extreme psychosis or schizophrenia. As a sanguine person learns more about the sanguine temperament she is better able to control her emotions instead of them controlling her. If surrounded by nurturing, loving people, friends, places, and food, she will grow to be more and more balanced.

A sanguine person is the most misunderstood type because of her seasons. A person who meets her when she is in "spring" will be constantly searching for that "spring" after "winter" arrives. When "spring" comes again the other person will once again think they have a handle on the sanguine, only to encounter "fall" and "winter" once again. This paints a picture of inconsistency and fragmentation to the outside world when really the friends and family of the sanguine need to understand that she is composed not of one season, but of many and "that" in itself *is the sanguine.*

A sanguine person needs a guide - a gardener and the sun, so to speak. She needs a spiritual path in life (sunshine) and someone (the gardener) to tend and guide her in her growth to make sure she gets the proper nutrients. A sanguine's growth becomes unruly and uncontrolled without a "gardener" and she will die without the "sun."

Affirmations & Cautions for the Sanguine

A sanguine must get to know herself and appreciate and love those traits which are positive and constructive within herself. These include:

Charity
Candor
Cheerfulness
Adaptability

A sanguine must be cautious of the following traits and work to balance these:

Vanity
Tendency to Have Only One Close Friend
Sentimentality
Sensuality
Jealousy
Levity
Superficiality
Instability

41

In a situation where any of these traits becomes exaggerated, this exaggeration will completely suppress other temperament balances. Repeat the following affirmation daily and add to it as new ideas occur. This will strengthen the good qualities. Let these good qualities shine! Some of them may be weak now or yet undiscovered, but they are all there in potential.

Affirmation for the Sanguine

Like a hawk, I can soar or ride on the wind.
I am bold and seek adventure and action.
I am ambitious and powerful and decisive.
Seeking challenge, I push myself to the limit.
I enjoy and do well under pressure.

Like the willow, I am flexible and durable, yet strongly rooted.
I have motivation and capacity to grow and expand, and yet
I have the willpower to stay within defined boundaries.
I am intuitively alive and creative.
I renew my daily relationships each day the sun rises.

Physical Ailments of the Sanguine

Sanguines tend toward left-sided ailments and yeast infections. Because she has an ever-changing experience with life around her, she may try to control and balance this experience with the energy derived from sugar and caffeine, along with the calm that excess bread and baked goods give. However, by using these items in an unhealthy fashion to balance their temperament, a number of physical ailments may develop such as anxiety, fibromyalgia, lower back pain, upper back pain, cramps, and hypoglycemia or hyperglycemia among others.

The Sanguine Diet

Sanguine types or people with excess sanguine condition should eat greens daily in the form of Swiss chard, parsley, mint, coriander, chives, arugula, dark greens, and lettuce (dark green) and avoid rich or sugary foods. Although these guidelines are important for people of all types, the sanguine needs to make sure she consumes extra servings of greens and is especially careful when consuming sugar. The sanguine should never consume sugar as a snack. Sugary items should only be eaten for desert, with a meal or balanced by eating vegetables or drinking herbal tea. When given a choice between eating a salad or eating carrots, it would be healthier for the sanguine to choose the greens.

Symbols of the Sanguine

Each temperament relates to a different season of the year, time of day, animal, color and many other things. When looking for ideas on how to relate better to the sanguine child, it often helps to do exercises using these symbols. Choose one of the items listed below and compare it to one of the items listed under your own temperament. Mix shapes with animals, or seasons with times of day. There are hundreds of combinations to try and each one will reveal more depth in your relationship with the sanguine child. Also ask the child to participate in these exercises by drawing pictures, telling stories, or acting out different scenarios. For example, if you are of the melancholic type, which corresponds to a square and the child is of the sanguine type, corresponding to a squiggle, spend some time drawing these two geometric shapes on paper and observe how they interact.

The symbols of the sanguine are:

East
Dawn
Childhood
Spring
Wood
Air
Wind
The liver
An artisan
A squiggle (geometry)
A monkey
A pioneer

The Choleric Temperament

"The choleric temperament will show itself as active in a strongly pulsating blood. In this, the element of force in the individual makes its appearance in the fact that he has a special influence upon his blood. In such a person, in whom spiritually the ego, physically the blood, is particularly active, we see the innermost force vigorously keeping the organization fit. And as he thus confronts the outer world, the force of his ego will wish to make itself felt. That is the effect of this ego. By reason of this, the choleric appears as one who wishes to assert his ego in all circumstances. All the aggressiveness of the choleric, everything connected with his strong will-nature, may be ascribed to the circulation of the blood." – Rudolf Steiner, 1908-09

The choleric is famous for their strong and assertive ego. Sometimes the choleric person is described as pushy, egotistical, selfish, greedy, loud, annoying and/or self-centered. However, for those that understand the true inner motivations of the choleric these words are transformed. The choleric person is actually assertive, self-respecting, intentioned, without boundaries, vibrant, enthusiastic and determined.

The Physical Traits of the Choleric

The choleric person may display some of the typical outward traits of the choleric temperament or they may display only a few of these traits. A classic choleric person would have a lean body, hollow eyes and/or protruding bone structure, yellowness of skin, a propensity to headaches, a swift and strong pulse, warm and dry skin, dark brown or red hair, a very hairy body, a short or average stature, overactive digestion, orange urine and dry or yellow bowel movements. These traits may become more or less noticeable as the choleric fluctuates between the more balanced and the more extreme states of their temperament.

The Choleric in Social Situations

The choleric is very comfortable in social situations and usually seeks them out. When around people the choleric is usually animated, enthusiastic and full of life. Choleric people are often the "life of the party" or the motivator in the relationship or the classroom. Although their energy may create disharmony or discomfort for some people in social situations, the choleric is undeniably the spark that keeps things interesting.

Cholerics have an uncanny ability to know what others are thinking and feeling. This ability goes beyond the intuition of the sanguine and has more to do with the realm of "knowing" than "sensing". The choleric simply knows what is going on around them as if it is clearly written on the surfaces of every wall, object and person in the room. In the world the choleric lives in, such things are clearly visible. For this reason, a choleric may be skilled at knowing the right thing to do or say in social situations, may have a very good sense of fashion and trends, and may be overly concerned with how they appear in social situations. To someone of another temperament, running out of the house in their casual clothing may be a simple act of efficiency. To the choleric this may represent a tear in the very fabric of reality and create a feeling of great discomfort between him and his surroundings.

The choleric enjoys physical contact and intimacy with the people around them. This works well when their friends and family are similarly inclined. However, many times friends or family members will feel their space is being invaded by the choleric, who does not have many space issues himself. When observing the choleric, one notices that he will most always welcome a hug, he will rarely tell someone to leave the room, and he is usually open to interruptions of any kind as long as they involve social interaction. When these same rules, however, are applied to the people around him, they may create feelings of irritation and annoyance to other people. Simply put, the choleric's door is always open and he may assume everyone else's is too.

This innocent tendency to occupy the space that others consider their own also shows itself in the verbal realm. Just as the choleric can be unaware of the physical boundaries of those around him, the choleric person can also be unaware of the emotional boundaries of those around him. A choleric person is always happy to share their innermost feelings and desires and has a hard time hiding their sentiments. The choleric may not realize that these emotions are not always appropriate to share or that sharing them may make people feel uncomfortable or hurt. Because the choleric is always open to hearing the passions of others around him, they assume that others have the same capacity. However, this is not to say that the choleric is unfeeling. On the contrary, the choleric is incredibly compassionate, empathetic and responsive and can easily be hurt or feel another person's pain. Because they appear to be so immune to boundaries, others may not realize that he is so sensitive and may unintentionally hurt the choleric person.

The choleric considers eating merely a function of life and is always eager to get on with the next social encounter or creative endeavor. However, when presented with an eating situation that is social, such as a family meal or classroom snack time, he can focus more easily on the task of eating and may eat large quantities with great speed. Of course the choleric will also talk while they are eating and may have a difficult time following the rule of "chewing with your mouth closed". When left to his own devices, the choleric may graze casually, but will not eat large amounts without the social environment to encourage him.

The Personal Life of the Choleric

The choleric person is full of passion and is rarely satisfied with anything ordinary, but must create situations in which everything is extraordinary. Because of this drive a choleric may be extremely creative and be able to create things that others could not have even begun to imagine. For a choleric, however, these creations come quite naturally and fulfill an important purpose in their life. A choleric is happiest when things are "larger than life" because for him this is a normal state of existence. The choleric's vision is 60/20 – it is as if they put a magnifying glass on life and enlarge everything so it is easier to experience and see. When others try to "correct the vision" of the choleric, however, he can become depressed or, alternately, anxious to get "their vision" back.

The choleric enjoys being alluring and charismatic and will cultivate talents and traits that they feel will bring them more recognition. For this reason, a choleric will shine equally in any culture or situation he is put into. This is because a choleric does not necessarily take inspiration from inner desires for certain objects or actions, but from the inner desire to be attractive to others. This brings about what may seem like a contradiction in the choleric's personality for those that do not understand his true inner motivations. If a choleric is put into a society where ownership of various objects is popular, such as the desire to own many stuffed animals among children, then the choleric may appear to be quite greedy in their need to own more and more stuffed animals. If, however, the choleric is put into a situation where people around them are giving instead of taking, he may actually become overly generous and forget his own needs. However, because the choleric lives in the here and now and does not often worry about the future or dwell on the past, he can quickly shift between these two states of being materialistic and charitable.

Above all, the choleric enjoys the pleasure of his senses. The choleric enjoys physical contact with other people, the taste of food, the feeling of the wind in their hair, the warmth of the sun on their skin, sparkling gems, cold firm stones, soft blankets, warm puppies and furry rabbits. Everything in life is richer when it comes with a pleasant sensation; and memories, for the choleric, are often wrapped up in the memories of certain physical sensations.

The choleric's vibrant way of living puts him at risk for feeling they are superior to their fellow man/woman. Because everything in their life is "larger" the choleric may start to see this as "better" and may feel that everyone else is inadequate compared to him. The choleric may even try to bring other people "on board" by telling them that they "need" to be a certain way or do certain things. When engaged in imaginary play they may often insist on directing the play.

Spiritual Practices for the Choleric

Meditation on the Simple Things in Life
A choleric is often drawn to all that is exciting in life. The choleric child needs to learn to focus on things that are not glamorous and stimulating. This can be practiced by the choleric taking walks in nature, spending regular time with family, caring for a family pet on a regular basis, making his own toys or tools and other activities that encourage meditation on simplicity.

Patience

A choleric lives in the now and often wants things in the now. A choleric needs to learn patience by waiting for things to happen. One way to help this to happen is to create a schedule for some of the choleric's favorite foods or things to do. Certainly one does not want to restrict everything in the choleric's life but restricting a few on a regular basis can help teach the choleric patience and discipline. For example, if the choleric loves ice cream it would be a good practice for him to have ice cream only on Tuesdays and Fridays. Another way to practice patience is for the choleric to practice having a savings account. To some this may seem obvious, especially if one is an adult. However, there are many adults who don't have savings accounts. A choleric would benefit from having one even if it is a small one. Another good way to practice patience is for the choleric to engage in long term projects as well as the short term ones he loves.

Feeling Boundaries

Because a choleric views the world without boundaries he needs to learn to feel the boundaries of others so he does not step over them too much. One good game for learning about boundaries is one called "Mine Field".

Mine Field

In this game you create an easy obstacle course on the floor of a living-room or outdoor area. The choleric person must take turns with his partner leading the person through the maze. The person being led must be blindfolded. This game helps the choleric person be more aware of space. It also helps the choleric person experience what issues the other person may have with space. If the exercise is discussed afterwards between the two participants it is an even more effective teaching tool.

Giving

Because a choleric has a limitless ability to give, he also has a limitless ability to ask for what he needs. However, the latter often comes more readily than the former. Without the inspiration to give, the choleric will naturally focus more on taking. It is important for the choleric to practice giving of their time, possessions and money on a weekly basis.

Humility

The choleric is very self confident and aware of their own vibrancy and value. This is a lovely trait that is a healthy part of self-love and spiritual development. However, the choleric also needs to develop the ability to see others in that same light. For this reason, a choleric needs a hero, a spiritual leader or a person they can look up to and admire. The more people a choleric can feel this admiration for, the healthier and more balanced they will become. A choleric should interact with people they respect, should read biographies, and should be told stories of heroes and saints from the time they are in second grade and continuing on into the later grades.

Nurturing the Choleric

The choleric person needs ample physical contact and interactions with other people. Most likely one person will not be able to fulfill these needs. Therefore, a choleric needs to be provided with an adequate social network and the opportunity to be close with different family members and friends. The choleric child will often be the one that requests to sleep with the adults at night and seems unwilling to sleep in his own bed. A choleric child will enjoy overnights with friends and extended family members. These activities may seem frivolous to the outsider, but they are essential to the choleric child's development.

A choleric has a great need to explore his visions and should be provided with the tools to do so. A choleric may need extra sets of colored pencils, extra walks in the woods, extra stories at bedtime or any number of tools to help encourage them to expand their imagination.

Educating the Choleric

A spiritual center is very important for the choleric person and is an essential part of his education. Any educational program for the choleric must nurture the soul as well as the mind, and the spirit as well as the body. The choleric person needs space to move in and people to interact with as he learns, because this enriches the learning experience. If a choleric is being schooled at home, he may benefit from study trips to a café, library or other public location. If a choleric is at school, he needs to be in a classroom where frequent movement is permitted and perhaps even encouraged. If a choleric is studying online, he may need to engage in live chats and take the computer outside or to public locations to remain captivated with his studies.

Relating to the Choleric

Friends and relatives need to understand that the choleric person contains a strong element of fire and may be inclined to "burn up" those around him. However, any harm that comes of this intensity is completely unintended. The choleric is very free in giving and taking emotion, things and support. Since he is very free in giving, very enthusiastic and generous, the choleric does not feel they ask too much of others. What the choleric may not realize is that others, lacking the same element of fire, do not have the choleric's burning passion and energy and are actually unable to give what the choleric is able to give.

The result is that the choleric person may "burn up" friends and family with requests and needs, but at the same time always feels unsatisfied because his own needs are not met. He needs to understand that other people are willing to give them what he wants and that they are loved. The choleric needs to realize it is not the fault of their family and friends that they are unable to provide the fuel that the choleric fire needs. Nor does it mean their friends and family are shallow, unloving or unworthy of the choleric person. The choleric person also needs to understand that the demands he puts on their friends and family may be too much for them. For when the choleric person asks for too much and is constantly disappointed, he will be hurt and sad and will withdraw. Instead, they need to expect less from the individual people around them and seek fulfillment from society as a whole.

When speaking to a choleric person bear in mind that they are won over by calm elucidation of reasons and motives, but are hardened and become hard-headed by harsh commands. In addition, a choleric child may actually become fearful and anxious when he encounters harsh commands and may become clingy or desperate for attention.

Affirmations & Cautions for the Choleric

A choleric must get to know himself and appreciate and love those traits, which are positive and constructive within himself. These include:

The Ability to Express Oneself through Physical Movement
Joyful at Heart
Giving and Generous
Expressive
Quick to Laugh and See the Bright Side of Life
Optimistic
Communicative
Charismatic
Empathetic
Dedicated
Alive and Alert to the World
Enthusiastic and Energetic

A choleric must be cautious of the following traits and work to balance these:

Talkativeness
Inability to Follow Through
Vanity
Interrupting Others
Materialism or Over-consumption
Obsession

In a situation where the choleric type becomes exaggerated, it will completely suppress the balance of the other temperaments. It is useful for the choleric to have affirmations to repeat daily to keep him balanced. These affirmations are most effective when written by the choleric himself, however, I have included some examples below.

The choleric should repeat the following affirmation daily and add to it as he thinks of new things. This will strengthen the good qualities in the choleric person that already exist. As the choleric lets these good qualities shine and appreciates them within himself, others will too! Some of these qualities may be weaker or stronger at different times in the life of the choleric.

Affirmation for the Choleric

I am like a campfire – dancing, warming,
Brilliant, glowing and vibrant.
I give and receive love easily
And provide a space for the spirit to be set free.
I am joy in times of tribulation.

I am like the cherry tree – ripe, mature,
Blooming, bearing fruit, colorful, inviting and expansive.
My fruits speak my heart
And the color red laughs among my many tongues that are leaves.
I am hope in a faded garden.
I renew my beauty each spring and summer.
I can captivate and color a drab day.

Physical Ailments of the Choleric

The choleric temperament may experience problems with anxiety, agitation, and temper tantrums and may frequently suffer from nervous exhaustion and/or insomnia. A choleric person will either have trouble getting to sleep or may suddenly fall asleep after he has completely worn himself out for the day. A choleric's body is a bit like a wind-up toy. His body will be full of energy one moment and completely lacking the next. Because of this the choleric person needs to be careful not to push himself too hard and to take breaks even if he does not feel like it. Because of this constant drive on the body, the choleric person may experience palpitations, circulation problems, hypoglycemia, rashes, restless leg syndrome or other nervous and metabolic disorders. Because a choleric experiences constant movement within themselves, they may easily get motion sick when traveling in a car, plane or boat.

The choleric can drift toward the usage of mind-altering substances in his pursuit of a life that is larger and more vibrant. The choleric may indulge in anything from coffee or sugar to illegal or prescription drugs. The choleric should limit exposure to such substances to avoid any damage that could come from the inevitable abuse of these substances. An adult of a choleric child should limit their intake of sugar, chocolate, fast foods and any other items that have the potential to become addictive.

The choleric should avoid engaging in hot activities too frequently like arguing, fighting, intense sports or running, and should instead focus on cooler activities such as tai chi, yoga, swimming, walking, reading and singing.

The Choleric Diet

The choleric is healthiest when he consumes things that are cool and moist. These foods help them balance their hot and dry temperament. Some examples of good foods for the choleric are juicy fruits, greens, vegetables, warm soups, water, root vegetables, sea vegetables, legumes, carrot-celery juice, chives, duck, eggplant, corn, figs, olives, pears, walnuts, basmati rice, brown rice, millet, and fish. When a choleric is feeling worn down and tired, they can consume more hot foods and drinks to rebalance their heat. For example, warm foods, extra protein and spicy teas, like chai or cinnamon tea, can help stimulate the choleric's natural warmth. When a choleric is feeling overly stimulated and excited, he can consume more raw foods to help him cool down. Cholerics should rarely use ice cream, spicy condiments, yogurt, or icy drinks. Adult cholerics need to avoid overindulging in curry, sugar, alcohol, caffeine, tea, chili, and salt. Choleric children need to avoid colas, sugar and processed foods.

Symbols of the Choleric

Each temperament relates to a different season of the year, time of day, animal, color and many other things. When one is looking for ideas on how to relate better to the choleric person, it often helps to do exercises using these symbols. To do an exercise with a person of the choleric temperament, one must choose an item listed below and compare it to one of the items listed under his own temperament. When doing this, shapes can be mixed with animals or seasons with times of day – one does not need to restrict the lesson to comparing shapes or comparing colors. When one combines the different symbols between the two temperaments there are hundreds of combinations a person can try and each one will reveal more depth in the relationship between the temperaments. Asking the other person to participate in these exercises can also intensify this exercise. When people of two different temperaments can act out stories together, draw pictures together and tell stories together, it can be very therapeutic. Take for example, a person of the melancholic type, which corresponds to a square, and his child of the sanguine type, which corresponds to a squiggle. The melancholic adult could spend some time drawing these two geometric shapes on a paper and observe how they interact.

The symbols of the choleric that one can use in the exercises are:

Summer
Noon
Youth
South
Fire
Heat
The heart
A triangle
A bear

The Relationships

Melancholic Adult - Melancholic Child

- ## General Relationship

This pairing is a "force to be reckoned with." Together they can do anything and accomplish much! The melancholic child will be happy to have a system to follow and fit into and the melancholic adult is the perfect person to provide that system for her. One will be thrilled to have a child around who understands and appreciates her system of organization, order and the "way things should be."
However, they should be careful not to form a "tribe of two," shutting out other students, family members or friends. Their synergy is obvious to everyone around them and may cause jealousy with siblings or classmates.

Appreciate the chemistry one has with this child but be careful not to set the bar too high for other children. Remember – the synergy of this pairing occurs because both adult and child are of the same temperament. Although this can feel personally affirming, it does not mean that the melancholic's system is right for everyone. It just means it is the right system for her. One will still encounter situations with other children that offer the opportunity for personal growth and reaching outside of one's comfort zone.

This is the child that will guarantee family traditions are passed on. This is the student to put in charge of the class when one must leave to visit the bathroom. This is the child that affirms everything the melancholic adult *is*. However, everything she *could be* will come from other children and people.

- ## Helping the Melancholic Adult Understand the Melancholic Child

Understanding this child will be relatively easy for the adult who, as a melancholic, assumes everyone should be following her system and that everyone views or experiences the world in the same way she does. This is correct, in the case of the melancholic child.

One emotion this pairing will share in common is melancholy. A child of this temperament will spend so much time thinking about the past and the future that she can often become troubled by the weight of her thoughts. This is a normal and comfortable state for the melancholic child. The adult will be able to understand such comfort with this way of thinking because she also sees the time spent on contemplating the past and future as useful work in the process of learning and planning. Because this is a healthy part of being melancholic, this heaviness of emotion should not be discouraged but rather channeled into positive and useful tasks. As a melancholic adult, however, one may be liable to encourage the child's contemplative state of mind toward a depth of exploration that could prevent healthy action from taking place. Understand that the melancholic child needs to be able to move from her thoughts into the realm of action. If unable to do this, she can become depressed or overburdened with worries.

A melancholic child has a natural fear of the darkness and dark places, including any person, emotion or place that is unknown or dark. A melancholic child may also have a fear of crowds or crowding and may even prefer to wear lose clothing. As you have grown into a balanced melancholic adult you have most likely grown out of these fears or learned to push them into the back of your mind and either ignore or deny them. As you get to know your melancholic child your own fears will come to the surface again and you will need to face them. As a melancholic adult you appreciate strength in the people around you and may feel that you need to discourage your child's fear of the dark and unknown. However, before you can do this you need to come to terms with your own fears of the same.

A melancholic child desires order. This will not seem like an unusual or outstanding trait to the melancholic adult since she expects the world and people in it to maintain order. However, this is a unique strength that the melancholic temperament possesses and should be encouraged in a healthy way. Try to understand that, although the melancholic child and adult both desire order and organization in the world around them, not everyone may agree with their point of view. Teach the melancholic child to pursue her desire for order in a way that is respectful of other people's boundaries and feelings.

One familiar trait to recognize in the melancholic child is her sense of righteousness and inclination to judge people. If the adult has not yet come to terms with this trait in herself, she may be very proud of the melancholic child for being so outspoken, confident and assured of her own values and traditions. Without realizing it, she may be teaching the child to be less tolerant of other people's traditions, values and needs. Recognize that the child is just learning to master these strong emotions and may need some guidance through this passage in her life. The adult's goal is to nurture and balance the child's temperament and not to alter it. To help the melancholic child stay balanced in this area, make sure she has ample opportunity to state opinions on various topics and people in a healthy way. She may benefit from practicing debate, giving public presentations, writing reports, writing letters to the editor of the newspaper and other actions that have positive outcomes. When the melancholic child has an outlet for the desire to evaluate people and events, she will likely feel less need to target this skill at family and friends. However, as the child engages in more activities in which this skill can be practiced, she may be *more* apt to practice on family and friends until reaching the understanding that there are appropriate situations in which to express her sense of justice, and there are some situations in which she must allow others to have a voice as well. A melancholic adult will need to come to terms with these challenges, herself, before understanding the child's needs in this area.

The melancholic child also has a great desire to master tasks, lessons, activities and even people. As this is usually the melancholic adult's goal, as well, she will have no problem relating to this desire within them and will be happy to encourage them.

- ## Helping the Melancholic Child Understand the Melancholic Adult

The young melancholic is all about understanding things and figuring things out. Having the same temperament, she will be able to easily understand why the adult does things and how the adult sees the world.

The melancholic child will most likely find great comfort in who her melancholic adult is. Because the adult likes to maintain a neat and orderly personal life and control over her environment, the child will feel safe in that environment and should not have any problems comprehending the arrangement of the home or classroom.

The melancholic adult is often strongly committed to moral principles and standards. However, the melancholic child is just learning to identify what those standards are within herself. Because of this, she may initially view the adult's style as very strict and may feel unsettled by the firm style. Although melancholic children can be very firm, themselves, and develop a moral code very early in life, they need the adult to display gentleness to them during these early years. This will help them learn to feel safe exploring their emotions instead of feeling fearful of them. The melancholic adult should keep this in mind when communicating with the melancholic child. Because she is so similar to the adult in many ways, it may not occur to the adult that the child could develop anxiety over the firm parenting style. She may view the child's potential rather than who she actually is, and not realize the need to be very gentle with the melancholic child.

As a melancholic adult or adult, one may be inclined to focus more on order and procedure and less on people. As long as everyone is following proper procedure she feels confident and that all is well with the world. However, the melancholic's focus on form instead of emotional attachment does not mean that she does not need other people. Because the melancholic child also has the same tendency to focus on order and goals rather than personal relationships, both child and adult may find themselves passing like ships in the sea of life – both on very orderly and straight courses, but never meeting. The adult should take some time to connect on a personal level with the melancholic child every day. This will not be something that comes naturally to either of them, although it will come more naturally to the young melancholic. So, the adult may take a cue from their needs – give them hugs when they need them and take time to interact, personally. As the child learns about the adult or adult, she is learning about herself and needs to understand that personal connections also have an important place in their orderly world.

A melancholic adult will most likely put principles before pleasure and may often say "work before play" is the rule. However, the melancholic child is still in the early years when the sanguine element is the strongest, so she may want to play more. This should be encouraged since this desire will diminish as she grows older. When allowed to experience more play during childhood, she can grow into being a more balanced melancholic. As the child strives to understand the melancholic adult or adult, she needs to be able to also understand that although the adult prefers to put work before play, it is OK for them to experience the freedom of childhood, put play before work and even turn play into her work.

Another trait that follows this same path is the way in which the melancholic does her work. The melancholic adult is often systematic and methodical in work. Because the melancholic child has these same predispositions, there is the danger that she will have these traits come to the surface in her temperament too early. The adult can help the child to understand that the adult's methodical methods are more suitable for the child as she grows older. The adult can encourage the child to enjoy the appropriate play for her age.

- ## Discipline

Good discipline always stems from a sense of trust, love and harmony between the adult and child. The more the adult and child understand and respect each other, the more discipline happens naturally. To have a healthy discipline relationship with the melancholic child the melancholic adult should first read the sections above on how to best understand the child and how to help the child understand the adult.

Discipline in the early years should be relatively easy. A melancholic will most likely have a set schedule or plan for the home or classroom. As long as one is communicating this clearly to the child, she will be happy to follow along and cooperate. However, if one is not communicating her system well, then the child may find another system to follow and it may become difficult to bring her back over to the adult's system. The adult or adult should make sure to communicate expectations, rules and schedule to the child in a clear way that she can understand based on her age and abilities. One may need to write it down for a visual child or take time to talk to a more verbal child about these issues. If one has a toddler, she will need more repetition.

Whatever else the adult may do, she must also remember to communicate expectations clearly before embarking on any disciplinary relationship with the child. Some of the most common problems of the melancholic adult are due to the lack of clear communication of needs, wants, schedule and/or rules. She may think these are communicated clearly, but will still need to check with the child or children to make sure. One may ask them, "What do you understand the rules to be?" or "What do you think my expectations are?"

When a melancholic child is young they will happily follow the system that is put into place by an influential person in their life – either an adult or adult or both.

As the melancholic ages, however, they may seek out new systems. Melancholics migrate towards the most popular system. When they are little, their mother's system is usually the most familiar to them so they follow that. When they are at school, their adult's is the most familiar so they follow that. However, as they venture farther and farther out into society, they may find that there are many other different systems than their mother's or adult's and, if they feel that one of these systems is more popular, they may want to try it out. This may cause some misunderstandings and changes in the adult-child relationship. The melancholic adult may not understand why the child wants to try out a new system. However, keep in mind that the child needs to find her own path in life and that this path may take her to new places outside of home and family. The adult need not worry that the child will leave all that she was taught behind. Melancholics are keepers of tradition and honor the past. Even if they do adopt a new system, it will be integrated with the old one or in addition to it.

One must be careful not to play favorites with this child. Because she may be such a "model child," the melancholic adult might wonder why all her other children are not the same. If siblings or other students sense this attitude, then they may feel anger or resentment toward this child. This anger or resentment will adversely affect the relationships the adult has with the other children, with this child and even the relationships that this child has with other children. One must remember that this child is like the adult and may seem "ideal" at times, but the other children are just as good and amazing, though perhaps not in the way the melancholic adult expects them to be. Keep an open mind and an open heart with this child.

Because both adult and child feel largely that they are impeccable in their ethics and above reproach in many ways, it may be hard for either of them to communicate disappointment in the other without becoming defensive. The adult must bear in mind that both adult and child have this trait and must be willing to consider that she may be wrong now and then. When the child sees that the adult is willing to admit fault and apologize now and then, she will also learn to do this. This skill will help the child in all her future relationships and will help balance her temperament as a melancholic.

- ## The Teaching Relationship

This student will excel when given clear guidelines, rules and expectations. Melancholics are very good at giving clear guidelines and rules but often do not let the people around them clearly know what their expectations are. The adult must keep in mind that the melancholic student, although she understands her more readily than others do, may still need some help in understanding what the exact expectations are. Because the melancholic tends to assume everyone is (or should be) thinking like herself, she may not realize that people really do not know what the expectations are. She may get frustrated with them for not doing as requested or for not respecting her. However, the melancholic may not realize that the listeners simply didn't understand to begin with.

In a teaching relationship with the melancholic student, it is essential that one makes sure she understands because this is the basis of the melancholic's success. The melancholic student will not need a lot of help beyond understanding the guidelines, rules and expectations because they thrive when given those three things. As long as the adult can clearly communicate those to the student, these two will make a good teaching-student team!

The only drawback with this teaching relationship is that, although it can be harmonic and peaceful, it does not provide some of the growth elements that a melancholic needs to learn. Harmony is useful for regular work habits and everyday learning. However, to really expand their horizons and go beyond "normal," your melancholic will need to be exposed to and learn from other temperaments, too. Make sure there are other students in the class to learn from or that the student has another mentor. Even having a piano adult or sports coach of a different temperament can help them learn beyond their current horizons.

A melancholic student learns best by using her sense of touch. When one can provide something solid for the melancholic student to grasp she will be able to learn more quickly and understand concepts more readily. Since the adult also learns by touch and by exploring solid ideas and concepts, she will naturally include these elements in lesson plans.

In geometry, the melancholic is like a square. In math, the melancholic relates most to the action of adding. In language, the melancholic relates most to the process of structure and grammar and in science, they relate most to the area of Physics. This does not mean that one should focus only on these skills or that one should assume she will grasp these skills quickly. One should merely be aware of the special relationship the melancholic student has with these areas of learning. By watching how they process their relationships with adding and drawing squares, the adult can learn more about her and she will learn more about herself as well.

The melancholic student will thrive when given tasks that require logical and analytical thinking or problem solving. Happily, these are probably the easiest lessons for the adult to create since she also loves puzzles and problem-solving.
The melancholic student will work easily and efficiently in situations where the adult has put forth well established goals and guidelines. Use charts, schedules and other written methods of displaying these guidelines to make sure the student understands what is expected from her in the realm of learning. The melancholic will often assume people understand her, so she may not always take the time to ask them if they do. By writing down expectations and guidelines for the student, the adult is helping herself to learn clearer ways of expression while providing the student with the immediate benefits of that expression.

- A Story to Share

In this traditional tale from Germany, a melancholic King with a sense of order interacts with the melancholic young gentleman who seeks to please him and win the hand of his daughter. His daughter, also being of the melancholic type, is quite agreeable to the rules her father has set down for her and agrees to marry the prince that wins the competition.

The Three Tasks Assigned by the Melancholic King

Traditional German Tale

Once there lived, in a great city, a mighty king. He had an only daughter. When she had reached her eighteenth year and no bridegroom had offered himself, the king thought it would be best to give his daughter to any man who would perform the tasks assigned to him by the king. To this end, the king caused the tower, which stood in his city and was famed for its immense size and height, to be decked with banners. It was so high that all his subjects could see it.

At first people did not know what the banners on the old tower meant, but when they asked about it, they were told so. Then the three sons of a peasant, Mathias, Jacob and Hans, decided to try their luck. They set out, and in passing through their father's garden, the eldest said to the youngest, "Shut the garden door."

Hans thought he said, "Take the door." So Hans took the door off its hinges, and carried it on his back.

The two others went in front and did not trouble themselves much about Hans, and did not once notice that he was carrying the door on his back. When the night came on, they had to look out for a place to sleep in, and decided after some discussion to climb a tree, so that they might be safe from the wild beasts. Now the brothers noticed for the first time that Hans had brought the garden door along with him. They scolded him for this, and told him he must carry the door up the tree, so that no trace of a human presence was to be seen on the ground. And they pushed and pushed till they had got the door up.

The brothers now stretched themselves out and soon fell asleep. But they were awakened by some shots, and to their great horror, they saw some robbers approaching the tree, and then arriving to camp underneath it. Although the brothers kept quite quiet, the robbers soon observed that someone was above, and loaded their guns to fire at the strangers. Hans, seeing these preparations, was so terrified that he let the door fall, and by its fall it killed the robbers.

The two elder brothers now perceived that they were saved by Hans, and behaved more kindly to him. The three wanderers remained sitting on the tree all night, and waited the break of day to continue on their way.

As soon as the first streak of dawn appeared, the three brothers came down and went on their way singing. After some hours they had reached the royal court, asked for entrance, and told why they had come.

Then the king said, "Two of you may go, for I have only one daughter, and she only needs one groom."

None of the brothers wanted to give way, and it even came to a quarrel, till at last the king commanded the eldest of the brothers, Mathias, to stay. The king then asked him about his situation and gave him the following task:

"You are to come sailing to me on a golden ship, but not on the water. The ship must not have wheels, but must sail through the air."

When Matthias had heard this, he went sadly home, and quite alone, for the other brothers had already gone before.

Next day Matthias went into the forest, and in the hope that the king would consider the task done if the ship was made of wood, he hit a fine tree and worked day and night on the ship. On the third day he felt very tired and could not help falling asleep. When he woke up, an old man came to him and asked for a piece of bread.

Matthias drove him off roughly. The man walked away and said: "Matthew, Matthew, you'll regret it."

Hardly had he uttered these words, when he was gone and the tree that had almost assumed the form of a ship was in its former glory again before the astonished Matthias.

Gradually his surprise gave way to anger because his three day's work was for nothing. He went home and told his misfortune to his adults, but they could give him no explanation of it.

The deadline had passed, and Matthias was still at home. Two days after the expiry of the time there came messengers, and sadly Mathias went to the royal castle. He could not excuse himself, and so was condemned to death.

When his adults heard of this they were greatly troubled, and forbade the two younger brothers to woo the king's daughter. But the brothers had not in mind to obey, and the second went into a dense forest and selected a fine tree. He then began, like his brother, to hew the trunk into a ship. When in his weariness he fell asleep, there came a woman, woke up the sleeper, and begged for money. Jacob treated her harshly, and she went away, saying, "Tree, stand up!" and at once the tree stood up again in its full glory.

So Jacob fared no better than his brother, for he had not accomplished the task.

And now came the turn of the youngest brother. Hans went into the forest, hewed down a fine tree, and built out of it a ship. He finished his task singing and when it was done, there came to him a hideous old woman who demanded a kiss. Hans did not hesitate, but hugged and kissed the old woman, not once, but several times.

Then she said to him, "The victory is yours!" She then repeated something over the ship, and suddenly the ship was changed into pure gold and began to move. It carried Hans to a great mountain, and here it rested. Hans waited till the ship should again begin to move. But this lasted too long, for he had already eaten the bread that his mother had given him.

When the third day had passed and the ship was still at rest, he cried in despair, "Woman, come to me!" All at once he then heard a rustling well. He went up to it and said, "Dear fountain, help me!" And suddenly Hans read these words on the surface of the brook: "Not far from me lies a pipe. Take it on your ship."

He sought the pipe and found it too. Then he went into his boat and began to whistle. A man appeared and asked: "What do you want?"

Hans told him his trouble, and the man told him than when Hans urgently needed water, he should just whistle and he himself would come and get him some.

Soon after the ship began to move and carried him to a field. Here, it stopped. A hunter came and gave Hans a trumpet with the remark, "Only blow if you need anything, and you will see what an expert hunter can do for you."

Then the ship began moving again and carried him to the castle of the king.

The king looked with astonishment on the man and the ship that could fly so cleverly and admirably through the air. Hans stepped out of the ship, and the king invited him to a merry feast. Then Hans asked the king for the second task, and the king answered, "Get me just a jug of water the moment you stand up from your chair by this table."

Hans remembered his pipe and whistled, at once. Then the pitcher was on the table when he stood up.

The third task was to call together all the sheep in the world, and let the king see them. Hans blew on his trumpet, and suddenly there was a multitude of sheep, including all those that kings owned in other countries.

The next day, the betrothal ceremony was to take place. But the princess, who loved rules and order more than anything, begged the king to set him some further tasks.

The king refused, saying, "Hans has performed his three tasks." So nothing helped against it; the princess had to become his wife, and as luck would have it, lived long and happily with him.

When stories are told they speak to the child on a basic level. The reason one tells stories instead of explaining things to a child is because stories have the ability to adapt to the child's needs. When a person explains a situation to a child she is putting forth a concept that the child needs to grasp at or reach to understand. When one simply *tells* a story the child is given permission to understand the story in any way she wishes and to gain wisdom and knowledge from it in the way that best suits her at that moment. For that reason, it is not recommended that the story be explained to the child or that the child be provided with the ubiquitous "moral" at the end. Rather, it is best to give them a chance to enjoy the story for what it becomes to them and provide them with numerous chances to hear the story told. The stories in this book help the different temperaments understand each other. If the adult or adult would like to explore this understanding on a deeper level they can ask questions once the story is finished. However, one must be sure to ask open questions and allow the child to express her feelings.

Melancholic Adult - Phlegmatic Child

- ## General Relationship

The melancholic adult will often admire the phlegmatic child for his strong will and will appreciate the way the child is able to listen without arguing - for a melancholic likes to be respected and listened to. Phlegmatics and melancholics both honor tradition, which is another aspect one will have in common. There is potential here for a very harmonious relationship if both respect each other's differences. The melancholic may get frustrated with the slower pace of the phlegmatic and view that as a lack of motivation and order. The phlegmatic may feel pushed and pressured by the melancholic and push back with a quiet, but strong will. This can create a cycle of pressure and resistance between the two, which can provide fantastic learning experiences, but might come at the expense of the relationship if too much tension is allowed to remain between them. Working through temperament differences together can help prevent that from happening.

- ## Helping the Melancholic Adult Understand the Phlegmatic Child

The first thing to be aware of in the phlegmatic child is his comfort zone. It is very easy to push the phlegmatic child out of their comfort zone. The phlegmatic and melancholic both have a smaller comfort zone than the expansive choleric or the versatile sanguine. When the phlegmatic is pushed too far, he will most likely respond in a direct way, perhaps even with anger. Because of this response in oneself, the melancholic may expect that other people will be just as direct. One may confidently make requests of the phlegmatic child assuming he will communicate his opinion about those requests. However, a phlegmatic child instead will either agree with the request and perform the task quietly or dislike the request and not perform the task at all. The child will usually not let the adult know that he is not planning on doing the task. When the child has avoided enough tasks, there might even be a build-up of resentment at all the requests. Also, the phlegmatic child might take a much longer time to fulfill requests or tasks that are outside of his comfort zone as opposed to the tasks he feels comfortable with. Being aware of one's child's comfort zone will help the adult understand how to communicate more effectively. One will also be able to understand better why the child may seem resistant, angry or nervous about some of the adult's requests. One will learn which requests or topics are within easy reach and which ones need more time, patience, and extra care.

I counseled Stacey, the melancholic adult of Matthew, usually a very agreeable child. Matthew would always take out the trash and walk the dog when asked. He was always happy to lend his mom a helping hand when she needed help at home. However, whenever Stacey asked Matthew to take care of tasks at school, they would never get done and he would say "I forgot". She sent lunch money to school with him one day and he "forgot" to give it to the cashier. She asked him to get a sign-up form from the front office for baseball team and he "forgot". After exploring Matthew's comfort zone, she discovered that he was actually very uncomfortable performing any tasks which involved people he did not know well. Once she realized this, she was able to help him overcome his fear of talking to and interacting with new people. Matthew did not necessarily become comfortable with these tasks right away, but he did at least develop the ability to complete them.

• Helping the Phlegmatic Child Understand the Melancholic Adult

While the phlegmatic child is steady and thoughtful in his decisions and actions, the melancholic adult tends to be quick and decisive. Since speed and efficiency are admired traits in today's computer age, the phlegmatic child may be painfully aware of his tendency to take life at a slower pace and may feel inadequate. Because the adult seems to fit so well into the modern pace of life, the child may feel intimidated by his adult. It may seem to the child that the entire world, including the adult is part of a club he was not invited to. The better the phlegmatic child can learn to understand this difference in the adult's style, the less the child will fear the modern pace of life, and the more he will feel comfortable with his own style.

Because a phlegmatic child may feel like the "odd one out", he may be extra sensitive or protective of who he is. Having a melancholic adult may increase this feeling. However, the phlegmatic holds an important cornerstone of our society. The more one can teach this child about the importance of his unique qualities, the more he will have the ability to understand the adult. For the phlegmatic child will have trouble understanding others if he lacks the confidence to first understand himself. An essential characteristic of the phlegmatic is to protect oneself and keep a protected and rich inner world. As long as the phlegmatic is stuck in his inner world, he will not have the capacity to see beyond it. The adult will need to draw this child out of his inner world; only then can one help the child understand who you are as the adult. To draw a phlegmatic out of his inner world, he needs to feel safe, loved, and successful.

When the phlegmatic child finds himself in a comfortable situation, he will naturally start to observe the adult and learn about the adult's style. It is important to allow this child numerous opportunities to observe the adult interacting with others. Eventually, this child might know the adult better than the adult knows himself.

Part of the phlegmatic child's "protection program" is to become as familiar with the people around them as is possible. The child will watch how his adult disciplines other children and will learn from that. He will observe what makes the adult angry and happy and will learn from that. Even when it seems as if the child is not watching - he most likely is. However, this does not necessarily lead to the child "knowing" you. This merely brings forth a "knowledge" by which this child knows how to keep the adult happy and stay within a safe zone when interacting with the adult. A phlegmatic child will go to great lengths to stay within a safe zone of interaction. For this reason, it is important that the adult takes some extra time to explain one's actions to the phlegmatic child – especially during times when one has been extra forceful, angry or frustrated. Even if one was interacting with another person or another child, the phlegmatic child will observe that and will take it in as information. It is important that this child gets the information that one wants him to have.

One phlegmatic child, Sara, with whom I worked, confused her melancholic mother, Sue, by always appearing as if she was hiding her cereal when eating. When Sue would walk into the room, Sara would look guilty and pretend not to see her. As we talked more about the bigger picture at home, it was revealed that Sue's other child, Miranda, was allergic to milk. Sara had often observed Sue becoming frustrated with Miranda when she would sneak milk into her cereal. Sara had observed those interactions and decided that, when she ate cereal, it would be best if her mother was not around. When Sue took the time to explain to Sara that her sister had allergies and why she could not drink milk, Sara's nervousness about eating her snack vanished over-night.

- Discipline

Good discipline always stems from a sense of trust, love and harmony between the adult and child. The more one understands and respects one other, the more naturally discipline happens. To have a healthy discipline relationship with the phlegmatic child, please first read the sections above on how to best understand this child and how to help the child understand the adult.

The first rule to follow when disciplining the phlegmatic is to be gentle. Even if one is speaking in a normal voice and have asked the phlegmatic child a fair question or made a simple request, he may perceive this as being harsh. The melancholic is usually decisive about what one wants and firm and direct about requesting it. Since a phlegmatic is more indirect, he can sometimes perceive any direct requests as aggressive – even if they are not.

The second rule to follow is to give the phlegmatic child more time. The melancholic tends to enjoy a sense of order and proper procedure and appreciates hearing that the requested tasks will get done. However, a phlegmatic child will not always respond as quickly or as clearly as the melancholic adult would like. Because of this, the adult may perceive that the child is ignoring his adult or does not want to help or even listen. One may even feel like disrespected. However, none of these are the case. The phlegmatic child simply needs extra time to absorb the request. If the adult makes the mistake of becoming angry with the phlegmatic child for the "improper" response, the child most likely will become resistant. This could result in a heated battle and frustration for both – even over the simplest things.

The third rule to follow with the phlegmatic child is to remember that the phlegmatic is very fair. The melancholic adult has a very direct and firm way with discipline and this can work if one is also fair. However, in order to do so, one needs to include the phlegmatic child in the discipline process. If you perceive they have done something wrong you need to first ask them what their view of the situation is. Before one ventures into discipline, it is important to truly understand what has happened. Giving the child a chance to explain himself, is quite crucial.

The phlegmatic child is usually very honest when he knows that his voice will be heard and really listened to – even if he has done something wrong. Because a phlegmatic child is also very fair, one might also consider consulting with the child about possible consequences.

The fourth thing to remember is the deep honesty of the phlegmatic child. He does not like to lie. This makes it easy to tell whether the child is actually lying or not. As long as there is the feeling that the person speaking to him is fair and will listen, this child will almost always tell the truth. The child will only lie to protect himself from disappointing the adult or from unfair punishment. This will usually result in a guilty feeling later.

The child may then come to the adult and confess, or, if being asked later, the child will tell the truth. However, it is usually best not to accuse a phlegmatic child of lying, even if it is clear that he is. It would hurt this child deeply, since honesty is such an important value to the phlegmatic. If one is talking to a choleric and one implies that one does not really believe what the other is saying, the choleric may laugh it off and tell the truth. Accusing a phlegmatic of lying will make that person very upset. He will defend himself profusely instead of admitting he didn't tell the truth. The phlegmatic will also, most likely, over-react to whatever the conversation is about.

The fifth thing to remember with a phlegmatic child is that he has a very strong will – just as the melancholic adult has. When engaging in conversations or giving instructions, remember that these conversations could easily become a battle of "wills". Since you are the adult you will need to be the one to "back down" from these battles and re-start the conversation. As your child grows you can also teach him how to do this. However, when they are younger, and even as they grow and are learning, you must be the one to do this. They will learn from your example, so as you back up from the situation and reposition yourself, explain to them what you are doing so they can learn.

Harry, a melancholic father, was often head-to-head with Steve, his phlegmatic boy. Sometimes these conflicts would go on for days and result in Steve crying and Harry yelling. Once Harry learned to recognize the battle of the wills they were having, he was able to stop the battle and provide a good example to Steve on how this was done.

Whenever a battle of the wills would start Harry would stop and say "I would really like to talk to you about this. It looks like both of us have become frustrated so let's take some time to think about this and talk about it in an hour. OK? I would really like to talk to you about this." Other times, when the conversation could not be delayed or when Steve looked nervous about waiting, Harry would say, "I am really sorry we are not communicating well with each other now. Can we start over? Can we start by you telling me what you need?"

When the melancholic adult finds himself in a battle of wills with the phlegmatic child the adult needs to find out what was not clear to the child, what the child felt was not honest or fair, and how the conversation fit into their comfort zone.

- ## The Teaching Relationship

The phlegmatic student will benefit from the melancholic adult's motivation and organizational skills. The student will feel comforted by the learning system the adult creates and the melancholic's ability to stay on track and keep a regular rhythm.

However, the phlegmatic may have trouble with the pace the adult wants to keep with the lessons. Melancholics are sometimes driven "like a train" in the way he performs tasks. The adult may want to forge ahead with the next concept in math when the phlegmatic student is still trying to grasp the first lesson. Because the melancholic is accustomed to working and thinking in this way and he finds it comfortable and easy the adult may not understand that the student is having a hard time keeping up. Instead, the adult may perceive the student as slow, stubborn, or lacking in motivation. However, in reality, the phlegmatic student simply needs more time to absorb concepts. One must not worry about the phlegmatic student taking longer – once a phlegmatic has absorbed a concept one does not usually need to repeat oneself or re-teach the concept as one might with the choleric or sanguine student, who grasps things more quickly, but may retain less without repetition and reminders.

When a melancholic runs up against a problem he tends to push through it and out to the other end. Melancholics are so driven that they may hit their heads against the proverbial wall and actually knock it down. Because melancholic approach problems in an orderly and then forceful manner they may expect others to do the same. Even if the melancholic knows another person is not like him, he may still assume that if the person "tried hard enough" or "wanted it enough" the person would be able to be more driven and motivated to complete hard tasks. However, a phlegmatic does not function like this. A phlegmatic is like the turtle in the fable *"The Tortoise and the Hare"* – he gets through hardships at a slow and steady pace – and never gives up. If one lets a phlegmatic student have the time and encouragement he needs to solve a problem he will persevere. The adult should make and effort not only to cheer on the "rabbits" but also the "tortoises" in the classroom!

Phlegmatics are most receptive to learning when they are in familiar places and situations. Melancholics are motivated by function and purpose and as long as they have a purpose they can function in any environment. Because this is the way the melancholic functions he may become frustrated with the phlegmatic student who seems to do very well on math problems at home but has trouble with them in the car, or the phlegmatic student who spends hours in his room writing, but has trouble writing even a few sentences in class.

It may take a phlegmatic a few times to become familiar with a new place and a new situation but once he is they should be able to learn quite easily. If the melancholic adult enrolls the phlegmatic student in Tai Chi lessons at the local gym keep the adult should keep in mind that it may take the student the first six weeks of lessons just to get used to the environment. For this reason phlegmatic students do best in long term learning situations such as year-long classes or long-term study groups rather than short term learning situations like mini-courses at a local art institute or a three-day summer camp. If one wants them to be able to experience these shorter learning situations and benefit from them he needs to be patient enough to allow the student to "just listen" and not do much participating the first time they are enrolled.

I always remember Foster when I think about long-term learning versus short-term learning situations. Foster's mom, Joy knew he was interested in drawing so she enrolled him every summer in drawing classes at the local art institute. However, each summer Foster would complain he didn't want to be in the classes and would be on the verge of tears when she dropped him off. After two years of this experience and paying a few hundred dollars, Joy finally decided to give up and let him stay at home. However, when the third summer came around and he was not enrolled in the same art classes he had been the past two years Foster become visibly upset and insisted that he be allowed to participate. Joy felt like he was being uncooperative and purposefully argumentative. However, when I explained to her how the phlegmatic student needs time to get used to places and people she understood and enrolled him in the art classes for the third year in a row. Foster was very happy and didn't give his mother any trouble that summer when she dropped him off.

Not only do phlegmatics learn best in familiar situations, they also learn best when allowed to become familiar with a situation or task. When something is repeated over and over a phlegmatic will learn the task – often using the simple skill of observation. Phlegmatics can also be very private about their learning and will not display their knowledge in an obvious way. They love to be challenged and to win games and challenges. However, they will not voluntarily show off their skills. For this reason it may appear that a phlegmatic does not understand a lesson or is not listening. The only way to tell is to directly test his skills after giving the student a few days to observe and practice. A phlegmatic will most often surprise those around him with how completely he has understood new concepts when given the time and freedom to do so. However, when pressured or put on the spot the phlegmatic student's learning centers will close down causing him to be unable to learn or recall information.

- A Story to Share

With time many fables have been changed to suit the needs of the era. When Aesop took his fables and wrote them down with morals and lessons he removed an essential element from the fable – the ability to explore different angles and meanings and to honor the differences between the different characters rather than labeling one as "bad" and the other as "good". In this familiar fable of the lion and mouse the lion is often portrayed as a strong and unfair character and the mouse is often portrayed as a weak and hapless character. Additionally, the moral of the story is given in a perfunctory manner at the end of the story. What would happen instead if the story were told and each listener was allowed to explore the feelings of the lion and the mouse and allowed to justify or try to explain the actions of each? What would happen if neither the lion nor the mouse was bad and they are simply both characters in the story?

The Melancholic Lion and the Phlegmatic Mouse

Traditional Fable Adapted by Kristie Burns

There once was a Lion who loved to sleep under the same oak tree every day. He felt that it was important to take a nap at the same time every day and upon waking he would gather the animals in the jungle together and hold a meeting. Because he was so organized and filled with authority the animals of the jungle had made him king. In this same jungle there was a mouse who spent his days collecting fluff for his home and food for his family. He was a regular and peaceful presence in the forest and the other animals often smiled at how industrious and steady he was with his work. Once when the Lion was asleep, Mouse happened to run across his particular tree looking for food and without even being aware of what he was doing he began running up and down upon him, which soon awakened the Lion. The Lion placed his huge paw upon him, and opened his big jaws to swallow him.

"Pardon, O King," cried the little Mouse: "forgive me this time, I shall never forget it: who knows but what I may be able to do you a turn some of these days?"

The Lion was usually not one to let tradition go so easily. Wasn't he the king of the jungle and weren't mice meant for him to snack on? But he was so tickled at the idea of Mouse being able to help him that he lifted up his paw and let him go. Some time afterward, the Lion was caught in a trap and the hunters, who desired to carry him alive to their leader, tied him to the big oak tree while they went in search of a wagon to carry him on. Just then the Mouse happened to pass by, and seeing the sad plight in which the Lion was, soon gnawed away the ropes that bound the King of the Beasts.

When stories are told they speak to the child on a basic level. The reason one tells stories instead of explaining things to a child is because stories have the ability to adapt to the child's needs. When a person explains a situation to a child he is putting forth a concept that the child needs to grasp at or reach to understand. When one simply *tells* a story the child is given permission to understand the story in any way he wishes and to gain wisdom and knowledge from it in the way that best suits him at that moment. For that reason, it is not recommended that the story be explained to the child or that the child be provided with the ubiquitous "moral" at the end. Rather, it is best to give them a chance to enjoy the story for what it becomes to them and provide them with numerous chances to hear the story told. The stories in this book help the different temperaments understand each other. If the adult or adult would like to explore this understanding on a deeper level they can ask questions once the story is finished. However, one must be sure to ask open questions and allow the child to express his feelings.

Melancholic Adult · Sanguine Child

- ## General Relationship

The best relationships between a sanguine and melancholic are one of mutual understanding and balance. This relationship has great potential for both of them – but only if they are both open to learning from the other one. If the melancholic adult can keep her mind open to learning from the sanguine child the two can have a wonderful relationship.

The best thing about the relationship between the sanguine and the melancholic is the balance they provide each other. The sanguine seeks external balance and the melancholic provides that balance. The melancholic often can get stuck in the past and the future and the sanguine can help bring their focus back into the now. The sanguine often has trouble focusing on just one task. However, the melancholic can steer the child towards focusing on their best abilities and bring out those abilities in them. Left to her own devices the sanguine may spread herself too thin and not get a chance to focus on one or two things she could develop great skill at.

In an ideal relationship the sanguine child will enjoy the organized nature of having a melancholic adult and will thrive in that atmosphere. The child will feel secure with the adult that has set rules and values that are unchanging and easy to identify and the child will admire and perhaps even become inspired by the adult's ability to focus and become skilled at one activity. The melancholic adult will find herself doing things they may never have done before they met this sanguine child. The child will be able to bring the adult out of her world and experience new things. The melancholic will learn from the sanguine that although schedules are good, learning to "go with the flow" is sometimes the best solution and the melancholic adult will admire the sanguine's ability to regenerate and renew herself and their ability to have such diverse interests. The adult may even be inspired to try something new herself.

The main conflict between a melancholic adult and sanguine child is one of communication. Melancholics are very organized and usually traditional in their customs and habits. Because of this they are very confident when it comes to their needs and wants and they do not have any trouble communicating these needs and wants. A sanguine, on the other hand, is always growing and changing to match the current situation in their environment. The sanguine child is on a constant path of self-growth. Because of this she may not seem as confident as the adult seems. However, the sanguine can actually be very confident. Because the sanguine child is in a constant learning process the child sometimes struggles to convey this confidence or communicate who she is and what her needs are because she is spending so much time discovering that for themselves. Another trait that the sanguine has is that she loves to make people happy and to please people.

Sometimes trouble can occur when these two temperaments are combined. The melancholic adult has a very strong outwardly confident temperament who knows what her needs are and is not afraid to communicate these needs. When interacting with the sanguine child the adult will find that the child may often take the adult's requests and fill them without considering her own needs first. This is because it is of utmost important to the sanguine for those people around them to be happy so instead of taking time to think through their decision she may often say "yes" more often than She should. This can get the sanguine and melancholic into some sticky situations. A melancholic could make a large number of requests from a sanguine. As the sanguine fulfills request after request the melancholic does not notice that the sanguine is becoming or experiencing less and less of herself and more and more of the melancholic. The melancholic does not even think to ask because she may see this development as being a blessed changed in their child who is now more like her!

Over time this can create distance between the melancholic and sanguine and cause the sanguine to feel misunderstood and eventually angry. Then the melancholic can become confused by the sanguine's anger and wonder why she is angry. The adult may even feel anger towards the child because she feels that the child's anger towards her is unfair. From the adult's point of view she has been patient with the child's "strange" way of doing things and have given them a lot of leeway. The adult may even feel like the child has been holding back a little anger herself. However, once the child lets the adult know she is not happy the adult may feel indignant and angry towards the sanguine child.

This can be avoided if both adult and child work on one thing. The sanguine needs to work on identifying her needs and communicating those to others. A sanguine also needs to learn to say "no" and learn that people will still love them if they say "no". The adults may need to lead the child into learning this. When the child says "yes" the adult may need to figure out if that "yes" is really the best thing for the child. The melancholic adult can then ask the sanguine child if she really means "yes". Then the adult can communicate with the child that she needs to practice being honest about her feelings. Because the melancholic adult is so strong willed and confident the child may interpret this as frightening and may be scared to say no.

Additionally, some melancholics do err on the side of firmness and can often be frightening to many people when they become angry or determined. The melancholic may view herself as firmly standing by her standards and being motivated and true to her word. However, sometimes the behavior of the melancholic may be too intense for the other temperaments. This is not necessarily true for all melancholics but it is something to watch out for.

The melancholic person should watch out for signs that the person she is talking too feels apprehensive or frightened. If this happens the melancholic must ask herself why or ask a friend why and try to learn what mannerisms and word choices she is making that may be frightening. As the sanguine needs to take responsibility for being more direct and firm in their communication, the melancholic needs to take responsibility for providing an easier forum for the child to do this. The melancholic can learn to listen more and instruct less. If this can happen the relationship with the sanguine child will be much more enriching for both the adult and child.

- ## Helping the Melancholic Adult Understand the Sanguine Child

The sanguine child lives in the now and follows her own rhythm. A melancholic is accustomed to exploring experiences of the past and planning diligently for the future. However, to a sanguine, the only thing that is "real" is what is happening now or in the near future. A melancholic, on the other hand, has a natural rhythmic clock that is somewhat like a steady tempo or drum beat. The melancholic person may even go to sleep at the same time every day and eat at the exact same time every day. However, a sanguine's rhythm is deeply connected to nature itself. The sanguine rhythm follows that of the seasons as well as the moon. The sanguine may have more or less motivation depending on the time of month, the time of day or the season. She may have a lot of energy one day and less the next day. This may see completely random to the likes of the steady melancholic. However, if this is seen as random it only creates more frustration for the melancholic adult and less understanding.

To best understand the sanguine child it is most efficient to try to understand what her cycles are and how they work. Usually a sanguine is affected by outside influences quite easily. A sanguine may change moods due to a food they ate or a party they attended. If the melancholic adult can make a list or observe when and why these changes happen in the child, she is not only on the road to understanding the child better, but also on the road to helping the understand herself better.

Remember, a sanguine child lives in the now, so it often takes her some extra time to get to know herself because each time she is in a different mood she thinks that mood is who she is or she thinks that mood is "forever". By observing patterns in the sanguine child the adult will start to see that there is a method to the outward appearance of constant change. The sanguine child may appear to change randomly, however, in reality, there is usually a reason.

It is a good idea to start helping a sanguine child guide themselves at a young age. For example, if the adult notices that the sanguine child becomes moody every time they eat bread (perhaps they cannot digest it well) then the adult would want to mention that to the child so that over time, the child is able to make better nutritional decisions. A sanguine loves to be in control and learn her own lessons in life so it is usually better to gently guide her over a long period of time rather than suddenly trying to teach her something in a short period of time.

If the melancholic notices that the sanguine child is always less motivated in the winter time the adult may want to plan fewer extracurricular activities for that child during this time. If the adult notices that the child usually needs a lot of time alone after attending a party the adult may want to plan this into the schedule as well and make sure she doesn't plan for the child to attend two social events in a row. If the adult notices that the sanguine is always more active in the evening time she may also want to take that into account. As the melancholic adult makes these observations it is useful to share them gently with the child. After age seven the adult can start by simply sharing the observation. She can say, "Did you notice that every time it is evening time you are very active? What do you think of that? Have you noticed that?" After a year of sharing observations the melancholic adult can start asking her to share some observations as well. The next step is to integrate these observations into action. The adult could say, "You are usually pretty tired after attending a party. How about we plan to go shopping another day?" or "You usually have a lot of energy during the springtime – would you like to plan to build something with me then?"

At this point, any melancholic adult reading this is probably loudly protesting and thinking about how life cannot always be adapted to the needs of the sanguine and how life just doesn't work like that. They are right. Learning about the sanguine child needs to be a balance between teaching oneself and others to understand the child and also teaching the child to function with the expectations of a fast-paced schedule-based society. The way to do this is to provide an outside structure for the sanguine. Because her inner structure is so in-tune with nature, emotions and events around her, she actually responds quite well when someone else provides her with an external structure or system of organization.

• Helping the Sanguine Child Understand the Melancholic Adult

Because the sanguine child lives in the now and is motivated by inspiration rather than time, the child may interpret the melancholic's way of functioning as very harsh and demanding. Because a sanguine child does not hold onto emotions for a long time the child may not understand why the melancholic does and may be confused as to why the adult is angry in the evening when "what the child did" happened in the morning. The sanguine child may even have forgotten about it by then. Because a sanguine is very eager to please and wants people to be happy she may not understand why the melancholic adult demands so much of her. The overall impression a sanguine has of a melancholic adult or adult can be one of harshness.

To help the child understand the melancholic adult, the melancholic will need to know what things about her may frighten the child, confuse the child or frustrate the sanguine child and take the time to soften those parts of herself or explain those parts of herself in a language the child can understand. This is very important – the melancholic must explain it in a language the sanguine child can understand – not just explain it.

Ted, a melancholic father and Katie, a sanguine daughter, benefited from reflecting on this concept. Ted always insisted that Katie bring home good grades. Ted felt that Katie became frightened and stressed by this demand but did not know what to do. It confused him that Katie seemed scared of him. Ted didn't think he was very scary at all!

I explained to Ted that the right thing to do was to explain to Katie why he insisted on such good grades. So Ted took Katie aside one day and said, "I want to let you know why I have been so hard on you. I want you to be well educated and have opportunities in the future and have more choices in life." Katie, of course, didn't relate to what Ted was saying at all because he was talking about the future. The sanguine person lives in the now. I explained to Ted that a better way to explain the caring and concern he had as an adult would be to say something like, "I know you have really been working hard on this paper you wrote. You have done such a good job and I really want the adult to reward you with the grade you deserve tomorrow. Can I take a look at the paper and help you with some final edits? Perhaps I can catch something you didn't. I could be a pretend editor just like if you worked as a journalist for a magazine (sanguine always like the element of play)." This way, Ted is still accomplishing what his goal is, while at the same time relating to Katie, the sanguine child, in a more effective way. Ted wanted to help Katie get better grades but she didn't need to see the big picture that he saw as a melancholic – Katie only needed to see each incident as it happened along the way.

Speaking to the sanguine in terms of the "now" will help keep her focused and enthusiastic. This will also help her self-confidence. When the melancholic adult focuses on each issue as it comes up the sanguine child has a chance to succeed each time the adult talks to them and this is very important to the sanguine as they thrive with verbal acknowledgement and reward.

In the case of Ted and Katie he was asking his child to bring home A's at the end of the semester. This only gave Katie one chance to be congratulated. For a sanguine this is not enough and the wait is too long. If one were to ask the sanguine child to succeed each time she has an assignment this provides numerous opportunities for the child to be complimented on her work as well as a shorter wait time in-between those feedback interactions the child so desperately needs.

Another way the melancholic adult can help the sanguine child to understand her/him is to share what she loves with the child. The sanguine child may not understand that the adult actually loves organization and order. The child may not understand the melancholic adult has a love for a certain religion, culture or tradition. All the sanguine child sees is that the melancholic adult insisting on the child becoming involved in those. However, if the child can see the adult's emotional attachment and enthusiasm for those things the child will be able to relate to them more easily and may even be more inclined to participate and become part of the melancholic adult's world. A sanguine relates to things on an emotional level in many ways. If one can attach an emotion to a request and desire this can help the sanguine understand more clearly. Of course, for a melancholic, this is not the usual way of thinking. The melancholic does not usually attach emotion to everything. However, the adult can choose to think of this as a spiritual practice or a self-growth exercise. The melancholic adult may not be comfortable attaching emotions to different things she enjoys or does. To a melancholic, much of life one "just does" and that is the way it is. However, the melancholic may find that exploring those emotions she has for the people and traditions in her life may help her relationships with everyone – not just the sanguine child.

- ## Discipline

Good discipline always stems from a sense of trust, love and harmony between the adult and child. The more the adult and child understand and respect each other, the more discipline happens naturally. To have a healthy discipline relationship with the sanguine child the melancholic adult should first read the sections above on how to best understand the child and how to help the child understand the adult.

To the melancholic adult it may often seem "logical" that certain things need to be done. Melancholics often follow tradition in some way. Perhaps she does things the way her adults did or the way her religion does or perhaps the melancholic follows social rules carefully. Whatever system the melancholic follows it is most likely she does follow a system. This is why it may be hard for her to understand that the sanguine does not necessarily follow this same system. An essential part of discipline is the understanding of why a child does what she is doing. It is only then that one can attempt to communicate with the child about the topic.

An essential part to getting along with the sanguine child is the understanding that she does not, will not and will most likely never follow the melancholic system. The sanguine *can* learn the system and learn to respect it. If the adult requires the child to perform certain tasks (like attending religious services every Sunday or wearing ties to certain events) she can certainly require this of the child and if done in a respectful manner, the sanguine child will be happy to comply. However, she will most likely not be enthusiastic or inspired or self-motivated into following these expectations. This is where the two keys to sanguine discipline come in:

1. One must realize that the sanguine child is not naturally going to follow another system. The melancholic adult should not take offense by this or think the child is being difficult or defying the melancholic on purpose. Instead, the adult can realize that she will need to let the sanguine know what the rules are (of the system) and let her know which rules she needs to follow (if the adult expects the child to wear a dress to Sunday School or to always shake hands when greeted, for example). The melancholic adult should let the child know that it would really mean a lot to the adult if the child could follow some of these rule.. A sanguine loves to make people

happy and especially loves to be told someone is proud of them. If the melancholic expects the sanguine to follow the rules and then is shocked and upset when the child does not, the child will wilt and become depressed and perhaps angry and defiant. If the melancholic simply asks nicely the sanguine will fall over herself to please the adult.

2. The second tip is that one must learn to respect the natural rhythms of the sanguine and learn to "choose her battles". For example, if the child would rather wear pants to Sunday school instead of a dress, which is traditional in the melancholic adult's mind, the melancholic must ask herself if that is something she wants to argue with the child about or if she would you rather save her special requests for another topic?

A sanguine has a mind of her own and her own way of doing things. She is happy to please others and this is one of her pleasures in life. However, the sanguine does have limits. If asked to do too many things using a different system than her own the sanguine will become frustrated and feel trapped. If a sanguine becomes uncooperative then the melancholic adult should take a look at the demands she has been making of the sanguine child. Usually, a sanguine is very cooperative. When she is not, it usually means they are overwhelmed in some area of her life.

- ## The Teaching Relationship

The sanguine naturally functions very well when given unlimited amounts of time and resources. However, if there are time-based expectations (for example, the student needs to finish an assignment by a certain time) the student will not do well setting those deadlines for themselves. However, the student will excel if the melancholic adult sets those deadlines for the student. One should not expect a sanguine to say "I will finish that assignment by Friday." A sanguine will say "Oh yes! I will finish that assignment." When the student does finally finish it, it may be a year later, but it will be the best assignment anyone has ever seen and the student will have enjoyed every inspired moment of doing it. If the adult actually wants to see the assignment by Friday she needs to say "Please turn in this assignment by Friday" and the student will happily do so. Understanding this can save a lot of anguish for the melancholic adult. The melancholic is accustomed to creating her own schedule and may think that the sanguine is being lazy, unmotivated, or not very committed to her ideals when she refuses to create schedules and set deadlines. This is not the case. A sanguine is a very hard worker, is very motivated and is very dedicated. However, only when a gentle external schedule is set or when completely allowed to move and function according to her own internal rhythm.

Another important thing to remember with a sanguine student is that she is more motivated by the now than the future. It will be easier for the melancholic adult to get them to participate and work if the adult says "let's do this now!" rather than "let's do this in two weeks". So, for example, if the melancholic adult purchased tickets to an amazing show in two weeks but plans on going to the library today, the sanguine student may actually seem to be more excited and motivated about the trip to the library. This is not because the student likes the library better than the show, it is simply because the sanguine student likes anything that is happening "now" better than anything that will happen in the future or has already happened.

- ## A Story to Share

When stories are told they speak to the child on a basic level. The reason one tells stories instead of explaining things to a child is because stories have the ability to adapt to the child's needs. When a person explains a situation to a child she is putting forth a concept that the child needs to grasp at or reach to understand. When one simply *tells* a story the child is given permission to understand the story in any way she wishes and to gain wisdom and knowledge from it in the way that best suits her at that moment. For that reason, it is not recommended that the story be explained to the child or that the child be provided with the ubiquitous "moral" at the end. Rather, it is best to give them a chance to enjoy the story for what it becomes to them and provide them with numerous chances to hear the story told. The stories in this book help the different temperaments understand each other. If the adult or adult would like to explore this understanding on a deeper level they can ask questions once the story is finished. However, one must be sure to ask open questions and allow the child to express her feelings.

The following story is about a sanguine child who has a melancholic mother and grandmother. What can you tell about the differences between the sanguine and the melancholic temperaments from this story? What can the mother and grandmother learn from Little Red? What can Little Red learn from her mother and grandmother?

Little Red-Cap

Grimm's Fairytales

Once on a time there was a dear little girl who was loved by everyone who looked at her, but most of all by her grandmother, and there was nothing that she would not have given to the child. Once she gave her a little cap of red velvet, which suited her so well that she would never wear anything else; so she was always called "Little Red-Cap."

One day her mother said to her, "Come, Little Red-Cap, here is a piece of cake and a pot of herbal tea; take them to your grandmother, she is ill and weak, and they will do her well. Set out before it gets hot, and when you are going, walk nicely and quietly and do not run off the path, or you may fall and break the pot, and then your grandmother will get nothing; and when you go into her room, don't forget to say, 'Good-morning,' and don't peep into every corner before you do it."

78

"I will take great care," said Little Red-Cap to her mother, and gave her hand on it.

The grandmother lived out in the wood, half a league from the village, and just as Little Red-Cap entered the wood, a wolf met her. Red-Cap did not know what a wicked creature he was, and was not at all afraid of him. On the contrary – she was curious! Little Red Cap loved to explore the woods and discover all the different animals and plants that lived there. She considered all the animals and plants in the woods her friends and would often stop to discover new ones on her walks.

"Good-day, Little Red-Cap," said he.

"Thank you kindly, wolf."

"Where away so early, Little Red-Cap?"

"To my grandmother's. She is not feeling well and yet she is accustomed to having her lunch at the same time each day so I must bring her a meal or she will not eat and she will feel even more ill."

"What have you got in your apron?"

"Cake and tea; yesterday was baking-day, so poor sick grandmother is to have something good, to make her stronger."

"Where does your grandmother live, Little Red-Cap?"

"A good quarter of a league farther on in the wood; her house stands under the three large oak-trees, the nut-trees are just below; you surely must know it," replied Little Red-Cap.

The wolf thought to himself, "What a tender young creature! what a nice plump mouthful — she will be better to eat than the old woman. I must act craftily, so as to catch both."

So he walked for a short time by the side of Little Red-Cap, and then he said, "See Little Red-Cap, how pretty the flowers are about here — why do you not look round? I believe, too, that you do not hear how sweetly the little birds are singing; you walk gravely along as if you were going to school, while everything else out here in the wood is merry."

Little Red-Cap raised her eyes, and when she saw the sunbeams dancing here and there through the trees, and pretty flowers growing everywhere, she thought, "Suppose I take grandmother a fresh nosegay; that would please her too. It is so early in the day that I shall still get there in good time;" and so she ran from the path into the wood to look for flowers. And whenever she had picked one, she fancied that she saw a still prettier one farther on, and ran after it, and so got deeper and deeper into the wood like a little butterfly following a delicious trail of nectar.

Meanwhile the wolf ran straight to the grandmother's house and knocked at the door.

"Who is there? Do you have an appointment?"

"Little Red-Cap," replied the wolf. "She is bringing cake and tea; open the door."

"Lift the latch," called out the grandmother, "I am too weak, and cannot get up. However, be sure to close the door after yourself and make sure you do not track in any muddy footprints."

The wolf lifted the latch, the door flew open, and without saying a word he went straight to the grandmother's bed, and devoured her (don't worry she comes out alive later ;) Then he put on her clothes, dressed himself in her cap, laid himself in bed and drew the curtains.

Little Red-Cap, however, had been running about picking flowers, and when she had gathered so many that she could carry no more, she remembered her grandmother, and set out on the way to her.

She was surprised to find the cottage-door standing open. Her grandmother was always very organized and always made sure things were in order and done correctly. Furthermore, when she went into the room, she had such a strange feeling that she said to herself, "Oh dear! how uneasy I feel today, and at other times I like being with grandmother so much."

She called out, "Good morning," but received no answer; so she went to the bed and drew back the curtains. There lay her grandmother with her cap pulled far over her face, and looking very strange.

"Oh! grandmother," she said, "what big ears you have!"

"The better to hear you with, my child," was the reply.

"But, grandmother, what big eyes you have!" she said.

"The better to see you with, my dear."

"But, grandmother, what large hands you have!"

"The better to hug you with."

"Oh! but, grandmother, what a terrible big mouth you have!"

"The better to eat you with!"

And scarcely had the wolf said this, than with one bound he was out of bed and swallowed up Red-Cap.

When the wolf had appeased his appetite, he lay down again in the bed, fell asleep and began to snore very loud. The huntsman was just passing the house, and thought to himself, "How the old woman is snoring! I must just see if she wants anything."

So he went into the room, and when he came to the bed, he saw that the wolf was lying in it.

"Do I find you here, you old sinner!" said he. "I have long sought you!" Then just as he was going to fire at him, it occurred to him that the wolf might have devoured the grandmother, and that she might still be saved, so he did not fire, but took a pair of scissors, and began to cut open the stomach of the sleeping wolf. When he had made two snips, he saw the little Red-Cap shining, and then he made two snips more, and the little girl sprang out, crying, "Ah, how frightened I have been! How dark it was inside the wolf," and after that the aged grandmother came out alive also, but scarcely able to breathe. Red-Cap, however, quickly fetched great stones with which they filled the wolf's body, and when he awoke, he wanted to run away, but the stones were so heavy that he fell down at once, and fell dead.

Then all three were delighted. The huntsman drew off the wolf's skin and went home with it; the grandmother ate the cake and drank the tea which Red-Cap had brought, and revived, but Red-Cap thought to herself, "As long as I live, I will never by myself leave the path, to run into the wood, when my mother has forbidden me to do so."

It is also related that once when Red-Cap was again taking cakes to the old grandmother, another wolf spoke to her, and tried to entice her from the path. Red-Cap, however, was on her guard, and went straight forward on her way, and told her grandmother that she had met the wolf, and that he had said "good-morning" to her, but with such a wicked look in his eyes, that if they had not been on the public road she was certain he would have eaten her up.

"Well," said the grandmother, "we will shut the door, that he may not come in."

Soon afterwards the wolf knocked, and cried, "Open the door, grandmother, I am little Red-Cap, and am fetching you some cakes."

But they did not speak, or open the door, so the grey-beard stole twice or thrice round the house, and at last jumped on the roof, intending to wait till Red-Cap went home in the evening, and then to steal after her and devour her in the darkness. But the grandmother saw what was in his thoughts. In front of the house was a great stone trough, so she said to the child, "Take the pail, Red-Cap; I made some sausages yesterday, so carry the water in which I boiled them to the trough." Red-Cap carried till the great trough was quite full. Then the smell of the sausages reached the wolf, and he sniffed and peeped down, and at last stretched out his neck so far that he could no longer keep his footing and began to slip, and slipped down from the roof straight into the great trough, and was drowned. But Red-Cap went joyously home, and never did anything to harm anyone.

Melancholic Adult - Choleric Child

- ## General Relationship

The general relationship between the melancholic adult and the choleric child is one of mutual respect and admiration mixed in with a bit of apprehension about the other person. Each is aware of the other's confidence and strong will. However, the two temperaments are different in so many ways that they each present a puzzle to each other. How they choose to solve that puzzle will determine how their relationship progresses.

One particular thing that the melancholic adult appreciates about the choleric child is that he is very clear with his needs, wants and opinions. The melancholic adult may not agree with the child but he cannot help admiring the child's dedication to the path he has chosen. Similarly, the choleric child may disagree with much of what the melancholic adult says, but will always maintain a healthy level of respect for his confidence.

- ## Helping the Melancholic Adult Understand the Choleric Child

The Melancholic adult usually expects that people around them will perform their duties and tasks without complaint and as a matter of fact. In the world of the melancholic there is little room for emotion in the completion of these tasks. A task is completed because it must be done and not because one feels like doing it or because one is inspired in some way. Thus, when the melancholic adult observes the choleric child's high energy, skillful social demeanor and ability to accomplish many tasks, the adult may assume the child's motivations are similar to hiss. A melancholic adult may then speak to the choleric child in the language of the melancholic, assuming the child will understand. However, the choleric child is motivated by inspiration and not by a sense of duty. The melancholic adult will be able to understand and communicate with the choleric child more effectively when they appeal to the child's sense of inspiration instead of his sense of duty.

The choleric child is very confident and certain about his needs, wants, desires, and opinions. One choleric child I worked with was actually able to shop for her own clothing when she was only two years old and verbalize the reasons for her fashion choices. Another choleric child I had in one of my first classes always knew exactly which craft she wanted to work on when she came to class and would head straight for her craft basket when she arrived.

Choleric children express themselves most often through the emotion of delight or elation. However, when he is imbalanced or experiencing an exaggeration of his temperament he can also express anger in the form of temper tantrums. A melancholic adult may struggle to understand this as the emotion of delight is a frivolous one to the melancholic adult and not an emotion that can motivate or inspire. For the melancholic adult, joy is the frosting on the cake. For the choleric child joy *is* the cake. The melancholic adult needs to recognize the validity of the choleric child's emotions and realize that his expressions of joy are important and essential to whom the child is and not just extra emotions that happen in passing. This realization will help the melancholic adult understand the choleric child on a much deeper level. Without this essential understanding the melancholic adult will just be skimming the surface.

The melancholic adult is fulfilled by completing tasks and often feels fulfilled when those tasks have been completed. The choleric child, on the other hand, does not often feel satiated and instead, seems to be constantly seeking fulfillment.

The choleric child is naturally charismatic because he sincerely enjoys other people and is often very intuitively tuned in to the social environment he is in. The melancholic adult may observe the child charming so many people, however, and may view him as manipulative rather than sincere. The melancholic adult finds more pleasure in seeking people like himself, rather than seeking to fit into a social group. He feels that all actions should have meaning. Because of this, the melancholic adult may assume that the choleric must be purposefully saying and doing certain things to get what he wants. The melancholic adult can rest assured that the choleric child is completely sincere and is not being manipulative. The choleric simply has an instinctive skill which allows him to easily discern a person's needs, and he has an innate desire to meet those needs.

The choleric child is often seeking excitement. This may upset the melancholic adult, as they feel that excitement is an extreme emotion that upsets the balance of things. The melancholic adult prefers to live a life of moderation, so the energy seeking choleric may make the adult uncomfortable. The melancholic adult feels that it is always best to seek the moderate ground concerning actions and emotions. However, he needs to realize that the choleric will find his own moderate ground by balancing experiences and emotions, rather than keeping them at an even keel. For example, a choleric may attend a noisy party with friends, and then return home and read a book quietly in his room. This is the choleric's natural way of balancing.

Another intense choleric trait, often disturbing to the melancholic adult, is the child's propensity to explore space. To the well-earthed melancholic, the choleric child may seem like an earthquake. This trait may seem less disturbing to the melancholic adult if he can understand that the choleric child is actually learning about people, places and things through where they are in space. The movement of the choleric is not a destructive force, but rather movement with the purpose of gathering sensory input.

This need the choleric has to explore space is also apparent in the way the child uses the space around himself. The melancholic has a strong sense of organization, but may perceive that the choleric does not because he can often be seen with papers strewn around himself or several projects spread out on the table before them. The choleric child may have a room crowded with knick-knacks, books, clothing and school supplies that seem to be strewn all around carelessly. However, this stems from the same process mentioned above – the choleric child learns through exploring space and must organize things out in the open where they can be seen. The piles that appear to be disorganized actually look orderly to the choleric child who perceives the world from a different point of view. If one asks the choleric child where a paper is in what appears to be a disorganized desk, the child will most likely be able to find the paper immediately. My favorite quote from a choleric child is, "I didn't leave my coat on the floor of my bedroom. That is the corner where I keep it. It belongs there!"

The choleric child always freely shares his emotions and feelings. Because of this transparency, the melancholic adult may be tempted to use the information he gathers to try to "fix" the choleric child in some way. After all, the choleric child has been very open about everything so now, the melancholic adult has all the information he needs to create an improvement program – right? The melancholic adult may also feel that the emotions being expressed by the choleric child cannot be genuine as they appear so exaggerated and numerous.

However, the choleric child does not need to be fixed and will feel betrayed if his feelings are used in such a manner. The melancholic adult should be respectful of the choleric child's emotions and feelings and treat them with great care. It may seem that they are not as valuable as those which are kept safely hidden and protected. However, the choleric does not share openly because he does not value his emotions. The choleric shares freely because that is how he connects with people around him.

The melancholic adult experiences life through physical touch and can often connect more deeply with someone or something when he uses the sense of touch. The choleric child enjoys physical contact and will usually be receptive to hugs, tickle games and snuggles. This physical rapport can help foster a deeper connection between the melancholic adult and the choleric child. The melancholic adult should be careful not to miss these opportunities to connect as this form of communication may be the one that the adult and child have most in common. The melancholic adult can make a further effort to connect in this way by touching the child's shoulder when talking to him, and displaying other signs of affection such as ruffling the hair or giving goodnight kisses on the cheek.

The choleric child is often able to see the humorous side of life and may respond to many statements with a joke, a giggle or a funny comment. This is the choleric's way of processing information and does not indicate that he is not taking the statements seriously.

The choleric child is truly compassionate, empathetic and emotionally sensitive to those around him. Because these emotions are mixed in with so many other emotions the melancholic adult may not recognize these gems. In fact, some of these expressions may even be difficult for the melancholic to comprehend. In the melancholic adult's world it is hard to imagine that the quality of compassion can exist side by side with the quality of self-centeredness and that the attribute of empathy can exist along with covetousness. However, in the world of the choleric all these are real. The melancholic adult must be careful not to feel that one negative attribute of the choleric "cancels out" the more positive aspects of the choleric child's temperament.

• Helping the Choleric Child Understand the Melancholic Adult

A choleric child can often be overheard saying, "that is not fair" about something the melancholic adult does. That is because fairness in the world of the choleric child is defined by how often he receives what he wants, while the melancholic adult is not one to cater to desires. The choleric does not define fairness in such a way because he is greedy. The choleric child simply sees the world as a limitless place where everyone gives and receives generously and cannot understand, therefore, why everyone cannot have what they want at all times.

Additionally, the melancholic adult always strives to be fair. If the choleric child uses this phrase it may upset the adult. The choleric child may have a better understanding of the adult if he can understand that the melancholic adult has a different definition of "fair". To the melancholic adult "fair" means equal. A melancholic adult will always strive to make sure that each person in his life receives equal attention, gifts and consideration. If a melancholic adult sees that there is a greater need in a person, such as a relative who has lost a job or a child that is ill, the melancholic adult will feel obliged to focus his attention on that person in need. This does not mean that the melancholic adult is not considering the needs of the choleric child. The choleric child can benefit from trying to understand this different concept of fairness, as it could help him balance his own temperament.

The melancholic adult may appear very serious and stern to a choleric child. This is because the choleric child defines goodness as laughter, joy and smiles. However, the melancholic adult does not often laugh or express great delight as he is more moderate with emotion. Additionally, the melancholic adult most easily identifies with the emotion of melancholy. Thus, if the choleric child expresses grief, disappointment or sadness those emotions will register more clearly with the melancholic adult than the emotions of joy and happiness the child expresses. The end result may be that the melancholic adult feels that the choleric child is "always complaining" or "never happy". The choleric child will be confused at these accusations and feel insecure about expressing emotions if he does not understand the adult's method of digesting information. The choleric child may not have the ability to alter his method of speaking at such a young age. However, the simple understanding of the melancholic's point of view can help the child not take the accusations so personally. Additionally, a choleric child can often be very empathetic and may actually be able to adapt his way of speaking at a very young age once he becomes aware of how the melancholic adult is hearing him. The skill of social adaption is very prominent in choleric children, even in children as young as the age of three.

The melancholic adult considers order and organization of the utmost importance. The melancholic adult is also most at ease when he is in control of the environment he is in. Thus, the choleric child's visual way of organizing items may be disturbing to the melancholic who prefers to organize things in a compartmentalized manner. Throughout his life, the choleric child may often find this resistance to his non-traditional method of organization. For this reason it is healthy to let the choleric child know from a young age that it is OK to have a different method of doing things. There are many folk-tales and fairy-tales that have this theme. My favorite is a traditional African tale called, *"Ten for the Princess"*.

Ten for the Princess

Traditional African Tale Adapted by Kristie Burns

The lion, the king of the jungle, needed to find a suitable successor for his crown and thus a suitable husband for his daughter. Many a lion had come to court his daughter but he had been disappointed in each one and none seemed suitable for leadership.

One day it occurred to him that perhaps he would find suitable leadership outside of the lion clan. So much to the shock and chagrin of the lion community he declared that he would hold a contest for his daughter and for his position on the throne.

All of the jungle animals arrived on the appointed day and each were eager for a place in the contest. When they arrived the king requested that each animal clan choose the best leader among them to compete. After some decision making one rhino, one giraffe, and one elephant came forward. The remainder of the jungle animals declined to enter the contest as they were intimidated by the larger animals that had entered before them. However, right before the king announced the beginning of the contest a small jungle mouse came forward and declared his intentions. All the jungle animals chuckled but it did make the contest at least more amusing.

The king then announced the rules:

"I will toss the royal crown into the air and whoever can count to ten before it falls may keep the crown and the princess."

The giraffe laughed. He was certain that being the tallest he would win the contest because he would be able to catch the crown so easily with his long neck so he decided to volunteer to go first so as to end the contest early.

The king tossed his crown in the air and the giraffe elegantly bent his neck to catch it while counting, "1-2-3-4-5-6...." Then the crown fell to the ground. The giraffe looked visibly surprised and walked away quickly to allow the next contestant to try.

The rhino was sure he would win since his horn provided such a great way to catch the crown and he had seen that the giraffe was so tall that although he had a long neck he had actually been too high to catch the crown in time.

The king tossed the crown a second time. The rhino counted more quickly than the giraffe and waited, "1-2-3-4-5-6-7..." Then the crown fell to the ground. The rhino stormed off through the forest, knocking over a couple trees in the process. The princess sighed with relief.

The elephant stepped forward next with a knowing grin. He would use his trunk to catch the crown as close to the ground as possible. So the elephant put his trunk on the ground and started counting as soon as the crown was tossed, "1-2-3-4-5-6-7-8...." Then the crown fell. The elephant was devastated.

The king then nodded to the small mouse and tossed the crown one last time. The mouse placed himself under the path of the falling crown, hoping it would fall around him and not on him, and counted, "FIVE-TEN!" The crown fell with the mouse exactly in the middle of it and the king exclaimed he was the winner.

The animals protested loudly, "But he CHEATED! He didn't say all the other numbers."

The king replied, "Ah, but my instructions were not to say all the other numbers. I simply said that one must count to ten. And there is more than one way to count to ten. The mouse counted by 5's."

The melancholic adult is very careful and methodical in his actions. The melancholic adult is also very moderate and careful in the way he speaks. To the choleric child this may seem distant or it may seem as if the adult does not have emotions at all. The choleric child is very expressive and open about actions and emotions so, subtle ones may not register on his scale. The choleric child needs to meditate on the actions and expressions of the melancholic adult to better understand him. There are a number of games that can be used to foster this ability and practice between the choleric child and melancholic adult. One such game is called "Two Truths and a Trick". This game will help foster an open mind and sense of humor in the melancholic adult and will help the choleric child learn the skill of listening more carefully. It will also teach the choleric child a lot about the adult. The choleric child will love the creativity and humor of this game.

Two Truths and A Trick

The adult and child can take turns being the storyteller in this game. The first storyteller stands up or sits on a chair and tells the listener three things about himself. Three examples may be:

"Once when I was a little girl I ate a worm."

"When I was five years old I liked to drink coffee when my mom accidentally left it on the table."

"As a child I could eat more than any of my older brothers and sisters and never gain any weight."

One of the above is a trick to see if the other person can figure out that it is just a silly story that was made up. The listener needs to guess which story is a trick.

The melancholic adult is motivated by the process of transformation and making things the best they can be. The choleric child may understand this to mean that he is not good enough and it may even seem that the melancholic adult is impossible to please! However, this is not what the adult intends. The choleric child can feel more secure with the melancholic adult if he can understand that each word the melancholic adult says has great significance. Thus, if a melancholic adult says that they enjoyed the piano piece played by the choleric child this means that the adult enjoyed it immensely and will always enjoy every time the child plays it for the next few weeks. The choleric child may find it useful to keep a memory notebook called "Things my Mommy Loves about Me". The melancholic adult can create this notebook for the child and encourage him to add to it with pictures, colors, words and poems when he is inspired to do so.

A melancholic adult's strength lies in his ability to care for and protect the family. This story is a delightful example of that strength and may help the choleric child appreciate this trait in his melancholic adult. Stories such as this are important for the choleric child to hear. The choleric child naturally appreciates those things that are expressive and sensational. Stories that lend glamour to basic parental functions are helpful to the choleric child. For example, one does not usually applaud an adult for saying, "Be careful crossing the street". This statement is not full of a lot of glamour. However, in the following story, statements like this make the adult a hero.

The Wolf and the Seven Young Kids

Grimm's Fairytales

There was once on a time an old goat who had seven little kids, and loved them with all the love of a mother for her children. One day she wanted to go into the forest and fetch some food. So she called all seven to her and said, "Dear children, I have to go into the forest, be on your guard against the wolf; if he come in, he will devour you all — skin, hair, and all. The wretch often disguises himself, but you will know him at once by his rough voice and his black feet."

The kids said, "Dear mother, we will take good care of ourselves; you may go away without any anxiety."

Then the old one bleated, and went on her way with an easy mind.

It was not long before some one knocked at the house-door and called, "Open the door, dear children; your mother is here, and has brought something back with her for each of you."

But the little kids knew that it was the wolf, by the rough voice; "We will not open the door," cried they, "you are not our mother. She has a soft, pleasant voice, but your voice is rough; you are the wolf!" Then the wolf went away to a shopkeeper and bought himself a great lump of chalk, ate this and made his voice soft with it. The he came back, knocked at the door of the house, and cried, "Open the door, dear children, your mother is here and has brought something back with her for each of you."

But the wolf had laid his black paws against the window, and the children saw them and cried, "We will not open the door, our mother has not black feet like you; you are the wolf."

Then the wolf ran to a baker and said, "I have hurt my feet, rub some dough over them for me."

And when the baker had rubbed his feet over, he ran to the miller and said, "Strew some white meal over my feet for me."

The miller thought to himself, "The wolf wants to deceive someone," and refused; but the wolf said, "If you will not do it, I will devour you."

Then the miller was afraid, and made his paws white for him. Truly men are like that.

So now the wretch went for the third time to the house-door, knocked at it and said, "Open the door for me, children, your dear little mother has come home, and has brought every one of you something back from the forest with her."

The little kids cried, "First show us your paws that we may know if you are our dear little mother."

Then he put his paws in through the window, and when the kids saw that they were white, they believed that all he said was true, and opened the door. But who should come in but the wolf! They were terrified and wanted to hide themselves. One sprang under the table, the second into the bed, the third into the stove, the fourth into the kitchen, the fifth into the cupboard, the sixth under the washing-bowl, and the seventh into the clock-case. But the wolf found them all, and used no great ceremony; one after the other he swallowed them down his throat. The youngest, who was in the clock-case, was the only one he did not find. When the wolf had satisfied his appetite he took himself off, laid himself down under a tree in the green meadow outside, and began to sleep. Soon afterwards the old goat came home again from the forest. Ah! What a sight she saw there! The house-door stood wide open. The table, chairs, and benches were thrown down, the washing-bowl lay broken to pieces, and the quilts and pillows were pulled off the bed. She sought her children, but they were nowhere to be found. She called them one after another by name, but no one answered. At last, when she came to the youngest, a soft voice cried, "Dear mother, I am in the clock-case."

She took the kid out, and it told her that the wolf had come and had eaten all the others. Then you may imagine how she wept over her poor children.

At length in her grief she went out, and the youngest kid ran with her. When they came to the meadow, there lay the wolf by the tree and snored so loud that the branches shook. She looked at him on every side and saw that something was moving and struggling in his gorged belly.

"Ah, heavens," said she, "is it possible that my poor children whom he has swallowed down for his supper, can be still alive?" Then the kid had to run home and fetch scissors, and a needle and thread, and the goat cut open the monster's stomach, and hardly had she make one cut, than one little kid thrust its head out, and when she cut farther, all six sprang out one after another, and were all still alive, and had suffered no injury whatever, for in his greediness the monster had swallowed them down whole. What rejoicing there was! They embraced their dear mother, and jumped like a sailor at his wedding. The mother, however, said, "Now go and look for some big stones, and we will fill the wicked beast's stomach with them while he is still asleep."

Then the seven kids dragged the stones there with all speed, and put as many of them into his stomach as they could get in; and the mother sewed him up again in the greatest haste, so that he was not aware of anything and never once stirred.

When the wolf at length had had his sleep out, he got on his legs, and as the stones in his stomach made him very thirsty, he wanted to go to a well to drink.

91

But when he began to walk and move about, the stones in his stomach knocked against each other and rattled. Then cried he,

"What rumbles and tumbles
Against my poor bones?
I thought 't was six kids,
But it's naught but big stones."

And when he got to the well and stooped over the water and was just about to drink, the heavy stones made him fall in, and there was no help, but he had to drown miserably. When the seven kids saw that, they came running to the spot and cried aloud, "The wolf is dead! The wolf is dead!" and danced for joy round about the well with their mother.

- Discipline

Good discipline always stems from a sense of trust, love, and harmony between the adult and child. The more they understand and respect each other, the more naturally discipline happens. To establish and maintain a healthy relationship with the choleric child, including the art of discipline, the melancholic adult should first read the sections above covering how to best understand the choleric child and how to help the child understand him.

In discipline and communication it can often seem like the melancholic adult is constantly trying to "rein in" the choleric child. The image that comes to mind is one of puppies in a basket. The melancholic adult is struggling to keep all the puppies inside of the basket but each time one puppy is restored to the cozy interior of the container, the next one is wiggling out the back flap. Therefore, the choleric child may often feel like that little puppy – fearless, curious, eager to get out and explore the world, to give kisses and hugs and affection to everyone around. When the choleric "puppy" is put back into the basket he will usually keep trying to get out. He has a great capacity for optimism, just as the eager little puppies do. Usually it will be the choleric child's spirit, then, that "wins" the game. This can often cause the melancholic adult great frustration and can result in increased efforts at keeping the child "under control".

Thus, the melancholic adult must be careful in the methods of communication and discipline he uses with the choleric child so the child does not lose his desire to "leave the basket" but instead, learns to moderate his temperament in a healthy manner while still retaining his natural joy, energy and passion.

Because the choleric child is so optimistic the melancholic adult can often mistake this optimism for durability or determination. This can cause the adult to assume that the choleric needs stronger discipline in the form of more punishment, stronger words or stricter rules. However, the melancholic adult needs to be able to distinguish between durability and optimism. The choleric child simply keeps trying because he has a strong spirit and desire to experience life. However, if the child experiences strong words or too much resistance he can eventually feel defeated and turn the energy inward or outward in damaging ways. This can result in a choleric child becoming intensely angry at himself or others in the form of temper tantrums or by trying to harm himself in some way.

Because of this innocent optimism the choleric child may easily break down in arguments or confrontations with the adult that get out of control. The melancholic adult may then feel as if the child may be attempting to manipulate him with tears or emotions. However, the choleric child is usually being very sincere in his emotions. When the choleric child begins displaying emotions during a discussion with the adult it is a sign to the melancholic adult to lighten up, back up and reevaluate the conversation and not an invitation to become stricter to avoid "giving in". This does not mean that the melancholic adult should bow to every whim of the choleric child. This simply means that the adult can respond to those emotions without giving into what may be an unreasonable request from the child.

However, the choleric child does need defined, regular rules and guidelines to help him feel secure and to make it easier for him to follow instructions. Although the melancholic adult should be responsive to the emotional needs of the choleric child, they should also be careful to keep the regulations of the household clear and unwavering. If the choleric understands the expectations of the melancholic adult and the rules of the household and/or classroom the child will naturally be more cooperative and pleasant. When new rules are being introduced or guidelines are not clear and steady the choleric child will need many reminders and much repetition. However, once the standards are clear, the choleric does not require a lot of discipline from the melancholic adult. A choleric child is very intuitive and since the melancholic puts out very strong non-verbal emotional cues, the choleric will usually pick up on those.

The melancholic adult must be especially careful with the choleric child to not dole out criticisms or penalties based on the child's temperament. Many aspects of the choleric temperament could qualify as "punishable offenses" in the world of the melancholic. However, the melancholic adult must make an effort to understand the magnificence within the choleric rather than trying to enhance him. For example, the choleric child enjoys extravagance while the melancholic enjoys moderation. The melancholic adult will restrain emotional expression while the choleric will seek it out. The melancholic adult usually puts principles before pleasure. However, for the choleric child pleasure and joy are the essential principles of existence. As the melancholic adult begins focusing on the positive aspects of the choleric's personality traits rather than the negative ones, he will find this problem easier to avoid.

Here are some examples of how those traits can be transformed. One must remember that most negative traits also have a positive aspect.

Extravagance can easily transform into extreme generosity.

Nagging can translate into the persistence to get a problem solved.

Constant chatter can turn into the ability to express oneself eloquently.

- ## The Teaching Relationship

The teaching relationship between the choleric student and the melancholic adult can be quite challenging for both the adult and the student. However, if a balance can be found there is amazing potential for growth in both people.

The melancholic adult has an aptitude for running an organized classroom with defined limits and expectations. This is exactly what the choleric student needs to balance his temperament and to help him be able to develop beyond the limits of his temperament. The choleric student's own point of view of the world is one without limits. However, this expansive vision can often make the choleric student feel overwhelmed, lost, scattered, or anxious. Clearly defined limits help the choleric student organize his unrestrained ideas into more manageable plans. In this atmosphere the choleric student will accomplish more and feel more confident and secure.

The melancholic adult must also make sure, however, that the natural talents of the choleric student are not lost in this contained environment. The choleric student should also be given ample opportunity to expand his ideas and explore new ideas. The melancholic adult does not necessarily need to create these opportunities. It is sufficient if the melancholic adult simply supports some of those ideas the choleric student has on his own.

An ideal classroom day would follow a regular rhythm and schedule but would also allow for at least a couple hours of unrestrained time in which the choleric student can explore anything his mind and body wants to explore. All that the melancholic adult needs to provide during this time are the tools for exploration. A choleric student will thrive when he is provided with these tools which may include drawing paper, books, colored pencils, boxes, craft supplies, musical instruments and more.

Although the choleric student needs and enjoys structure in the classroom, this does not mean that the classroom must be immovable. Structure can be built into an active learning experience as well. The melancholic adult should make the effort to build movement into the classroom rhythm. This can happen naturally if the adult bases his lesson plans on the concept of head, heart and hands. To follow this plan one lesson should incorporate all of these aspects or the adult can plan the day so that the day covers all these aspects of the learning experience. Lessons that work with the hands include handiwork, gardening, art, building, yoga, bread making, cooking and circle time. Lessons that use the head include grammar, spelling, phonics, math problems, geometry lessons, and botany. Lessons that evoke the heart include storytelling, singing, music, sharing, giving and painting.

The choleric student thrives when he works with others but can also become distracted in this process. A good way to guarantee balance in the choleric's educational experience is to create a lesson plan that follows a "breathing in-breathing out" rhythm. This rhythm is actually beneficial to all the temperaments so will be useful for classrooms with more than one student as well. "Breathing out" activities involve more extroverted activities in which the student connects with others. These activities are not limited to but may include circle time, games, free play, snack time, theater, working in pairs, and other group activities. "Breathing in" activities may include silent reading, painting, math calculations, writing, and other forms of more introverted or individual work.

The choleric student lives in the world of today. The melancholic adult needs to make an effort to design lessons that are relevant to the choleric student's current world. Because the melancholic adult often considers the future and is accustomed to planning for it, he can be motivated by striving towards a future benefit or goal. The choleric student, on the other hand, wants to see the immediate benefit of what he is doing. So, for example, math lessons may seem a logical part of school as the melancholic sees with great clarity how those lessons will benefit him in the future. The choleric, however, will ask, "Why do I need long division? What good is math doing for me now?" The more successful the melancholic adult can be in answering those questions, the more enthusiasm the choleric student will have for the lessons the adult plans.

- A Story to Share

When stories are told they speak to the child on a basic level. The reason one tells stories instead of explaining things to a child is because stories have the ability to adapt to the child's needs. When a person explains a situation to a child he is putting forth a concept that the child needs to grasp at or reach to understand. When one simply *tells* a story the child is given permission to understand the story in any way he wishes and to gain wisdom and knowledge from it in the way that best suits him at that moment. For that reason, it is not recommended that the story be explained to the child or that the child be provided with the ubiquitous "moral" at the end. Rather, it is best to give them a chance to enjoy the story for what it becomes to them and provide them with numerous chances to hear the story told. The stories in this book help the different temperaments understand each other. If the adult or adult would like to explore this understanding on a deeper level they can ask questions once the story is finished. However, one must be sure to ask open questions and allow the child to express his feelings.

In this story the King is melancholic and the youngest son is choleric. Together they accomplish great things.

The Golden Bird

The Brother's Grimm

In the olden time there was a king, who had behind his palace a beautiful pleasure-garden in which there was a tree that bore golden apples. When the apples were getting ripe they were counted, but on the very next morning one was missing. This was told to the king, and he ordered that a watch should be kept every night beneath the tree.

The king had three sons, the eldest of whom he sent, as soon as night came on, into the garden; but when midnight came he could not keep himself from sleeping, and next morning again an apple was gone.

The following night the second son had to keep watch, it fared no better with him; as soon as twelve o'clock had struck he fell asleep, and in the morning an apple was gone.

Now it came to the turn of the third son to watch; and he was quite ready, but the king had not much trust in him, and thought that he would be of less use even than his brothers; but at last he let him go. The youth lay down beneath the tree, but kept awake, and did not let sleep master him. When it struck twelve, something rustled through the air, and in the moonlight he saw a bird coming whose feathers were all shining with gold. The bird alighted on the tree, and had just plucked off an apple, when the youth shot an arrow at him. The bird flew off, but the arrow had struck his plumage, and one of his golden feathers fell down. The youth picked it up, and the next morning took it to the king and told him what he had seen in the night. The king called his council together, and everyone declared that a feather like this was worth more than the whole kingdom.

"If the feather is so precious," declared the king, "one alone will not do for me; I must and will have the whole bird!"

The eldest son set out; he trusted to his cleverness, and thought that he would easily find the Golden Bird. When he had gone some distance he saw a Fox sitting at the edge of a wood, so he cocked his gun and took aim at him. The fox cried, "Do not shoot me! and in return I will give you some good counsel. You are on the way to the Golden Bird; and this evening you will come to a village in which stand two inns opposite to one another. One of them is lighted up brightly, and all goes on merrily within, but do not go into it; go rather into the other, even though it seems a bad one."

"How can such a silly beast give wise advice?" thought the king's son, and he pulled the trigger. But he missed the fox, who stretched out his tail and ran quickly into the wood.

So he pursued his way, and by evening came to the village where the two inns were; in one they were singing and dancing; the other had a poor, miserable look.

"I should be a fool, indeed," he thought, "if I were to go into the shabby tavern, and pass by the good one."

So he went into the cheerful one, lived there in riot and revel, and forgot the bird and his father, and all good counsels.

When some time had passed, and the eldest son for month after month did not come back home, the second set out, wishing to find the Golden Bird. The fox met him as he had met the eldest, and gave him the good advice of which he took no heed. He came to the two inns, and his brother was standing at the window of the one from which came the music, and called out to him. He could not resist, but went inside and lived only for pleasure.

Again some time passed, and then the king's youngest son wanted to set off and try his luck, but his father would not allow it.

"It is of no use," said he, "he will find the Golden Bird still less than his brothers, and if a mishap were to befall him he knows not how to help himself; he is a little wanting at the best."

But at last, as he had no peace, he let him go.

Again the fox was sitting outside the wood, and begged for his life, and offered his good advice. The youth was good-natured, and said, "Be easy, little Fox, I will do you no harm."

"You shall not repent it," answered the fox; "and that you may get on more quickly, get up behind on my tail."

And scarcely had he seated himself when the fox began to run, and away he went over stock and stone till his hair whistled in the wind. When they came to the village the youth got off; he followed the good advice, and without looking round turned into the little inn, where he spent the night quietly.

The next morning, as soon as he got into the open country, there sat the fox already, and said, "I will tell you further what you have to do. Go on quite straight, and at last you will come to a castle, in front of which a whole regiment of soldiers is lying, but do not trouble yourself about them, for they will all be asleep and snoring. Go through the midst of them straight into the castle, and go through all the rooms, till at last you will come to a chamber where a Golden Bird is hanging in a wooden cage. Close by, there stands an empty gold cage for show, but beware of taking the bird out of the common cage and putting it into the fine one, or it may go badly with you."

With these words the fox again stretched out his tail, and the king's son seated himself on it, and away he went over stock and stone till his hair whistled in the wind.

When he came to the castle he found everything as the fox had said. The king's son went into the chamber where the Golden Bird was shut up in a wooden cage, while a golden one stood hard by; and the three golden apples lay about the room.

"But," thought he, "it would be absurd if I were to leave the beautiful bird in the common and ugly cage," so he opened the door, laid hold of it, and put it into the golden cage. But at the same moment the bird uttered a shrill cry. The soldiers awoke, rushed in, and took him off to prison. The next morning he was taken before a court of justice, and as he confessed everything, was sentenced to death.

The king, however, said that he would grant him his life on one condition namely, if he brought him the Golden Horse which ran faster than the wind; and in that case he should receive, over and above, as a reward, the Golden Bird.

The king's son set off, but he sighed and was sorrowful, for how was he to find the Golden Horse? But all at once he saw his old friend the fox sitting on the road.

"Look you," said the fox, "this has happened because you did not give heed to me. However, be of good courage. I will give you my help, and tell you how to get to the Golden Horse. You must go straight on, and you will come to a castle, where in the stable stands the horse. The grooms will be lying in front of the stable; but they will be asleep and snoring, and you can quietly lead out the Golden Horse. But of one thing you must take heed; put on him the common saddle of wood and leather, and not the golden one, which hangs close by, else it will go ill with you."

Then the fox stretched out his tail, the king's son seated himself on it, and away he went over stock and stone till his hair whistled in the wind.

Everything happened just as the fox had said; the prince came to the stable in which the Golden Horse was standing, but just as he was going to put the common saddle on him, he thought, "It will be a shame to such a beautiful beast, if I do not give him the good saddle which belongs to him by right."

But scarcely had the golden saddle touched the horse than he began to neigh loudly. The grooms awoke, seized the youth, and threw him into prison. The next morning he was sentenced by the court to death; but the king promised to grant him his life, and the Golden Horse as well, if he could bring back the beautiful princess from the Golden Castle.

With a heavy heart the youth set out; yet luckily for him he soon found the trusty Fox.

"I ought only to leave you to your ill-luck," said the fox, "but I pity you, and will help you once more out of your trouble. This road takes you straight to the Golden Castle, you will reach it by eventide; and at night when everything is quiet the beautiful princess goes to the bathing-house to bathe. When she enters it, run up to her and give her a kiss, then she will follow you, and you can take her away with you; only do not allow her to take leave of her adults first, or it will go ill with you."

Then the fox stretched out his tail, the king's son seated himself on it, and away the fox went, over stock and stone, till his hair whistled in the wind.

When he reached the Golden Castle it was just as the fox had said. He waited till midnight, when everything lay in deep sleep, and the beautiful princess was going to the bathing-house. Then he sprang out and gave her a kiss. She said that she would like to go with him, but she asked him pitifully, and with tears, to allow her first to take leave of her adults. At first he withstood her prayer, but when she wept more and more, and fell at his feet, he at last gave in. But no sooner had the maiden reached the bedside of her father than he and all the rest in the castle awoke, and the youth was laid hold of and put into prison.

The next morning the king said to him, "Your life is forfeited, and you can only find mercy if you take away the hill which stands in front of my windows, and prevents my seeing beyond it; and you must finish it all within eight days. If you do that you shall have my daughter as your reward."

The king's son began, and dug and shoveled without leaving off, but when after seven days he saw how little he had done, and how all his work was as good as nothing, he fell into great sorrow and gave up all hope. But on the evening of the seventh day the fox appeared and said, 'You do not deserve that I should take any trouble about you; but just go away and lie down to sleep, and I will do the work for you."

The next morning when he awoke and looked out of the window the hill had gone. The youth ran, full of joy, to the king, and told him that the task was fulfilled, and whether he liked it or not, the king had to hold to his word and give him his daughter.

So the two set forth together, and it was not long before the trusty Fox came up with them.

"You have certainly got what is best," said he, "but the Golden Horse also belongs to the maiden of the Golden Castle."

"How shall I get it?" asked the youth.

"That I will tell you," answered the fox; "first take the beautiful maiden to the king who sent you to the Golden Castle. There will be unheard-of rejoicing; they will gladly give you the Golden Horse, and will bring it out to you. Mount it as

soon as possible, and offer your hand to all in farewell; last of all to the beautiful maiden. And as soon as you have taken her hand swing her up on to the horse, and gallop away, and no one will be able to bring you back, for the horse runs faster than the wind."

All was carried out successfully, and the king's son carried off the beautiful princess on the Golden Horse.

The fox did not remain behind, and he said to the youth, "Now I will help you to get the Golden Bird. When you come near to the castle where the Golden Bird is to be found, let the maiden get down, and I will take her into my care. Then ride with the Golden Horse into the castle-yard; there will be great rejoicing at the sight, and they will bring out the Golden Bird for you. As soon as you have the cage in your hand gallop back to us, and take the maiden away again.

When the plan had succeeded, and the king's son was about to ride home with his treasures, the fox said, "Now you shall reward me for my help."

"What do you require for it?" asked the youth.

"When you get into the wood yonder, shoot me dead, and chop off my head and feet."

"That would be fine gratitude," said the king's son. "I cannot possibly do that for you."

The fox said, "If you will not do it I must leave you, but before I go away I will give you a piece of good advice. Be careful about two things. Buy no gallows'-flesh, and do not sit at the edge of any well." And then he ran into the wood.

The youth thought, "That is a wonderful beast, he has strange whims; who is going to buy gallows'-flesh? and the desire to sit at the edge of a well it has never yet seized me."

He rode on with the beautiful maiden, and his road took him again through the village in which his two brothers had remained. There was a great stir and noise, and, when he asked what was going on, he was told that two men were going to be hanged. As he came nearer to the place he saw that they were his brothers, who had been playing all kinds of wicked pranks, and had squandered all their wealth. He inquired whether they could not be set free.

"If you will pay for them," answered the people; "but why should you waste your money on wicked men, and buy them free."

He did not think twice about it, but paid for them, and when they were set free they all went on their way together.

They came to the wood where the fox had first met them, as it was cool and pleasant within it, the two brothers said, "Let us rest a little by the well, and eat and drink."

He agreed, and while they were talking he forgot himself, and sat down on the edge of the well without thinking of any evil. But the two brothers threw him backwards into the well, took the maiden, the Horse, and the Bird, and went home to their father.

"Here we bring you not only the Golden Bird," said they; "we have won the Golden Horse also, and the maiden from the Golden Castle."

Then was there great joy; but the Horse would not eat, the Bird would not sing, and the maiden sat and wept.

But the youngest brother was not dead. By good fortune the well was dry, and he fell on soft moss without being hurt, but he could not get out again. Even in this strait the faithful Fox did not leave him: it came and leapt down to him, and upbraided him for having forgotten its advice.

"But yet I cannot give it up so," he said; "I will help you up again into daylight."

He bade him grasp his tail and keep tight hold of it; and then he pulled him up.

"You are not out of all danger yet," said the fox. "Your brothers were not sure of your death, and have surrounded the wood with watchers, who are to kill you if you let yourself be seen."

But a poor man was sitting on the road, with whom the youth changed clothes, and in this way he got to the king's palace.

No one knew him, but the Bird began to sing, the Horse began to eat, and the beautiful maiden left off weeping. The king, astonished, asked, "What does this mean?" Then the maiden said, "I do not know, but I have been so sorrowful and now I am so happy! I feel as if my true bridegroom had come."

She told him all that had happened, although the other brothers had threatened her with death if she were to betray anything.

The king commanded that all people who were in his castle should be brought before him; and amongst them came the youth in his ragged clothes; but the maiden knew him at once and fell on his neck. The wicked brothers were seized and put to death, but he was married to the beautiful maiden and declared heir to the king.

But how did it fare with the poor Fox? Long afterwards the king's son was once again walking in the wood, when the fox met him and said, "You have everything now that you can wish for, but there is never an end to my misery, and yet it is in your power to free me," and again he asked him with tears to shoot him dead and chop off his head and feet. So he did it, and scarcely was it done when the fox was changed into a man, and was no other than the brother of the beautiful princess, who at last was freed from the magic charm which had been laid on him. And now nothing more was wanting to their happiness as long as they lived.

Phlegmatic Adult – Phlegmatic Child

- ## General Relationship

For the phlegmatic adult of a phlegmatic child the greatest relationship challenge will be struggling with seeing herself in the child. Because the phlegmatic type of temperament is not greatly supported by the modern fast paced diverse and multi-tasking modern world, the adult may have experienced some struggles in her personal relationships, school life or work life. Seeing the child go through these same struggles will be difficult for the phlegmatic adult and sometimes painful. The adult may feel guilty that it is perhaps "her fault" the child is that way and the adult may even try to pre-empt certain things from happening by forcing the child to do things both the adult and child are uncomfortable with (such as joining many different extracurricular activities).

The best thing the phlegmatic adult can do for this child is to take some time to really learn to love the phlegmatic temperament, learn to love herself deeply, and develop her own self confidence. Once the adult has done this then you will find it much easier to support your child through love of the temperament rather than through fear of the child experiencing the same problems the adult had in life.

- ## Helping the Phlegmatic Adult Understand the Phlegmatic Child

A phlegmatic child needs a lot of patience and luckily the phlegmatic adult has a lot of that to give. The adult also has the advantage of understanding why the phlegmatic child does what she does. However, the adult must make sure that this understanding does not cause her to assume things about the child. Just because the child is similar to the adult does not mean that she has the exact same thoughts and needs. One must also remember that the child needs to learn many things for herself so one should not try to overprotect the child from "making the same mistakes she did". There may be some phlegmatic traits that did not serve the adult well in life but they may serve this child well. Phlegmatic traits have great value and are especially needed in today's society. The phlegmatic adult must remember to guide this child gently but also let this child find his own way.

The adult should notice the traits that she has in common with the phlegmatic child and try to honor these and enjoy the child. Phlegmatics are honest and perhaps even have a tendency to be blunt. Both should both be able to communicate with each other very clearly and without too many misunderstandings. Both are cautious. Therefore the adult should make sure to let the child have some time to answer questions or venture into new things. The adult can recall the feelings she had when venturing into new topics of conversation or new projects and remember that the child naturally feels a similar feeling of caution.

The phlegmatic child enjoys time alone to think in her own world. Although the adult will understand this need, she may become frustrated due to having this same need. The phlegmatic adult may have a hard time finding times when both are feeling social enough to really "connect". Until the child has the wisdom to branch out from her natural temperament, the adult should make an effort to connect with her when she approaches rather than waiting until both feel "in the mood". The phlegmatic child has a tendency to keep her feelings to herself just as the adult does. However, this does not mean she does not need to share. The adult may have become accustomed to keeping feelings to herself over the years and not realize that she and the child do have a need to connect with others and share those feelings. The phlegmatic adult may just not be able to find the right times to do this. The child is more likely to open up to the adult when she is not "put on the spot" by questions. Playing a board game or having "tea" or taking a walk together may be the perfect time for a chat. When chatting with the phlegmatic one should ask only a few questions at a time and leave ample time for the child to consider the question and answer.

This child is, as the adult, usually content to be an observer at social events, unless she is very comfortable with the people present (like an intimate family gathering or having a couple close friends visit). Since both have the same tendency this may make it hard for the adult to encourage the child to go outside her social comfort zone. However, she needs to do this to prevent her from becoming isolated. She may not ask for social interaction. However, when invited by a friend or other person, she will usually be agreeable. The phlegmatic adult should her eyes and ears open for these opportunities and don't let them pass by. Since the child and the adult are not ones to seek gatherings out, when opportunities come they both should take as many as possible.

Also, like the adult, the child may enjoy being considered unusual or unique and may cultivate some unique traits. As a boy, he may enjoy growing his hair long. As a girl, she may want to double pierce her ears. Phlegmatic children may use unusual phrases or words that they create themselves. Most likely, although the adult also likes being unique, the child will not choose the same "unique" things that the adult has chosen. Some things she may choose to say, think or do may even alarm the adult. The phlegmatic adult must stay calm and not worry. The unique items the child chooses are very essential to the phlegmatic child. These unique traits are how she holds onto his public identity and feels safe. If she is asked to remove her chosen unique traits ("cut your long hair boy!") she may feel traumatized or upset and may retreat into herself even more. She feels that these unique traits are his safety net in social life.

This said, take note that if she develops a unique trait that is socially offensive, the phlegmatic adult should not be alarmed. The child may try on a number of unique approaches to social life before she finds the ones that fit him best. As phlegmatics are quick learners and learn by observation, it is best to let her discover what works and what does not work on his own. If the adult tells him what she thinks, the child is more likely to "buckle down" and do it even more.

The phlegmatic child has a great affinity for the truth and for fairness and will often defend truth when it is challenged.

This child is a "fighter". She does not give up easily and he likes the feeling of persevering even when things are difficult. The adult may worry about her because when the adult sees the child running up against a wall, frustration may set in that is reminiscent of times she felt frustrated as a child. The adult may even feel a sense of protectiveness. At these times the phlegmatic adult should recall how good it felt to overcome those challenges by herself and allow the child to do the same.

Because the child may prefer intellectual pursuits and time alone it will be healthier for her to have another influence in his life besides the phlegmatic adult. One must make sure the phlegmatic child spends enough time with siblings, her other adult, aunts, uncles, grandparents or even friends. She especially needs the influence of a sanguine or choleric to pull her out of his comfort zone and introduce her to new experiences. However, one should not worry if she only plays basketball when she is with that certain friend or she only does certain activities when inspired by others. She has her own agenda. It is good to get her out of her comfort zone from time to time and very healthy for her balance. However, she will pursue her own interests even if nobody else around her, including the adult, thinks those interests are worthy of pursuing. The point of having others to balance her is for balance only. The adult should not seek to change where the phlegmatic child's interests naturally lie because this would be like pushing up against a wall. She will find a way to pursue her interests despite any obstacles the adult may put in her way. This is why it is a good idea to make sure she is exposed to enough experiences at a young age that she has a good selection of healthy activities she may choose to pursue as she continues to grow.

One bond the adult and child will always have is that both consider family very important and both very faithful and dependable people. This is something the adult may admire in the child and the phlegmatic child needs to know this. A phlegmatic does not seek out attention or praise but she does appreciate it and it helps her gain confidence. One must try to find as many opportunities as possible to praise her and make an effort to do so. Because the adult also has a tendency not to express herself as often as some of the other temperaments and because the child has a tendency not to ask for praise and attention, the adult could easily fall into a pattern where the pair are not interacting very much or in a positive or meaningful way. The phlegmatic adult needs to watch out for this and – even if it takes writing herself reminders – must be sure to praise the child a few times a week.

The phlegmatic child is a very good listener. When the adult does try to communicate with her, the child will be more likely to just listen than to give feedback or nod her head or even to offer to participate a lot in the conversation. This may be frustrating to the adult because the adult is also a good listener and is accustomed to other people talking more and holding up more of the conversation. The phlegmatic adult needs to realize that the child is like her in this way and that she *is* listening and she *is* absorbing what the adult is saying, she just may not have the same frequent responses as another child or person may offer. Over the years the adult may have become attracted to more friends who are of the sanguine or choleric type so the phlegmatic adult may not be as familiar with dealing with the phlegmatic type and not be as comfortable with this as she could be.

The phlegmatic type, above all, is often underappreciated, since she does not have the glitter and glamour of some of the other temperaments. If the adult has more than one child she may notice that the other children get more compliments or comments from adults and friends. However, this does not mean there is something wrong with the phlegmatic child. One must remember that phlegmatics are steady, dependable and work at their own pace and be careful not to compare the phlegmatic child to other children. This is especially important for the phlegmatic adult as she is also of the phlegmatic type and may be attracted to types that compliment her and provide more excitement in life. The phlegmatic adult may unconsciously admire or seek out these other temperaments and thus not feel as much excitement about the nature of the phlegmatic child. It is natural for the adult to feel more at peace with the phlegmatic child than excited and energized by her. The phlegmatic would be more energized by someone of the opposite temperament. This does not mean the adult loves the phlegmatic child less. This just means that the adult has a different relationship with the child.

- ## Helping the Phlegmatic Child Understand the Phlegmatic Adult

As the phlegmatic adult understands her own temperament more and becomes more comfortable with it, the child will also be able to understand her similar temperament and become more comfortable with it as well. Because the child and the adult have the same temperament they should be able to understand each other easily. However, there will be some possible roadblocks in this process. Once they can overcome the roadblocks then they should both be able to live in peace, harmony and mutual respect. The balanced relationship between a phlegmatic and a phlegmatic will be one of peace and harmony. They will probably not provide each other with a lot of excitement or personal growth opportunities (outside of the phlegmatic element), however, in a healthy relationship they will both be able to feel peace, safety and security. The adult may find herself spending time with this child because it is comforting to the adult and the child may feel greatly comforted by the presence of the adult. They have the ability to form a very deep and intimate bond that will only be between them and will not be understood or felt by anyone else around them.

The roadblocks this pair needs to overcome are these:

The child and the adult, have the same tendency – to not want to admit or see her own faults. Thus, as the child gets to know the phlegmatic adult she will be extra sensitive to those "faults" or "weaknesses" that they both have in common. The child will be frustrated that the adult does not communicate with her easily and that the adult does not share emotion easily. The child may be frustrated that what she wants done does not get done as quickly as she want it done. These phlegmatic traits will frustrate her because she intuitively knows that, when presented with the same situation, she would react the same way.

To get beyond this roadblock the phlegmatic adult first needs to be aware of it. When a conflict involving similar temperaments happens, the adult and child should sit down and talk about it together. Instead of telling the child "well you are the same way" or telling her how the adult is, it is better to sit down with her and work on the issue together. One must ask the child what her needs are, listen to her and try to get beyond the struggle. If something needs to be done more quickly the phlegmatic adult should let the child know how the adult will resolve that. If the child needs more emotional connection the adult should let her know how the adult plans to work towards that with her. The adult phlegmatic should explain to the child what the adult struggles with and show her how she plans on overcoming these struggles. The child, who is also phlegmatic will observe this and learn. The phlegmatic learns greatly by example and does not do well in direct confrontation. So rather than butting heads with an argument – "well, you always take a long time to do things too" or "I don't have time right now", one should take some time to show her an example of what an adult phlegmatic is like, how the adult is comfortable with it, and what the adult is doing to be a better person.

The second road block the adult will encounter is that the child will recognize some things in the adult and will know her very well. It will be hard to hide some things from the child, even if revealing these things is painful. The phlegmatic child is already perceptive. However, when presented with a temperament she "knows", she can be even more perceptive. She may become so comfortable with quietly being "right" about the adult most of the time that she may fall into the habit of assuming she knows why the adult is doing things or what the adult is thinking. She may be painting a picture of the adult in her head that is inaccurate and the phlegmatic adult will never know because it will all be happening so quietly, behind the scenes. This is why it is essential that the adult communicate with the child on a regular basis. One should not wait for the child to ask questions. The phlegmatic adult should let the child know why the adult is doing certain things and making certain decisions. She will get a better picture of who the adult is and in the process will learn to ask more questions and not take for granted that she knows everything about the adult or another phlegmatic just because they have so much in common.

- Discipline

Good discipline always stems from a sense of trust, love and harmony between the adult and child. The more the adult and child understand and respect each other, the more discipline happens naturally. To have a healthy discipline relationship with the phlegmatic child the phlegmatic adult should first read the sections above on how to best understand the child and how to help the child understand the adult.

In general these two won't have a lot of confrontation. Phlegmatics prefer not to deal with problems in a confrontational way, but are more passive and thoughtful. The child or adult may be aware she is upset but decide that peace is more important than bringing it up. Or, she may not even be aware he are upset because she is so used to choosing peace over conflict it is hard for her to go into "problem solving" mode. When this happens her anger may come out in other ways. So, the first challenge that will present itself is that the adult will need to find ways to discover what the child's needs are.

One possibility is that the adult will most likely deal with conflict in the same way so she will not be angered or upset by the phlegmatic child's passive approach. The adult may even admire his way of being peaceful and indirect, as a form of courtesy.   If this is the case, then the adult will find it easy to find calm times when she can find out more about what the child is thinking and what she needs. One must learn to read the child's subtle messages and look for the sign that she is holding back tears or that she is avoiding a certain topic. One must listen for verbal cues in response to things that are said to her. She does not like direct confrontation – as this is almost painful to him – so the best way to talk about important topics with her is in a lighthearted manner or casually as the adult and child are doing something else. Playing a board game, having dinner or a snack together at a café or taking a walk are great ways to create a comfortable atmosphere for her to talk. One must also remember to keep the topics short and simple. She does not do well with complex problem solving on a personal level (although she may be great at logical problem solving and math) so it is best to tackle one problem at a time. For example, if the child has trouble with cleaning her room *and* finishing her homework, the adult should choose just one topic at a time to discuss.

Alternately, if the lack of direct communication has caused pain in the adult's own life and personal relationships, the adult may try to "fix" the child. This will just increase the child's own pain at his "lack" of direct communication skills. The phlegmatic child is very adept at communicating in a peaceful, passive and sometimes even intuitive way. She is also very adept at communicating through action and through touch. These are skills the adult will need to learn about herself, to come to terms with, and to learn how to use effectively. In turn the adult will then teach these skills to the child so she may also use and appreciate them.

Speaking about emotions is not a comfortable place for the phlegmatic adult to be in a relationship, for phlegmatics do not like to be "exposed". However, if the adult wants to have effective relationships with those around hi/her, she will need to learn to be direct from time to time. The adult will also need to be able to let people around her/him know that they should not take the silence personally. The phlegmatic adult should get to know herself and share who she is with others. Let the child know that the adult usually communicates through action and touch and help the child to see how actions and touch communicate feelings.

When conflict does arise, the phlegmatic should let people around her know that she works best in a structured conversational format or in one where the topic is focused. The phlegmatic can share that one of her greatest fears is to be exposed and to fail at something. This is one of the phlegmatic "buttons". So when someone criticizes a phlegmatic or tells her that something the phlegmatic does needs to be done differently or asks the phlegmatic "how you are feeling" the phlegmatic may respond very angrily or may withdraw from the conversation. The phlegmatic adult can find ways in which she can overcome this fear as well as communicate this with those who relate to her on a regular basis so they are aware that it may be more difficult to talk with her at times.

The phlegmatic adult should teach the child these same skills from an early age. The adult could set up a time to talk to the child at least once a week so she could get used to getting out of her conversational comfort zone. The phlegmatic adult could let the child listen to her discussing conflicts and have successful conversations with other people or let her listen in on other people doing this. This will help her learn, for the phlegmatic learns well by observation and gains confidence in that way – as if she had done it himself!

So what does all this have to do with discipline? Discipline is mostly communication. So to be able to understand what went wrong and how to communicate the consequence to the child, the phlegmatic adult needs to first to understand these basics.

The best way to communicate a consequence to a phlegmatic child is to ask her what she thinks would be a fair consequence. Phlegmatics are extremely honest and will, most of the time, come up with the perfect "consequence" for her action. She will also be very happy and satisfied with this proposed consequence as she has a very deep sense of "fairness" – even within herself. If a "wrong action" has a natural consequence, this is enough for a phlegmatic. She is very observant. She doesn't need to learn her lesson more than once like a sanguine or choleric may need. If the adult feels she must say something and point out the consequence to the child, the adult should do so gently, but not expect a response. She may nod or pretend she didn't hear you. Chances are she noticed it already and has already learned her lesson. If the action did not have a natural consequence and the adult needs to create one (for example, perhaps you have a rule that if a child doesn't finish the math work then she doesn't do painting afterwards) then one must make sure there is set standard for consequences and that this standard is posted somewhere. Phlegmatics are very fair, so the adult needs to let her know what the rules of the house/classroom are very clearly and let her know what the consequences are for breaking the rules. As long as she knows the guidelines, the adult will not have any trouble "reminding" the child and enforcing the rules. The child will naturally want to fit into this structure.

Although this pair will not experience a lot of conflict, the biggest challenge the phlegmatic adult will face with this child is that both have a very strong, quiet, will of steel. If the adult does "slip up" and end up in a confrontational situation or if the adult has pushed the child too far, or has doled out an "unfair" punishment, she will find herself against a wall of resistance or an angry person and the adult will most likely want to react in the same way. The adult's own walls may go up, her own anger may rise, and the pair will find themselves in a stand-off situation.

To overcome this, the phlegmatic adult will need to be able to step back from the situation and start again. This can be done with careful "time outs". Since people of the phlegmatic temperament are always happy to avoid conflict and believe in the power of time to heal all wounds, the concept of "time outs" comes naturally. However, these breaks must be done in a purposeful, respectful and clear manner to be effective. When taking a "time out" the phlegmatic adult must be sure to end the conversation with an encouraging word and make clear that the "time out" is not a punishment but is a mutually beneficial break from the conversation. Secondly, a time when the discussion will resume should be set. For example, if the phlegmatic adult is discussing something with the phlegmatic child before dinner and they need to take a "time out" the adult could say, "Let's eat dinner first and discuss this after the chocolate cake I made for desert!"

One should take note that the phlegmatic child responds most effectively to positive feedback rather than natural consequences or set rules. Although the child needs set rules to help them feel secure and to guide her, she will actually respond in a more positive manner if there is positive feedback to go along with these rules. One will see amazing results when the child is provided with positive feedback about the things she did "right".

Terry, a Phlegmatic adult found this out when she tried to motivate her son, Grant with natural consequences. When Grant woke up late he often ended up having to eat school lunch instead of bringing lunch from home. When Grant didn't finish his homework he had to do it on the weekend to catch up and when he forgot to take out the trash one week and the neighborhood raccoon spread it all over the garage Grant spent an hour cleaning it up. Terry was sure these natural consequences would motivate Grant to become more responsible so she pointed them out to him and said things like, "Hmm...if you had remembered to take out the trash you wouldn't be cleaning up the mess right now, would you?"

This didn't work for two reasons. First of all, when Terry highlighted the error Grant made it just made Grant even more determined to do what he wanted as he immediately felt Terry was being unfair. Secondly, Grant was not motivated by the natural consequences alone – he needed something else. In a phlegmatic person natural consequences work over a long period of time and sometimes are not very effective at all. The phlegmatic is like a river that rarely alters its course unless something highly unusual happens.

After consulting with me Terry started to use positive reinforcement with Grant instead of just the natural consequences. The next week Grant forgot to take his dog for a walk and it made a mess on the carpet. Terry asked him kindly if he would please clean up the mess and use the wet vacuum to clean the carpet. After Grant cleaned the carpet Terry focused on his success and said, "Wow. The carpet is so nicely done and smells so good. Thank you so much for doing that!" Grant beamed. Instead of feeling defensive he now felt very proud about what he had done. He also learned that when he made a mistake he had the ability to repair that mistake and still be successful.

- ## The Teaching Relationship

The phlegmatic person is usually motivated by factors outside herself. She is usually responsive rather than active about her learning. For this reason when one pairs a phlegmatic adult with a phlegmatic student they need some outside factor to "spark" the learning bond between them. In a classroom there would be other temperaments in the classroom and this would help. If the student has siblings that are of different temperaments this can also help. What the adult and student both need is an outside motivator to keep them going. If there are not siblings, classmates or a spouse around to add the "spice" the student needs to move forward, then the adult and student should join a local co-op, some local classes together or some group that meets at least twice a week so they can keep the movement going in the lessons.

The phlegmatic experiences life and learning through time. Numbers are important to her. So another way to keep both the adult and student on track is to make a schedule with certain hours for certain activities.

- ## A Story to Share

My favorite story with two phlegmatic characters is a story called *Who Will Talk First*. This is the quintessential phlegmatic story illustrating both their tendency to lock into a battle of the wills, along with their ability to stay silent for long periods of time and their comfort with small and familiar spaces. This story would never work if you changed one of the characters into a sanguine or a choleric. The punch line would never happen. I have included two versions of the story below. Both have been adapted by me.

The Phlegmatic Couple and the Chickens

Traditional Folktale Adapted by Kristie Burns

Once upon a time, a husband had the habit of sitting outside his home every day, while his wife cooked his meals, swept the floor, and washed his clothes. She was comfortable performing the same chores day after day but was not happy to see her husband sitting while she worked.

"Why do you sit there doing nothing?" the wife asked.

"I am thinking deep thoughts," the husband would reply.

"Did you get sunk in those deep thoughts?" the wife would retort.

One morning, the chickens were up clucking and the wife was not feeling well. She said to the husband, "Could you please go feed the chickens? I need some extra time for my work this morning."

"No," the husband declared, "I am already deep in thought."

"You are lazy!" the wife replied sharply.

"I inherited this home from my father and you live in it," the husband replied, "I provide for you quite well!"

The two glared at each other the rest of the morning and afternoon. Then, in the evening, the husband and wife both had the same idea at the same time.

"Whoever speaks first," they said simultaneously, "will feed the chickens from now on!" The two nodded in agreement, and said nothing more. They went to bed in silence.

The next morning, the wife knew that if she stayed home watching her husband do nothing all day, she would say something. So she decided to go for a walk to find some wild berries.

A short time later, a beggar came by the house and asked the husband for food and money. The husband was about to reply, when he stopped himself. This is my wife's trick! he thought. "She is trying to make me talk." So the husband kept silent. The beggar thought this meant the husband didn't care what he did and sure enough, when he ventured to open the door, the husband still did not say anything. No one was inside, but the cupboards were full of bread and cheese. So the beggar ate everything and left.

A traveling barber then passed by and asked the husband if he wanted his beard trimmed. The husband said nothing. This is another of my wife's tricks! thought the husband. The barber then started to trim the man's beard and he still said nothing so he figured it was the man's strange way of saying yes. However, when he wanted payment, the husband did not move. The barber demanded money again, and became angry. "I will shave off all your hair!" the barber threatened. The husband refused to stir, so the barber shaved off all the husband's hair and took his nice door knob as well for his payment.

As night fell, the woman was still out. She had become warmed by the sun while collecting berries and had fallen asleep under a beautiful oak tree watching the clouds pass by. A thief then approached the house. He thought the husband was a statue and confirmed this by speaking to him but receiving no reply. So the thief when into the house, which was filled full of Turkish rugs, expensive cookware and silk gowns, and packed everything in a bag.

I will punish my wife for her tricks, the man swore to himself. About that time his wife had woken from her nap and made her way home. When she saw there was no doorknob on the house and all the food and items in the home were gone she exclaimed, "what has happened here?!"

"Aha!" the husband sprang up. "You spoke first, so you must feed the chickens from now on!"

Another version of this story hinges around a door that neither of the couple want to close. You can easily change the relationships in either of these stories to that of two siblings or an adult and a child.

The Phlegmatic Couple and the Open Door

Traditional Tale Adapted by Kristie Burns

Once upon a time a poor farmer and his wife, having finished their day's labor and eaten their frugal supper, were sitting by the fire, when a dispute arose between them as to who should shut the door, which had been blown open by a gust of wind.

"Wife, shut the door!" said the man.

"Husband, shut it yourself!" said the woman.

"I will not shut it, and you shall not shut it," said the husband; "but let the one who speaks the first word shut it."

This proposal pleased the wife exceedingly, and so the old couple, well satisfied, retired in silence to bed.

In the middle of the night he heard a noise, and, peering out, he perceived that a wild dog had entered the room, and that he was busy devouring their little store of food. Not a word, however, would either of these people utter, and the dog, having sniffed at everything, and having eaten as much as he wanted, went out of the house.

The next morning the woman took some grain to the house of a neighbor in order to have it ground into flour. In her absence the barber entered, and said to the husband, "How is it you are sitting here all alone?"

The farmer answered never a word. The barber then shaved his head, but still he did not speak; then he shaved off half his beard and half his mustache, but even then the man refrained from uttering a syllable. Then the barber covered him all over with a hideous coating of lampblack, but the stolid farmer remained silent. "The man is under a spell!" cried the barber, and he hastily quitted the house.

He had hardly gone when the wife returned from the mill. She, seeing her husband in such a ghastly plight, began to tremble, and exclaimed, "Oh my! What have you been doing?"

"You spoke the first word," said the farmer, "so get on with it, woman, and shut the door."

When stories are told they speak to the child on a basic level. The reason one tells stories instead of explaining things to a child is because stories have the ability to adapt to the child's needs. When a person explains a situation to a child she is putting forth a concept that the child needs to grasp at or reach to understand. When one simply *tells* a story the child is given permission to understand the story in any way she wishes and to gain wisdom and knowledge from it in the way that best suits her at that moment. For that reason, it is not recommended that the story be explained to the child or that the child be provided with the ubiquitous "moral" at the end. Rather, it is best to give them a chance to enjoy the story for what it becomes to them and provide them with numerous chances to hear the story told. The stories in this book help the different temperaments understand each other. If the adult or adult would like to explore this understanding on a deeper level they can ask questions once the story is finished. However, one must be sure to ask open questions and allow the child to express her feelings.

For example, in these stories of the phlegmatic couples you could simply ask "what could they have done differently?" or "Do you agree with them?"

How your child interprets the story will help you understand how he is feeling. This story can also be used as a measuring tool for your child. As he grows and matures, he will interpret the story in different ways. Tell the story at different times in his life and observe how he interprets it each time. What he says will give you insight into areas he is developing in and areas he may still be challenged in.

Phlegmatic Adult – Melancholic Child

- ## General Relationship

The general relationship between the phlegmatic adult and the melancholic child is usually harmonious as the phlegmatic adult is usually respectful of tradition and keeps a simple and defined schedule around the home. The melancholic child finds these traits very comforting and will naturally feel nurtured by the phlegmatic adult.

- ## Helping the Phlegmatic Adult Understand the Melancholic Child

The melancholic child enjoys tradition and defined schedules. However, he has some needs that are not naturally filled by the phlegmatic adult unless the adult makes an effort to better understand the melancholic temperament.

The melancholic child often expresses himself in terms of what is "wrong" and may often seem depressed. This may upset the phlegmatic adult as he is happiest when everyone else is happy. If friends or family are upset in some way this upsets the phlegmatic who may even feel as if it is his fault. Because the phlegmatic adult tries so hard to keep harmony it is easy for him to assume it is his fault even if the event is far removed from anything he initiated. When the phlegmatic adult understands that the negative view of the melancholic is more reflective of a deep thought process than actual sadness then the adult can feel more relaxed. When the phlegmatic adult is relaxed, confident and secure in his role the relationship between the adult and child will improve.

The melancholic element corresponds to the time of old age and wisdom. The melancholic has an inherent need for order and usually keeps schedules, a clean room and an organized lesson book. The melancholic child also likes to feel in control of the social environment. Because the melancholic child is a master of order and organization, over time the melancholic may naturally migrate towards the role of the adult and the phlegmatic adult, without realizing it, may fall into the role of the child/student. I have seen this happen in many phlegmatic adult/melancholic child relationships from an early age.

Alice, a phlegmatic mother, and Adam, a melancholic child, are good examples of how this dynamic can work. Alice and Adam actually came to me as adults to work through some problems they were experiencing since Adam's father died. Alice felt as if Adam, now an adult with his own family, was treating her like a child. Alice wanted to let Adam know that she was able to run her own house, make her own decisions and have her own unique hobbies and interests. Adam, on the other hand, worried about his mother and felt she needed someone to guide her in life and help her run her home.

By listening to stories of his childhood I was able to see clearly that Adam and his mother had had this kind of interaction since he was a child. In one story that Alice told with a chuckle she described how Adam used to insist that the entire house be dark and quiet before he did his homework each day. Alice would shut all the blinds, tell Adam's sisters to work in peace and allow Adam to use the big desk in his adults' room with the door shut. When Adam was done with his work the entire house would go back to "normal". Alice had many more stories like this. Alice intuitively knew that by meeting some of the requirements of her melancholic child she could help him feel more comfortable and confident and enhance his educational experience. However, by agreeing to all of the needs instead of balancing her needs, his needs and the needs of the household, she had created a dynamic where she was the child and Adam was the adult.

By working through these stories I was able to help them to see how this dynamic between them was one of temperament misunderstanding. Once this realization was made Alice and Adam were ready to work on getting to know each other's temperament better, something they had never done when he was a child.

Additional characteristics of the melancholic include a need to feel he has mastered concepts, lessons and tasks in his life. A phlegmatic adult can be very protective in his efforts to maintain harmony in the house and may hold back the melancholic child without realizing what he is doing. A phlegmatic adult needs to let the melancholic child have freedom to make mistakes, work at his own pace and complete tasks on his own. This freedom should also extend to the physical realm. The melancholic child learns and experiences life through his physical body and sense of touch. A melancholic child may be the one that likes to see how high they can climb in the tree or to see what will happen if he jumps off of a ledge or off the swing at the playground.

To the cautious phlegmatic adult this can cause a lot of stress, however the melancholic temperament is very in touch with the physical realm and is also very careful. Although the melancholic enjoys exploring how far he can push the body, these experiments are always done with forethought and planning and are usually safe.

The melancholic has a strong sense of righteousness and tends to judge those around him. The melancholic child usually has a set list of standards and principles he follows. This is a common bond the phlegmatic adult and melancholic child share, so the adult needs to be careful not to indulge this trait too much but rather seek to balance it. There is a danger of the adult and child spending too much time discussing the "right" way to do things and how other people "should" do things the same way. This can help them both feel more confident and supported in their belief systems and methodologies. However, if indulged in it can also lead to prejudice, intolerance and discrimination in the child.

The melancholic is not usually comfortable sharing emotions and feelings and neither is the phlegmatic adult. This does not mean that the phlegmatic adult will not be able to understand or communicate with the melancholic child. Because the melancholic connects deeply to the physical world his emotions are often expressed in the physical realm, either through illness, action, facial expression or gesture, and because the phlegmatic adult is in tune with the subtle motions of people around him, the adult will actually be able to pick up on these emotions even if they are not expressed verbally. To the outside observer it can appear as if the phlegmatic adult and melancholic child have a psychic connection.

The melancholic child is comfortable with a few close friends as is the phlegmatic adult. For this reason the phlegmatic adult needs to make sure that the child has ample opportunity for social interaction, as this will not naturally happen if the child is usually interacting with the phlegmatic adult's environment. It is healthy and natural for the melancholic to desire only a few close friends. However, this longing must also be balanced with enough social experience that the melancholic does not become shy and socially challenged. Increased opportunity for social interaction also helps open up the melancholic child's mind to the beauty of different kinds of people and helps him cultivate respect for those that fall outside of his inner circle.

In social situations some people may comment that the melancholic child seems aloof. The phlegmatic adult may not notice this trait, but should be aware of it so he can help the child work through complex social situations and answer questions the child might have.

The melancholic child enjoys creating masterpieces and has a desire to transform situations, people and environments into the best they can be. The level of organization the melancholic child desires often requires quick and adaptive thought, inner motivation and a strong sense of purpose – traits that are not strong in the phlegmatic adult. The phlegmatic adult can learn to recognize this need in the melancholic and allow the child space and resources to create the masterpieces he wishes to create.

The phlegmatic adult will be pleased that the melancholic child always lets the adult know where he stands with the child. If the melancholic child is angry that anger will be expressed. If the melancholic child is saddened or frustrated by the adult, feels the adult is being unfair, is embarrassed by the adult, or has any other feelings about the adult, the child will be sure to express them. This will be reassuring for the phlegmatic adult as long as he is prepared for the direct way these feelings are usually communicated. A melancholic child's speech often has a tone of blame or judgment in it which can upset the adult if he is not prepared for the language.

- Helping the Melancholic Child Understand the Phlegmatic Adult

Because the melancholic child is often wise at an early age, very self assured, self confident about right and wrong and enjoys controlling his environment and the phlegmatic adult is more relaxed in his organization and does not enjoy conflict, the phlegmatic adult may find it easy to concede to the melancholic child's demands and requests.

In some ways this can make life easier. After all, the melancholic is quite capable, he usually does not make unreasonable demands, the plans he makes are usually well thought out and useful and the child is usually happy to execute and lead these plans on his own. For the phlegmatic adult this can create an ideal situation. Handing control over to the melancholic child takes pressure off of the phlegmatic adult, frees up more time for the adult to take life at an easy-going pace and prevents most arguments and conflicts from ever occurring. In fact, going back to the example I gave above with Alice and Adam, they don't remember arguing at all during his childhood years. Alice was always happy with Adam, and Adam felt in control of his environment and quite happy with life in general. The only conflicts in the household with Adam were between his sanguine sister and him and between his melancholic father and him.

Because this dynamic does work so well it is wise to keep some of it in place. However, the phlegmatic adult needs to be aware of this dynamic and make sure it does not become exaggerated or out of control. To prevent this from happening the melancholic child must learn to respect the strength, power and value of the phlegmatic temperament. This can be accomplished, first, by understanding the temperament itself.

The phlegmatic adult is committed to a path of knowledge and will often spend time pursuing that knowledge and find the pursuit of knowledge a valid goal in studying and lessons. However, a phlegmatic adult may express fear often. This can create a feeling in the melancholic child that the adult is not capable. Children in general, and especially those of the melancholic temperament, feel more secure when they feel confidence in their adults. The melancholic child needs to understand that this expression of fear in the adult does not indicate weakness or the inability to adult and protect the child. A phlegmatic adult expresses fear when he needs more time to think about something, when he needs time to adapt to a new situation and even when there is a disharmony in the environment either between people or between objects. A phlegmatic adult can help alleviate the melancholic's uncertainty in his adult's abilities by being aware of this trait within himself and making an effort to change some of the fear statements he makes into more positive and empowering statements.

Here are some examples:

Instead of the phlegmatic adult saying, "Please don't climb so high in that tree. I am afraid you will fall" he could say nothing and just watch or say, "Be sure that when you climb you stay on the branches that can hold your weight. If the branches are bending that indicates that they cannot hold your weight."

Instead of the adult saying, "I'm really not sure if we will be able to afford to repair the car this week," it would be better not to share that fear with the child. There are many pieces of information that the child does not need to know about that modern adults have made a habit of sharing with children.

Instead of saying, "I don't feel comfortable about visiting Aunt Linda in this heavy snow," the phlegmatic adult could simply say, "Our plans have changed and we have decided to visit Aunt Linda next week."

Once the phlegmatic adult works on changing the way he expresses himself it will become clear how often the element of fear enters into his statements. When a phlegmatic first becomes aware of this it is usually a surprise and may take some time to modify.

The phlegmatic adult experiences life in the dimension of time. For this reason it may take the adult longer to accomplish some tasks around the house or some extra time to fulfill requests. The phlegmatic adult may not be aware that this period of time seems like forever to the child or that the child may assume the task is not going to be done and may decide to do it himself. To reassure the child and help the child understand the adult more clearly, the phlegmatic adult can take the time to let the child know when certain tasks might be completed. The melancholic child will probably want an exact time and day which may be very stressful for the phlegmatic adult. A good compromise is to give the child a range of times in which the adult plans on fulfilling the request.

Another misunderstanding in this realm is in the way the phlegmatic adult expresses the intention to do something. A phlegmatic adult likes to indulge his creativity and imagination in the form of expressing intentions or dreams but not always following through with them. This may make the melancholic child feel that he has to help the adult finish these tasks. Instead the melancholic child needs to realize that the expression of ideas and dreams is the phlegmatic's way of venturing out of his comfort zone in a safe way and trying on new ideas. Because the phlegmatic enjoys thought and creativity but is also very cautious the end result is that he will come up with hundreds of ideas in one week but may decide that only a few of them are worth pursuing. The melancholic child, needing to experience things in the physical realm instead of the mental realm, may try many ideas only to discard them after trying them. It then appears that the melancholic does more than the phlegmatic, however, the end result may be the same.

The phlegmatic adult is often thought of as the ideal adult. One reason is because phlegmatic people consider the continuity of family as more important than daily happenings or personal goals. However, this does not mean that the phlegmatic adult does not have goals.

The phlegmatic adult tends to seek solitude and can easily feel invaded by emotions, actions or intense conversations. The adult also tends to keep thoughts and feelings to himself. This suits the style of the melancholic child quite well. However, because the melancholic tends to assume that people will make their needs known just as the child would, the child may start to assume the adult does not have needs or desires unless the adult starts to express those more often. A melancholic child can become more in touch with the needs of the phlegmatic adult by interacting with the adult in non-threatening ways such as by playing games, taking walks, playing sports together or reading together. If the phlegmatic adult has hobbies he should include the child now and then so the melancholic has more opportunity to understand him.

A phlegmatic adult is cautious and may be quiet while he thinks about the next move. The melancholic child may misinterpret this as meaning that the adult is unsure of what to do or that the adult has nothing to say and the child may jump in to take over the situation. The melancholic child needs to practice taking time to listen and give the adult time to express what he is trying to say. A good exercise is to practice mirroring the adult. This adaption of a familiar theater game will appeal to the melancholic's connection to the physical realm and the phlegmatic adult's comfort with indirect communication.

The Adapted Mirror Game

Adult and child sit facing each other on the floor. The adult and child take turns making movements. The rule is that the movement must be completed before the other person mirrors what they have seen. The movements can become more and more complex as the game continues. Another variation of this game is to clap a rhythm and have the second person copy the rhythm. Both of these reflection games are suitable for the melancholic child as they are very hands-on methods of interaction with the adult.

The phlegmatic will always pursue his own interests no matter what anyone else thinks. The melancholic child can understand the adult better when he takes the time to get to know what these interests are. The phlegmatic adult can help the child by sharing interests he has with the child.

The phlegmatic adult has a strong intellect and capacity for learning and often uses this intellect to pursue interests and knowledge. However, the phlegmatic temperament is usually most motivated by the enthusiasm of others and may have a hard time completing tasks without help or without joining a class or a group. Left to his own devices the phlegmatic adult may spend more time cogitating on the world around him instead of doing something. As discussed before, it is often best to allow the phlegmatic adult time to work through his thoughts and use this process of selection. It is acceptable for the melancholic child to offer to help, and, if the melancholic child finds he is interested in one of the ideas the phlegmatic adult mentions, it is also useful if the child expresses this to the adult and helps add energy to the idea.

For example, if the phlegmatic adult is musing about plans for the day he may say, "Hmm...I wonder what we should do. Should we fly a kite, go swimming, go for a walk or...."

The melancholic can allow the phlegmatic to work through the decision process or he can offer encouragement by saying, 'I would really like to go swimming, which is sometimes the only motivation a phlegmatic needs to bring thought into action.

The phlegmatic person is steady and loyal. Although the melancholic child shares these traits, he might take them for granted in the adult. The melancholic child would benefit by spending more time reflecting on those things he admires about the adult. Because the melancholic usually assumes and expects everything to work in a specific order or manner he tends to take ideal situations for granted. Since a melancholic child is famous for expressing only displeasure and forgetting to notice what is going well, a good practice for the melancholic child is to create a daily reflection box. The box aspect of the exercise will appeal to the melancholic temperament and the inner reflection aspect will appeal to the phlegmatic adult.

The Reflection Box

Make a box or cover an existing box with plain or decorated paper or old watercolor paintings. Cut a slit in the box that half an index card will fit into. Each day after dinner the melancholic child should write one thing he is thankful for on a paper and put it into the box. On Monday the theme should be the mother, on the second day the theme could be the Father, on Wednesday the theme could be siblings and so on. At the end of the week the box should be opened and shared or reflected on.

- Discipline

Good discipline always stems from a sense of trust, love and harmony between the adult and child. The more the adult and child understand and respect each other, the more discipline happens naturally. To have a healthy discipline relationship with the melancholic child the phlegmatic adult should first read the sections above on how to best understand the child and how to help the child understand the adult.

As I mentioned before in the previous two sections the main challenges between the phlegmatic adult and melancholic child are keeping the adult-child relationship balanced and helping the melancholic respect and admire the phlegmatic. As long as the melancholic child is able to respect the adult and the relationship is balanced discipline should come naturally and easily for this pair.

A phlegmatic adult is driven by a quest for the truth in everything and feels that honesty is one of the highest virtues. The melancholic child is also very dedicated to principles and standards, honesty often being one of those. However, because a phlegmatic adult is so dedicated to the truth this can often come off as blunt or lacking in diplomacy. The melancholic child is very sensitive to this blunt speech and may feel the adult is being too harsh. If the melancholic child seems to take a step back during a conversation the adult should consider that perhaps something in his speech seems harsh to the child. When this happens the phlegmatic adult needs to take a time out and reconsider how he is speaking. The pair may even need a "time out".

The melancholic child easily accepts authority and advice from someone with more competence, so the more often the phlegmatic adult displays competence in tasks the more likely the melancholic will listen to the adult's advice, requests and guidance. Sharing accomplishments does not come naturally to the phlegmatic adult, however, the effort it takes to communicate these accomplishments to the melancholic child is worth the result.

To help improve communication and cooperation the phlegmatic adult should be aware of some of the communication traits of the melancholic child.

The melancholic child often thinks of himself as above reproach. I once saw a melancholic child run into a wall, back up and state with absolute authority, "That wall hit me!" The phlegmatic adult will often have better results with requests or constructive criticisms if he cushions those statements in an indirect phrase. Instead of the phlegmatic adult saying, "You forgot to set the glasses of water on the table for dinner, can you do that please?" the adult could instead say, "I think one of the cats might have run off with the water glasses, can you tell them to bring them back?"

The melancholic child judges others by objective criteria and expects to be judged by the same. So, for example, if the phlegmatic adult says, "You need to apologize for hurting your brother's feelings," the melancholic child will not consider this as valid as, "What you said about your brother's shirt was inaccurate. His shirt is not old. I just purchased it three weeks ago." If the adult says, "The table you set needs to look nicer," the melancholic will be confused and unable to fully understand what the adult wants. It is clearer to the melancholic if the adult instead says, "You need to put a different table cloth on the table and new cups. The settings you have on the table now do not match."

Melancholic people are tolerant of many different types and temperaments of people. In fact, one could argue that melancholics are the least prejudice of all types as they see everyone in terms of performance rather than color, race, culture or creed. A melancholic is happy as long as everyone is fulfilling their roles and obligations. The melancholic expects compliance. He does not request it, but rather assumes that everyone will comply.

If the melancholic has a plan and it does not go well he can quickly become imbalanced and irritated. The phlegmatic adult, in an attempt to avoid conflict, may try to help the melancholic salvage the plan. However, this may not be the best approach. The melancholic child needs to learn his own lessons including the very important lesson of adaptability. It is often best to leave the melancholic to deal with his own anger until he can work out a solution.

- ## The Teaching Relationship

Once the authority of the phlegmatic adult is established, the teaching relationship between the phlegmatic adult and melancholic student should go smoothly. It will go even more smoothly if the phlegmatic adult can better understand the needs of the melancholic student.

The melancholic student feels most comfortable when there is a regular schedule in the home or classroom and when everyone is following the same schedule. If the classroom or home is well organized the melancholic will work efficiently. If the environment is not in order the melancholic person will spend time organizing his environment before he can complete any tasks. If the phlegmatic adult notices that the melancholic student is sorting things instead of working the adult should allow the student to finish so he can work more comfortably.

The melancholic student enjoys tasks that involve analytical thinking, logic and problem solving. The phlegmatic adult also enjoys thinking and exploring ideas, however, in a more flowing manner. The melancholic likes to encounter problems and solve them. The phlegmatic prefers to learn in a more passive manner. For example, the phlegmatic adult may enjoy researching different topics and writing reports, while the melancholic student may enjoy figuring out how to build the best bridge or how to combine different chemicals to induce different reactions. Because of this the phlegmatic adult may tend to use a more passive teaching method. The phlegmatic adult needs to make sure he also includes a lot of problem solving and analytical lessons to keep the melancholic student interested.

When completing his work the melancholic will often check it over again and again, making sure that everything is correct. Once this is done the melancholic student appreciates being recognized for his skill in precision and quality. The phlegmatic adult is not accustomed to giving out too many compliments or a lot of opinions, however, he will be able to motivate the melancholic more effectively by providing feedback on a daily basis.

- A Story to Share

When stories are told they speak to the child on a basic level. The reason one tells stories instead of explaining things to a child is because stories have the ability to adapt to the child's needs. When a person explains a situation to a child he is putting forth a concept that the child needs to grasp at or reach to understand. When one simply *tells* a story the child is given permission to understand the story in any way he wishes and to gain wisdom and knowledge from it in the way that best suits him at that moment. For that reason, it is not recommended that the story be explained to the child or that the child be provided with the ubiquitous "moral" at the end. Rather, it is best to give them a chance to enjoy the story for what it becomes to them and provide them with numerous chances to hear the story told. The stories in this book help the different temperaments understand each other. If the adult or adult would like to explore this understanding on a deeper level they can ask questions once the story is finished. However, one must be sure to ask open questions and allow the child to express his feelings.

The following story shows some interesting dynamics between the phlegmatic fisherman and the melancholic wife. There is no "bad guy" in this story, nor is one character better than the other. Instead, this story should be discussed with an older child or acted out with a younger child to let the child explore his feelings about each character's actions. Does the child think the fisherman was foolish, lazy or wise? Does the child feel the wife is demanding, unreasonable or simply ambitious?

The Fisherman and His Wife

Grimm's Tales

There was once on a time a fisherman who lived with his wife in a miserable hovel close by the sea, and every day he went out fishing. And once as he was sitting with his rod, looking at the clear water, his line suddenly went down, far down below, and when he drew it up again he brought out a large flounder. Then the flounder said to him, "Hark, you Fisherman, I pray you, let me live, I am no flounder really, but an enchanted prince. What good will it do you to kill me? I should not be good to eat, put me in the water again, and let me go."

"Come," said the Fisherman, "there is no need for so many words about it — a fish that can talk I should certainly let go, anyhow," with that he put him back again into the clear water, and the flounder went to the bottom, leaving a long streak of blood behind him. Then the Fisherman got up and went home to his wife in the hovel.

"Husband," said the woman, "have you caught nothing today?"

"No," said the man, "I did catch a flounder, who said he was an enchanted prince, so I let him go again."

124

"Did you not wish for anything first?" said the woman.

"No," said the man; "what should I wish for?"

"Ah," said the woman, "it is surely hard to have to live always in this dirty hovel; you might have wished for a small cottage for us. Go back and call him. Tell him we want to have a small cottage, he will certainly give us that."

"Ah," said the man, "why should I go there again?"

"Why," said the woman, "you did catch him, and you let him go again; he is sure to do it. Go at once."

The man still did not quite like to go, but did not like to oppose his wife, and went to the sea.

When he got there the sea was all green and yellow, and no longer so smooth; so he stood still and said,

"Flounder, flounder in the sea,
Come, I pray you, here to me;
For my wife, good Isabel,
Will not as I'd have her will."

Then the flounder came swimming to him and said, "Well what does she want, then?"

"Ah," said the man, "I did catch you, and my wife says I really ought to have wished for something. She does not like to live in a wretched hovel any longer. She would like to have a cottage."

"Go, then," said the flounder, "she has it already."

When the man went home, his wife was no longer in the hovel, but instead of it there stood a small cottage, and she was sitting on a bench before the door. Then she took him by the hand and said to him, "Just come inside, look, now isn't this a great deal better?" So they went in, and there was a small porch, and a pretty little parlor and bedroom, and a kitchen and pantry, with the best of furniture, and fitted up with the most beautiful things made of tin and brass, whatever was wanted. And behind the cottage there was a small yard, with hens and ducks, and a little garden with flowers and fruit.

"Look," said the wife, "is not that nice!"

"Yes," said the husband, "and so we must always think it, -- now we will live quite contented."

"We will think about that," said the wife. With that they ate something and went to bed.

Everything went well for a week or a fortnight, and then the woman said, "Hark you, husband, this cottage is far too small for us, and the garden and yard are little; the flounder might just as well have given us a larger house. I should like to live in a great stone castle; go to the flounder, and tell him to give us a castle."

"Ah, wife," said the man, "the cottage is quite good enough; why should we live in a castle?"

"What!" said the woman; "just go there, the flounder can always do that."

"No, wife," said the man, "the flounder has just given us the cottage, I do not like to go back so soon, it might make him angry."

"Go," said the woman, "he can do it quite easily, and will be glad to do it; just you go to him."

The man's heart grew heavy, and he would not go. He said to himself, "It is not right," and yet he went. And when he came to the sea the water was quite purple and dark-blue, and grey and thick, and no longer so green and yellow, but it was still quiet. And he stood there and said:

"Flounder, flounder in the sea,
Come, I pray you, here to me;
For my wife, good Isabel,
Wills not as I'd have her will."

"Well, what does she want, then?" said the flounder.

"Alas," said the man, half scared, "she wants to live in a great stone castle."

"Go to it, then, she is standing before the door," said the flounder.

Then the man went away, intending to go home, but when he got there, he found a great stone palace, and his wife was just standing on the steps going in, and she took him by the hand and said, "Come in."

So he went in with her, and in the castle was a great hall paved with marble, and many servants, who flung wide the doors; And the walls were all bright with beautiful hangings, and in the rooms were chairs and tables of pure gold, and crystal chandeliers hung from the ceiling, and all the rooms and bed-rooms had carpets, and food and wine of the very best were standing on all the tables, so that they nearly broke down beneath it. Behind the house, too, there was a great court-yard, with stables for horses and cows, and the very best of carriages; there was a magnificent large garden, too, with the most beautiful flowers and fruit-

trees, and a park quite half a mile long, in which were stags, deer, and hares, and everything that could be desired. "Come," said the woman, "isn't that beautiful?"

"Yes, indeed," said the man, "now let it be; and we will live in this beautiful castle and be content."

"We will consider about that," said the woman, "and sleep on it;" thereupon they went to bed.

Next morning the wife awoke first, and it was just daybreak, and from her bed she saw the beautiful country lying before her. Her husband was still stretching himself, so she poked him in the side with her elbow, and said, "Get up, husband, and just peep out of the window. Look you, couldn't we be the king over all that land? Go to the flounder, we will be the king."

"Ah, wife," said the man, "why should we be King? I do not want to be King."

"Well," said the wife, "if you won't be King, I will; go to the flounder, for I will be King."

"Ah, wife," said the man, "why do you want to be King? I do not like to say that to him."

"Why not?" said the woman; "go to him this instant; I must be King!" So the man went, and was quite unhappy because his wife wished to be King.

"It is not right; it is not right," thought he. He did not wish to go, but yet he went.

And when he came to the sea, it was quite dark-grey, and the water heaved up from below, and smelt putrid. Then he went and stood by it, and said,

"Flounder, flounder in the sea,
Come, I pray you, here to me;
For my wife, good Isabel,
Wills not as I'd have her will"

"Well, what does she want, then?" said the flounder.

"Alas," said the man, "she wants to be a king."

"Go to her; she is a king already."

So the man went, and when he came to the palace, the castle had become much larger, and had a great tower and magnificent ornaments, and the sentinel was standing before the door, and there were numbers of soldiers with kettle-drums and trumpets. And when he went inside the house, everything was of real marble and gold, with velvet covers and great golden tassels. Then the doors of the hall were opened, and there was the court in all its splendor, and his wife was sitting on a high throne of gold and diamonds, with a great crown of gold on her head, and a scepter of pure gold and jewels in her hand, and on both sides of her stood her maids-in-wait-ing in a row, each of them always one head shorter than the last.

Then he went and stood before her, and said, "Ah, wife, and now you are King."

"Yes," said the woman, "now I am King."

So he stood and looked at her, and when he had looked at her thus for some time, he said, "And now that you are King, let all else be, now we will wish for nothing more."

"Nay, husband," said the woman, quite anxiously, "I find time pass very heavily, I can bear it no longer; go to the flounder — I am King, but I must be Emperor, too."

"Alas, wife, why do you wish to be Emperor?"

"Husband," said she, "go to the flounder. I will be Emperor."

"Alas, wife," said the man, "he cannot make you Emperor; I may not say that to the fish. There is only one Emperor in the land. An Emperor the flounder cannot make you! I assure you he cannot."

"What!" said the woman, "I am the king, and you are nothing but my husband; will you go this moment? go at once! If he can make a king he can make an emperor. I will be Emperor; go instantly."

So he was forced to go. As the man went, however, he was troubled in mind, and thought to himself, "It will not end well; it will not end well! Emperor is too shameless! The flounder will at last be tired out."

With that he reached the sea, and the sea was quite black and thick, and began to boil up from below, so that it threw up bubbles, and such a sharp wind blew over it that it curdled, and the man was afraid. Then he went and stood by it, and said,

"Flounder, flounder in the sea,
Come, I pray you, here to me;
For my wife, good Isabel,
Wills not as I'd have her will."

"Well, what does she want, then?" said the flounder.

"Alas, flounder," said he, "my wife wants to be Emperor."

"Go to her," said the flounder; "she is Emperor already."

So the man went, and when he got there the whole palace was made of polished marble with alabaster figures and golden ornaments, and soldiers were marching before the door blowing trumpets, and beating cymbals and drums; and in the house, barons, and counts, and dukes were going about as servants. Then they opened the doors to him, which were of pure gold. And when he entered, there sat his wife on a throne, which was made of one piece of gold, and was quite two miles high; and she wore a great golden crown that was three yards high, and set with diamonds and carbuncles, and in one hand she had the scepter, and in the other the imperial orb; and on both sides of her stood the yeomen of the guard in two rows, each being smaller than the one before him, from the biggest giant, who was two miles high, to the very smallest dwarf, just as big as my little finger. And before it stood a number of princes and dukes.

Then the man went and stood among them, and said, "Wife, are you Emperor now?"

"Yes," said she, "now I am Emperor."

Then he stood and looked at her well, and when he had looked at her thus for some time, he said, "Ah, wife, be content, now that you are Emperor."

"Husband," said she, "why are you standing there? Now, I am Emperor, but I will be Pope too; go to the flounder."

"Alas, wife," said the man, "what will you not wish for? You cannot be Pope. There is but one in Christendom. He cannot make you Pope."

"Husband," said she, "I will be Pope; go at once, I must be Pope this very day."

"No, wife," said the man, "I do not like to say that to him; that would not do, it is too much; the flounder can't make you Pope."

"Husband," said she, "what nonsense! If he can make an emperor he can make a pope. Go to him directly. I am Emperor, and you are nothing but my husband; will you go at once?"

Then he was afraid and went; but he was quite faint, and shivered and shook, and his knees and legs trembled. And a high wind blew over the land, and the clouds flew, and towards evening all grew dark, and the leaves fell from the trees, and the water rose and roared as if it were boiling, and splashed on the shore. And in the distance he saw ships which were firing guns in their sore need, pitching and tossing on the waves. And yet in the midst of the sky there was still a small bit of blue, though on every side it was as red as in a heavy storm. So, full of despair, he went and stood in much fear and said,

"Flounder, flounder in the sea,
Come, I pray you, here to me;"
For my wife, good Isabel,
Wills not as I'd have her will.

"Well, what does she want, then?" said the flounder.

"Alas," said the man, "she wants to be Pope."

"Go to her then," said the flounder; "she is Pope already."

So he went, and when he got there, he saw what seemed to be a large church surrounded by palaces. He pushed his way through the crowd. Inside, however, everything was lighted up with thousands and thousands of candles, and his wife was clad in gold, and she was sitting on a much higher throne, and had three great golden crowns on, and round about her there was much ecclesiastical splendor; and on both sides of her was a row of candles the largest of which was as tall as the very tallest tower, down to the very smallest kitchen candle, and all the emperors and kings were on their knees before her, kissing her shoe. "Wife," said the man, and looked attentively at her, "are you now Pope?"

"Yes," said she, "I am Pope."

So he stood and looked at her, and it was just as if he was looking at the bright sun. When he had stood looking at her thus for a short time, he said, "Ah, wife, if you are Pope, do let well alone!" But she looked as stiff as a post, and did not move or show any signs of life. Then said he, "Wife, now that you are Pope, be satisfied, you cannot become anything greater now."

"I will consider about that," said the woman. Thereupon they both went to bed, but she was not satisfied, and greediness let her have no sleep, for she was continually thinking what there was left for her to be.

The man slept well and soundly, for he had run about a great deal during the day; but the woman could not fall asleep at all, and flung herself from one side to the other the whole night through, thinking always what more was left for her to be, but unable to call to mind anything else. At length the sun began to rise, and when the woman saw the red of dawn, she sat up in bed and looked at it. And when, through the window, she saw the sun thus rising, she said, "Cannot I, too, order the sun and moon to rise?"

"Husband," she said, poking him in the ribs with her elbows, "wake up! go to the flounder, for I wish to be even as God is."

The man was still half asleep, but he was so horrified that he fell out of bed. He thought he must have heard amiss, and rubbed his eyes, and said, "Alas, wife, what are you saying?"

"Husband," said she, "if I can't order the sun and moon to rise, and have to look on and see the sun and moon rising, I can't bear it. I shall not know what it is to have another happy hour, unless I can make them rise myself."

Then she looked at him so terribly that a shudder ran over him, and said, "Go at once; I wish to be like to God."

"Alas, wife," said the man, falling on his knees before her, "the flounder cannot do that; he can make an emperor and a pope; I beseech you, go on as you are, and be Pope."

Then she fell into a rage, and her hair flew wildly about her head, and she cried, "I will not endure this, I'll not bear it any longer; will you go?" Then he put on his trousers and ran away like a madman. But outside a great storm was raging, and blowing so hard that he could scarcely keep his feet; houses and trees toppled over, the mountains trembled, rocks rolled into the sea, the sky was pitch black, and it thundered and lightened, and the sea came in with black waves as high as church-towers and mountains, and all with crests of white foam at the top. Then he cried, but could not hear his own words,

"Flounder, flounder in the sea,
Come, I pray you, here to me;
For my wife, good Isabel,
Wills not as I'd have her will."

"Well, what does she want, then?" said the flounder.

"Alas," said he, "she wants to be like to God."

"Go to her, and you will find her back again in the dirty hovel."

And there they are living still at this very time.

Phlegmatic Adult - Sanguine Child

- ## General Relationship

The general relationship between the phlegmatic adult and the sanguine child is one of balance. However, this balance is not always appreciated by the adult and the child. More often than not, there are challenges to be overcome before both parties can understand and respect each other and realize the tremendous gift their relationship offers to both of them.

The phlegmatic adult and sanguine child relationship is especially challenging because as an adult enters their middle aged years they go through a phase of increased phlegmatic temperament. To make the situation even more challenging, childhood is the age of exaggerated sanguine temperament. In most cases, then, the phlegmatic adult – sanguine child relationship is actually an exaggerated phlegmatic – extreme sanguine relationship. These extremes can result in a very volatile and explosive experience or an amazingly complimentary relationship. The more each temperament understands about each other the more success and balance the relationship will have.

- ## Helping the Phlegmatic Adult Understand the Sanguine Child

The sanguine child is like the seasons or like a plant. She is always evolving, adapting and growing. To the phlegmatic adult it may appear that the sanguine child is unpredictable, inconsistent or even unreliable and capricious. However, it is essential that the phlegmatic adult recognize the syncopated rhythm of the sanguine. Since rhythm is an important part of the phlegmatic adult's life it is important that the adult understand the unusual rhythm that the sanguine child follows instead of being left to feel as if the sanguine has no rhythm at all.

The phlegmatic adult can understand the rhythm of the sanguine by considering the different rhythms that exist in music. The phlegmatic adult's natural rhythm follows the dependable 4/4 time signature such as one would find in rock, country music, blues, funk and pop. A sanguine child's natural rhythms follow complex time signatures such as syncopated time or "savage" time such found in music such as Igor Stravinsky's *The Rite of Spring* (1913). A sanguine child's rhythm can also be compared to musical pieces such as Vivaldi's *Four Seasons* where the listener is taken through different moods and paces, but within a single piece of music. Another possible rhythm associated with the sanguine child is "free time", a time signature that follows the mood and the pace of the musician. In "free time" a musician is free to play the piece of music in whatever way seems suitable to the occasion, mood or location in which she is playing.

Another way to view the sanguine child's rhythm is to consider her close relationship with the environment and the natural rhythms of nature. A sanguine child may become more animated in a noisy location. In a quiet forest, a sanguine child may become more contemplative and peaceful. In the winter time a sanguine child may spend more time in inner reflection; while in the summer time the sanguine child may spend more time with physical pursuits.

Without this vital understanding of the sanguine child's natural rhythms the phlegmatic adult may feel continuously frustrated and confused at what the adult perceives to be a lack of dependability in the sanguine child. The phlegmatic adult not being able to follow the rhythm of the sanguine child may feel like they cannot trust the child. This may result in the phlegmatic adult trying to change the sanguine child to fit more into the phlegmatic's view of the world. This can increase frustration for the phlegmatic adult and the sanguine child. The phlegmatic adult may question why the child cannot grasp "the simple concept of 4/4 time", while the sanguine child will feel unfairly accused of being irresponsible and unreliable. Having a very strong sense of responsibility and compassion towards other people and being very trustworthy, the sanguine child may be very hurt by the lack of faith the phlegmatic adult has in her abilities.

A sanguine child may often express anger, although usually full of joy, excitement, and energy. Sanguines are also very adaptable and enjoy "going with the flow". For this reason the sanguine's anger may surprise the phlegmatic adult who is more familiar with the steady flow of emotions in her own life. When confronted with the anger of a sanguine child the best approach is to allow the sanguine child to express herself and then allow the child to move naturally onto the next emotion. When allowed to express her anger in an open way, without judgment or defense by the phlegmatic adult, the anger will natural dissipate very quickly and the child will be able to move on to more positive emotions. Moments later the child may even have forgotten what the angry was about. When the phlegmatic adult can realize that anger, to a sanguine child, is a passing emotion rather than a state of being as it would be to a phlegmatic adult, then she can experience a more harmonious relationship with the sanguine child by not taking the anger and words that are said personally or too seriously.

The sanguine child often has a very strong sense of purpose, which may feel intimidating to the phlegmatic adult. Even though the relationship is that of an adult to a child the power of the sanguine's sense of purpose can transcend age and time and become an uncomfortable experience for the phlegmatic adult. Feeling the force of the sanguine's sense of purpose, the phlegmatic adult may start to feel inadequate and may start to doubt her abilities to provide enrichment, adequate lessons, or firm enough guidance as an adult or adult. The phlegmatic adult may fear that the sanguine child will find her lacking in some way. It is useful for the phlegmatic adult to understand that the sanguine's sense of purpose extends only to her own actions. A sanguine child is happy to let others be themselves as long as she is given the same freedom. A sanguine child who is allowed the freedom to move and experience life without criticism or blame, will not even notice that others are moving at a different pace. The phlegmatic adult need not worry that the sanguine child will find her wanting in some quality. A balanced sanguine child is happiest when others are doing their own thing since she enjoys the variety of different people in life.

The sanguine child enjoys taking risks and using her intuition. This behavior can seem dangerous and irresponsible to the phlegmatic adult, and even alarming. Since a person of the phlegmatic temperament depends on things in her life being predictable and dependable, she may feel apprehensive or uneasy when the sanguine child takes risks or uses their intuition to make decisions. To be able to understand the sanguine child more effectively and accept these traits, the phlegmatic adult may notice an inner fear of experiencing the unknown and is usually not related to any real peril of the sanguine child. Most of the time the intuition of the sanguine is very powerful and can get her through situations in which the phlegmatic adult would never even consider venturing.

A sanguine child likes to stay busy with a variety of things. Since the phlegmatic adult is more comfortable with the regular and steadily flowing routine of her daily life, the variety and intensity of experiences the sanguine engages in may cause the phlegmatic adult to become worried about the child's health. The phlegmatic adult may be tempted to judge the sanguine based on her own limitations and worries; however the sanguine child needs to experience whatever is desired. A phlegmatic adult is the perfect guide to help teach a sanguine child how to find a more moderate way of experiencing life. However, the phlegmatic adult must not insist that the sanguine give up her intensity. Instead, the phlegmatic adult can admire the child's intensity and help moderate it.

The sanguine child enjoys being seen as the best, first, unique or even as being a bit eccentric. The sanguine child is also very comfortable leading or directing others which the phlegmatic adult may often perceive as trying to tell others or herself what to do. This can be very upsetting to a phlegmatic adult who does not like being told what to do by anyone, especially someone younger than her. Conflicts can be avoided if the phlegmatic can understand that the sanguine is simply leading the situation because she feels most comfortable in that role. If the sanguine is given other options she would most likely consider those options as well.

The phlegmatic adult must also realize that not everyone has the ability to read feelings and energies across space and time as she does and that to the sanguine an emotion does not exist unless it is expressed.

• Helping the Sanguine Child Understand the Phlegmatic Adult

A sanguine child has a natural ability to understand all of the temperaments and be able to mimic each one. This, however, does not translate into the child being at peace with the differences. Although the sanguine child may be able to understand the phlegmatic adult the child may not understand the most crucial element of the phlegmatic temperament – that it has confined boundaries. Since the sanguine child does not have confined boundaries she may feel that once two people understand each other that they should easily be able to adapt to each other and communicate clearly. What the sanguine child may not understand is that this ability to deeply understand each of the temperaments is largely a sanguine trait. The ability to take this information and adapt it is a uniquely sanguine trait. Without this understanding the sanguine child may become frustrated with the phlegmatic adult.

As the sanguine child grows to understand the adult more thoroughly the child may assume that the adult is doing the same with her. One of the greatest gifts a phlegmatic adult can give a sanguine child is to teach an understanding of the unique talent of adaption and how she as a phlegmatic adult would appreciate learning from her. This simple piece of information relays confidence and respect to the sanguine child. It also helps the sanguine child practice patience and accept the responsibility that comes with her skill. In addition, this also lets the sanguine child know that even though she may need to initiate more understanding between the temperaments that the responsibility of adapting does not always need to fall on her shoulders.

A good first exercise to do with a sanguine child and a phlegmatic adult is to talk about the qualities of the wind and water. A sanguine child is like the wind – blowing in different directions – with the freedom to go up, down, to the side, over, under and above. The phlegmatic adult is like the water – always flowing but within the confined mold of the river bed - with the freedom to go forward only. Using this visual the sanguine child can start to comprehend many things about the phlegmatic adult. The sanguine child can understand that it may be difficult for the phlegmatic adult to reach back into the past and recall conversations or lessons and that she will tend to move forward in her words and actions. The sanguine child can perhaps grasp that the phlegmatic adult does want to understand, honor and respect her unique abilities but does not have a natural ability to look out of the path of the riverbed and may need some help in doing so.

The phlegmatic adult is most comfortable keeping emotions and opinions inside. The sanguine child will have a hard time understanding this since she enjoys sharing her ideas and exploring new ones with as many people as possible. The sanguine child will want to engage with the phlegmatic adult on a frequent basis and may be frustrated at the lack of response or enthusiasm. This may cause the phlegmatic adult to withdraw from interaction with the sanguine child, leaving the child to feel insecure and puzzled. If the phlegmatic adult can take the time to communicate her needs and intentions to the sanguine child confrontations and hurt feelings can be avoided. To help the sanguine child appreciate and accept the silence of the phlegmatic adult, the phlegmatic adult needs to contribute to this process. However, the sanguine child has such a natural ability to adapt that the phlegmatic adult will not even need to meet her halfway. The phlegmatic adult only needs to make the small effort of keeping the sanguine child informed. As long as the phlegmatic adult provides the sanguine child with a schedule and some general rules of engagement the child will feel secure enough to give the phlegmatic adult the space needed. It is only when the sanguine child feels abandoned or insecure that the insistence on engaging with the phlegmatic adult on a constant basis arises. The more the phlegmatic adult communicates her intentions and emotions to the sanguine child, the less need the sanguine child will have to seek the answers to those questions using fervent methods of interrogation.

The phlegmatic adult can be very objective and dispassionate about lessons, activities, relationships and events. Since the sanguine measures interest by a person's emotional reaction to an event or person, the child may wrongly assume that the phlegmatic adult is not interested in what she has presented. The sanguine child will be more confident when the phlegmatic adult reassures and perhaps even explains to the child the different ways of responding to the world around them.

The sanguine child is always eager to please others. However, if the child doesn't understand the needs of the phlegmatic adult, she may end up doing things that upset rather than please the adult. If the phlegmatic adult can recognize this desire within the sanguine child to delight others, then she can also realize that as the sanguine child is given more information, a more successful relationship will develop. Helping the sanguine child understand the phlegmatic adult is often just as simple as explaining the exact needs of the adult.

- **Discipline**

Good discipline always stems from a sense of trust, love and harmony between the adult and child. The more the adult and child understand and respect each other, the more discipline happens naturally. To have a healthy discipline relationship with the sanguine child the phlegmatic adult should first read the sections above on how to best understand the child and how to help the child understand the adult.

Since a sanguine child is comfortable with pressure and conflict, the phlegmatic adult may find it a challenge to engage the child. The sanguine child is comfortable with the process of disagreement and figuring out differences – and may even enjoy the process as it is yet another experience that encourages knowledge about the phlegmatic adult and the surrounding world. On the other hand, the phlegmatic adult is more inclined to focus on one topic and needs time to digest any information that involves discord. In general a person of the phlegmatic temperament does not enjoy disharmony and may even tolerate disagreeable situations in order to avoid it. The phlegmatic adult may see the sanguine child as argumentative whereas the sanguine child views herself as purely curious and willing to discuss differences.

A positive solution for this gap between the two modes of discourse is to set aside time (either at certain times of day or a few days a week) to discuss rules, differences, problems, and other issues. Doing this will help the sanguine child with the spiritual practice of patience, as well as offer reassurance that the phlegmatic adult is available. In addition, the phlegmatic adult will feel more secure within the structure of an organized and comfortable system instead of feeling constantly bombarded at unexpected times during the day or week.

Another difference to take note of is that the sanguine child often feels right, in word and action, even if others strongly disagree or disapprove. The sanguine child often needs to learn many lessons "the hard way". Observing this may be difficult for the phlegmatic adult whose own method of functioning is one of observation and carefully planned avoidance of difficulty. The phlegmatic adult must take time to observe the sanguine child learn from mistakes and gain confidence in the child's ability to do so. Instead of focusing on how difficult it is to watch the child struggle through situations the phlegmatic adult may feel are avoidable, it is more constructive to watch the process as an educational experience, with detached interest in the outcome. The more often the phlegmatic adult is able to observe the sanguine child succeed, the more confidence the adult will have with the child, and the less stress the phlegmatic will feel when the sanguine rushes into unknown situations or insists on pursuing impossible tasks. Additionally, the more often the sanguine child is allowed to learn from experience, the more she will learn and this will result in a much earlier balancing of the sanguine temperament. A sanguine child that is held back from this natural learning experience with too many worries, rules and fears of the adult, will take longer to balance her temperament and may experience greater difficulties in adult life.

Although the sanguine child learns through experience this does not always mean that advice is not appreciated. As part of the learning process, she eventually comes to realize that sometimes it is wise to listen to another person's advice. However, the sanguine child will rarely want to admit this. A sanguine adult might come to terms with this and be quite open to inviting advice; however, a sanguine child will rarely do so. The sanguine child may outwardly act with confidence and assurance regardless of what others think yet intuitively know that she may be entering into an uncomfortable or ill-advised state of affairs. It is therefore, prudent to gently suggest alternative solutions and paths to the sanguine child as long as the person suggesting them does not force them upon the child. As the child matures, taking advice will come more frequently, and often with the appearance of not having heard the advice. The phlegmatic adult can take comfort in knowing that the suggestions have been heard and may quite often be considered in silence as the sanguine child goes about daily life. A mistake often made by the phlegmatic adult is to attempt to force a result out of the advice or to insist that the sanguine acknowledge the guidance. This insistence can often create resistance in the sanguine child further impeding the ability to learn.

In raising or teaching a sanguine child, one's words must also be carefully considered. A sanguine often lives in the world of the mind and words rule that world. Many sanguine children are told by phlegmatic adults or adults things like "You are such a dreamer!," "Don't be so selfish," "Control your anger" or "Cool down, chill out!" or "Stop overreacting." These phrases represent the fears and confusion the phlegmatic adult feels with the sanguine child; however, for the sanguine child, these phrases sound unfair and confusing. The phrases below are alternative phrases that can be used with the sanguine child. These phrases will result in more positive feelings between the phlegmatic adult and sanguine child and will additionally affirm the relationship. In the process of hearing these phrases, the sanguine child will gain more confidence in who she is. In the process of saying these phrases, the phlegmatic adult will start to view the sanguine child in a more positive light and with a deeper understanding.

Instead of saying: "You are flaky, spacey or forgetful."
The phlegmatic adult can say: (Realizing the child has become distracted and needs to focus) "Why don't we go for a walk? You can finish that task later." or "Remember how we talked about regaining focus and centering? Would you like to do some yoga or meditation with me?"

Instead of saying: "Don't be selfish"
The phlegmatic adult can say: (Realizing the child may simply be seeing things from her own world view) "Let's play a game! Imagine you are someone else. What would they think of this situation? What would they do?"
The phlegmatic adult could even offer a specific example, saying "What would Winnie the Pooh do in this situation?" or "What would Uncle George be thinking now?"

Instead of saying: "Chill out. Control your temper!"
The phlegmatic adult could say: (Realizing the sanguine child is perhaps misdirecting her energies) "Let's take a walk (or paint, write, jump, dance, or exercise or get out of the house)." Another solution could be to change the activity as it could also be that in general the sanguine child needs more activities to do and is bored or under-stimulated.

To help prevent conflict, the phlegmatic adult needs to watch for a few key things. The first thing to watch for in the sanguine child is either over-stimulation (over watering the "plant") or under-stimulation. Overstimulation may create a selfish and dissatisfied attitude; whereas under-stimulation which creates an angry and dissatisfied individual. The sanguine child also needs to realize what state she is in and to learn to hold the tongue when they child is not in a balanced state. When a sanguine child becomes either under or over stimulated, she needs to seek balance in positive ways. A phlegmatic adult can teach the sanguine child this skill through living example but should not expect the child to develop this skill until much later. There are even some sanguine adults who are still working on this skill as they were not allowed to develop it during their youth.

The sanguine child thrives on structure and as an adult will crave organized spaces and situations. The sanguine child is often skilled at organizing her room, people or projects. Ironically, though, the child often has trouble staying within her own organizational bounds because of the constant need to seek balance. As a sanguine child becomes more aware and balanced, it becomes easier to stay within one's own boundaries. As the phlegmatic adult shares one's own experience with boundaries in a positive way with the sanguine child, the sanguine child can develop this skill more quickly. The best way to share this skill is through example and by providing comfortable boundaries and schedules that the sanguine child can follow around the home or in the classroom.

• The Teaching Relationship

The sanguine student has a great need for variety in the learning process; however, she may also have a propensity to become distracted with many different directions and options. The phlegmatic adult plays an important role in balancing the student's expansive predispositions without stifling the student's natural rhythms of learning.

A sanguine naturally learns by inspiration and intuition. As long as the sanguine can stay balanced and not become overly distracted, she learns best by following those inspirations and energy levels. A sanguine student could write an entire paper in one day but be unable to write for a few days after the completed task. A sanguine student might feel like working very quickly in the morning but more slowly in the afternoon. A sanguine student might become obsessed with butterflies one day and grasshoppers the next. As long as the student is able to finish the tasks started within a reasonable amount of time, it is productive for the student to follow her muse, switch back and forth between projects and pursue multiple projects at the same time.

• A Story to Share

When stories are told they speak to the child on a basic level. The reason one tells stories instead of explaining things to a child is because stories have the ability to adapt to the child's needs. When a person explains a situation to a child she is putting forth a concept that the child needs to grasp at or reach to understand. When one simply *tells* a story the child is given permission to understand the story in any way she wishes and to gain wisdom and knowledge from it in the way that best suits her at that moment. For that reason, it is not recommended that the story be explained to the child or that the child be provided with the ubiquitous "moral" at the end. Rather, it is best to give them a chance to enjoy the story for what it becomes to them and provide them with numerous chances to hear the story told. The stories in this book help the different temperaments understand each other. If the adult or adult would like to explore this understanding on a deeper level they can ask questions once the story is finished. However, one must be sure to ask open questions and allow the child to express her feelings.

In this traditional tale from China a phlegmatic king tried to confine a sanguine bird.

The Nightingale

Traditional Chinese Tale

The emperor's castle was so nice that you had to take great care how you touched it. In the garden were the most beautiful flowers. They were admirably arranged. Beyond the garden was a forest with great trees and deep lakes in it. The forest sloped down to the clear, blue sea. Large ships could sail under the boughs of the trees.

In these trees there lived a nightingale. She sang so beautifully "She'll be coming round the mountain when she comes" that even the poor fisherman, who had so much to do, stood and listened when he came at night to cast his nets. "How beautiful it is!" he said; but, he had to attend to his work, and he forgot about the bird. But when she sang the next night and the fisherman came there again, he said the same thing, "How beautiful!"

From all the countries round came travelers to the emperor's town, who were astonished at the castle and the garden. But when they heard the nightingale, they all said, "This is the finest thing after all!" The travelers told all about it when they went home, and learned scholars wrote many books on the town, the castle, and the garden. But they did not forget the nightingale; she was praised the most.

The books were circulated throughout the world, and some of them reached the emperor. He sat in his golden chair and tried to read a little. He nodded his head in approval, for he liked reading the accounts of the town, the castle, and the garden. "But the nightingale is better than all," he saw written.

"What is that?" said the emperor. "I don't know anything about the nightingale! Is there such a bird in my empire, and so near my garden?"

And the emperor called his minister to him and said "Here is a most remarkable nightingale! They say it is the most glorious thing in my kingdom."

"I have never before heard it mentioned!," said the minister. "I will look for it and find it! But where?"

"The book I read this in," said the emperor, "was sent to me from the Far East; so let me hear the nightingale this evening! She has my gracious permission to appear after supper!"

The minister started to run up and down stairs and through the halls and corridors, with half the court running with him. Everyone was asking about the wonderful bird that all the world knew of except those at court.

At last they met a little girl in the kitchen, who said, "Oh! I know the nightingale well. How she sings! When I am going home at night, I often rest for a little in the wood, and then I hear the nightingale sing."

"Little kitchen maid!," said the minister, "I will give you a place in the kitchen if you can lead us to the nightingale. She is invited to come to court this evening."

And so they all went into the wood where the nightingale was heard singing, but heard a cow mooing.

"Oh!" said the courtiers, "now we have found her!"

"No; that is a cow mooing! "said the kitchen maid.

Then the frogs began to croak in the marsh. "Splendid!," said the chaplain. "It is not wholly unlike a little church-bell!"

"No, no; those are frogs!" said the kitchen maid.

Then the nightingale began to sing.

"There she is!," cried the little girl as she pointed to a little dark-grey bird up in the branches.

"I should never have thought it!," said the minister.

"Little nightingale," called out the kitchen maid, "Our emperor wants you to sing before him!"

"With great pleasure!" said the nightingale as she sang a little song.

"She will be a great success at court," said the minister.

"Shall I sing once more for the emperor?" asked the nightingale, thinking that the emperor was there.

"He is not among us here. Come to the castle tonight and sing, and I am sure he will be enchanted with your lovely song!" said the minister.

"It sounds best in the green wood," said the nightingale; but, still she came gladly and was offered a golden perch to sit on. The whole court was there, and the kitchen maid was allowed to stand behind the door, as she was now a court-cook. Now the emperor nodded to the little grey bird, and she started singing so lovely that tears came into the emperor's eyes and ran down his cheeks. Then the nightingale sang even more beautifully. The emperor was so delighted by now that he said nothing at all. Then she sang again with her gloriously sweet voice. The nightingale was a real success.

She had to stay at court now; and was given twelve servants who each held a silken string which was fastened round her leg. The whole town was talking about the wonderful bird.

Then one day the emperor received a large parcel on which was written "The nightingale." "Here is another new book about our famous bird!" said the emperor. However, it was not a book, but a little mechanical toy in a box — an artificial nightingale that was set all over with diamonds, rubies, and sapphires. When it was wound up, it too could sing "She'll be coming round the mountain when she comes", and move its tail up and down. It glittered with silver and gold.

"This is magnificent!" they all said. "Now they must sing together; what a duet we shall have!"

And so they sang together, but their voices did not blend.

In the end, the artificial bird had to sing alone. When the singing was over, they all wanted the living nightingale to sing too, but where was she? No one had noticed that she had flown out of the open window away to her green woods.

"What shall we do!" said the emperor.

"But we still have the best bird!" they said, and the artificial bird had to sing again. That was the thirty-fourth time they had heard the same piece, but they did not yet know it by heart. The bandmaster praised it: "You see, with the real nightingale one can never tell what will come out, and just how!"

"That's just what we think!" said everyone. But the fishermen who had heard the real nightingale said, "This one sings well enough, the tunes glide out; however there is something wanting, but I don't know what!"

Later the real nightingale was banished from the castle, while the artificial bird was put on silken cushions. The bandmaster wrote a work of twenty-five volumes about the artificial bird. It was so learned, long, and little understood . . . But the emperor, the court, and all the people in time knew every note of the artificial bird's song by heart. They could sing along with it, and they did. It gave them great pleasure.

But one evening when the artificial bird was singing its best, and the emperor lay in bed listening to it, something in the bird went crack. The works inside it were nearly worn out it. It was found that from now on it must be very seldom used, only once a year, and even that was almost too much.

Five years passed, and then the emperor became ill. Cold and pale lay the emperor in his splendid great bed. The whole court believed him dead, and one after the other left him to pay their respects to the new emperor who had been chosen in his stead.

The old emperor longed for relief where he lay. The moon was streaming in at the open window but the night was silent.

"Music! Let there be music!" cried the emperor but the mechanical bird was silent. There was no one to wind it up.

All at once there came in at the window a wonderful burst of song. It was the little living nightingale who was sitting outside on a bough, and had heard the need of the emperor and had come to sing to him a little. As she sang the blood flowed quicker and quicker in the old, sulking emperor's weak limbs, and life began to return.

"Thank you!" said the emperor. "I chased you from the castle, and you have given me life again! Can I reward you?"

"You shed tears of delight the first time I sang, and thereby gladdened this singer's heart. Get strong again. I will sing you a lullaby."

The emperor fell into a deep, calm sleep. The sun was shining through the window when he awoke. He felt strong and well. None of his servants had come back yet, for they thought he was dead. But the nightingale sat and sang to him.

"You shall sing whenever you like, and I will break the artificial bird into a thousand pieces," said the old emperor.

"Don't do that!" said the nightingale. "He worked well as long as he could. Keep him. I cannot build my nest in the castle and live here, but let me come whenever I like. I will sit in the evening on the bough outside the window, and I will sing you something that will make you happy and grateful which otherwise lies hidden from you. I love your heart more than your crown. Promise me just one thing . . . "

"I think I can do that!" said the emperor.

"Don't tell anyone that you have a little bird who tells you things. It will be much better not to!" Then the nightingale flew away.

Now the servants came in to look at their dead emperor. He said, "Good-morning!"

Phlegmatic Adult – Choleric Child

• General Relationship

When looking at a choleric child, a phlegmatic adult's emotions will most likely fluctuate between awe and astonishment. Comforted by the steady and peaceful ways of the phlegmatic adult, the choleric child will feel balanced, secure and happy in the relationship, provided the child has other outlets for his high energy levels. The relationship between the phlegmatic adult and the choleric child is unique because middle age or the age of maturity also corresponds to the phlegmatic temperament. This means that the adult interacting with the child will be in the most phlegmatic state of being at this time in life. At the same time, as a child passes the age of seven he enters into the most choleric phase of his life. So, in this combination of adult and child there is the experience of having an extreme phlegmatic interacting with an extreme choleric.

• Helping the Phlegmatic Adult Understand the Choleric Child

The choleric child is represented by the element of fire while the element of water represents the phlegmatic adult. The phlegmatic adult can imagine how water would relate to fire to give him insight into the choleric child and some of the conflicts that the adult and child may struggle with. The water may fear the fire or be cautious of it because it knows that as the fire approaches, the water will become hot and perhaps even boil. This is uncomfortable for the water as the water prefers to be cool and flowing. However, the water may also notice how easy it is to put out the fire. The water does not need to make any effort at all. Just by being water, the fire will go out.

The choleric child is very intuitive and sensitive and will sense these emotions within the adult. The child will be confused by the adult's fear of him, leaving him feeling discouraged by the adult's reactions to his vibrancy. Yet the child will not know how to express these feelings. So, this may cause the choleric child to become even more energetic with the adult in hopes that that will bring the adult closer to him. What the child doesn't realize is that this increase in energy can push the adult even farther away and increase the feelings of fear. The following stories illustrate the dynamics between the phlegmatic adult and the choleric child. Using different points of view, the stories also show that the power of one is not necessarily better than the other. The story "The Sun and the Rain" will help one understand the point of view of the choleric child. The story "The Phlegmatic Rain and the Choleric Sun" will help the choleric child understand the adult more clearly. The second story is included under the heading "Helping the Child Understand the Adult".

The story *"The Sun and the Rain"* illustrates how the fiery choleric personality thinks, functions and communicates with others and the way he would motivate others to action. In this story, the choleric sun uses its enthusiasm, vibrancy and warmth to encourage the traveler to remove his coat. The choleric child shares the same understanding of the world as the sun in the story, using warmth and vibrancy to connect, motivate and show love to others. Sometimes the choleric child can be too warm and vibrant thus overwhelming others, which is illustrated in the second story.

The Sun and the Rain

By Kristie Burns

One day the sun noticed some lovely little raindrops hiding in a cloud. She was feeling quite bored that day so she decided to strike up a conversation with the little raindrops. However, she was quite frustrated when they refused to wake up. The raindrops were enjoying their cloud nap and didn't want to talk. So the sun shined brighter and brighter and finally the little raindrops could ignore her no longer.

"Wake up little raindrops!" said the sun.
"What do you want?" they said, feeling quite annoyed.
"I want to play!" said the sun.
But the little raindrops did not want to play.
So the sun said, "How about we sing?"
But the little raindrops did not want to sing.
So the sun asked, "Would you like to dance?"

But the little raindrops did not want to dance.

The sun knew what to do. Very few entities could refuse a challenge so she asked one last question, "Do you want to have a contest to see who is more powerful?"

Now the little raindrops were awake! They knew that they were definitely the most powerful on earth. They had flooded entire towns and brought down bridges. They could fill rivers and destroy trees in a hurricane. They laughed and said, "Sure! We are up to the challenge."

So the sun said, "Oh good! So let's see who can get that little boy to take off his coat."

The raindrops were confident and eager to prove their superiority so they enthusiastically started the challenge. They rushed from the clouds with such force that even the sun was surprised. The little boy was also surprised and ran under the awning of a house and wrapped his coat around him tightly. The raindrops came down harder. The little boy wrapped his coat around him even tighter.

Finally the raindrops said, "Well, we didn't lose yet. We are just taking a break and will try again later."

Now it was the sun's turn. The sun started to sparkle and shine and glow with warmth. The little boy was delighted. He felt the warmth and loved the way the sun's rays bounced off the earth and made everything brighter. He immediately took off his coat and lifted his head to the sky and smiled at the sun.

In this story the sun is doing what it knows best. This is what the choleric child will do as well, glowing and shining and giving warmth expecting that everyone will be so pleased. He does not always realize that the heat may disturb some people, as with the girl in the next story.

The choleric child will most often express himself with joy, laughter and giggling. The phlegmatic adult, being more stoically emotional, may perceive that the choleric child is not taking things as seriously as "he should" or that the child is laughing at him. A more accurate perception would be that the choleric child is simply expressing himself in the way that comes most naturally to him. When a choleric child laughs he could, at the same time, be taking something very seriously.

The phlegmatic adult may become worried or disappointed in the choleric child as the child seeks to fulfill his desires. A choleric desires many things and seeks different experiences with both people and objects. The phlegmatic adult, being satisfied to spend many hours alone in self reflection and not sharing the desire to own a great number of things, may worry that the choleric child is too dependent on others or that he is becoming greedy. Instead, try to appreciate that different forces of nature motivate the choleric child from within and that these are natural forces that are good and not bad. An exaggerated choleric can become greedy and dependent on others, but with the balance of a phlegmatic adult this is not likely to happen. To help the child maintain a balance, the adult can suggest ways in which the child can temper his desire for people and objects. One might encourage the choleric child to borrow books from the library instead of buying them, or to make stuffed animals and dolls instead of purchasing them. One could invite the choleric child on a peaceful nature walk and encourage him to enjoy activities on his own as well as with others. As long as the adult is accepting of who the child is, the child will be accepting of the adult's efforts at balancing. However, if he senses the adult is critical of his needs or desires, he will resist the adult's suggestions and become anxious. This may increase the child's desire to be with people and own more things as he may become fearful these things are soon to be taken away.

The choleric child may dazzle and overwhelm the phlegmatic adult so much, that one may have a hard time seeing the choleric child's beautiful inner peace. For the phlegmatic adult, inner peace is on the outside, however, the choleric child keeps his inner peace on the inside surrounded by glowing energy and light. A choleric child is very compassionate and often feels other people's emotions very deeply. The choleric child is often the child that is always asking for something new and for the adult to do something for him. However, he is also the child that will be the first to offer help when help is needed, or will be the first child to spend his allowance to buy a gift for a friend or family member.

The choleric child experiences life through space and is often seen moving around from room to room and place to place. This movement can be upsetting for the phlegmatic adult who prefers to remain in one location for a period of time. The phlegmatic adult experiences life through time, and he prefers to remain constant in his location, learning through the experience of time. If the phlegmatic adult can identify his experience with time as being similar to the choleric child's experience with space, he will gain a greater understanding of the choleric child. It is also important for the phlegmatic adult to realize that although the choleric child is often on the move, he enjoys physical contact and emotional intimacy. A phlegmatic adult may have a hard time understanding this aspect of the choleric temperament since he associates intimacy with resting and physical contact with remaining in one place.

The choleric child lives in a world with no limits that can often border on fantasy, becoming so wrapped up in his dream world that he will perceive parts of it to be true. In cases where the child realizes his thoughts are merely whimsy, he may still insist that the thoughts are true. Truth to a choleric child is based more on emotion and desire rather than reality. The phlegmatic adult places great value on honesty and truth and may not understand the fantasy world of the choleric child, thus becoming frustrated with what the adult perceives as consistent lying. The phlegmatic adult will have a greater understanding of the choleric child if the adult can interpret the intentions behind what the choleric child is expressing rather than focusing on the words used to communicate his message. At the same time the phlegmatic adult can guide the choleric child in ways to communicate more accurately and effectively.

Some see the choleric child as a bear or a triangle. Plato called choleric children the guardians. As the phlegmatic adult meditates on these symbols, he can gain a greater understanding of the choleric child, and special attention should be given to emotions evoked by these symbols. I have discussed this concept in more detail in the next section.

• Helping the Choleric Child Understand the Phlegmatic Adult

The worldview of the phlegmatic adult is very different from that of the choleric child. Just as the story *"The Sun and the Rain"* can help a phlegmatic adult understand a choleric child, the story of *"The Phlegmatic Rain and the Choleric Sun"* can help a choleric child understand a phlegmatic adult.

The Phlegmatic Rain and the Choleric Sun

By Kristie Burns

One time some resting raindrops passed the glowing sun in the sky. The sun saw them resting so cozily in the clouds and said, "Aha! You little lazy raindrops! I'll bet you don't accomplish anything today!"

Well, the little raindrops were quite offended. First of all the mighty and loud sun had woken them up from a lovely nap and secondly, they had felt quite satisfied with themselves before the sun pointed out that there was something wrong.

So they answered back in their little raindrop voices, "Oh, sun, we are quite capable of doing anything you ask! We can meet any challenge you put forth."

At this the sun was very happy. For, to tell the truth, the sun was a bit bored today. It was a mostly sunny day with only a few clouds in the sky and not a bit of wind. He felt fed up with nobody to play with. So the sun looked down on the earth to find a challenge for the little raindrops, and immediately his eyes fell upon a little girl sitting under a tree near a large meadow.

"I have a challenge for you!" he said to the little raindrops. "Whoever can get that little girl to play in the meadow will win the contest." The little raindrops had no idea how they would do this since they were way up in the sky and the little girl was way down on the earth, but they didn't want the sun to keep acting so boastful and proud, so they agreed to the challenge.

The Sun went first. He shined and shined and sent his rays of heat and light down on the meadow. The flowers sparkled and the grass glowed with the light. The little stones on the forest pathways looked like little stars shining out from the dark green moss. The sun, confident that he had won, hid behind a cloud and chuckled. How could anyone resist all of that beauty? The little girl became very hot and uncomfortable, however, and almost started to cry. It had become hot so quickly! She moved herself farther under the tree to shade herself from the burning rays of the sun. The sun was surprised. But just as he was about to attempt to lure her out of from under the tree again, something strange happened.

First the heat of the sun and then the rapid cooling of the sun, when it hid behind the cloud, caused the raindrops to start to fall from the sky. The little raindrops suddenly found themselves falling from their comfortable cloud pillow through the bright sky and onto the green earth. They fell on the flowers, on the birds, on the meadow and even on the little girl. The little girl was delighted! The raindrops were so soothing and cool and gentle. She ran out from under the tree and started skipping in the meadow.

The sun was quite angry when he saw that the little raindrops were going to win and started to shine quite brightly again, but the bright sun was no match for the cooling rain that fell on the earth. The earth was calmed, the flowers were happy and the little girl opened her mouth to the sky to catch as many of the tiny raindrops as she could in her mouth.

The phlegmatic adult is like the season of winter and the choleric child is like the season of summer. In geometry, the phlegmatic adult is like a circle, whereas the choleric child is like a triangle. The phlegmatic adult is like a dolphin and the choleric child is like a bear. The phlegmatic adult is like the color blue and the choleric child is like the color red.

The phlegmatic adult and choleric child can draw these symbols together and then talk about how they interact with each other. This simple exercise can deepen understanding between the two temperaments.

A phlegmatic adult can be very cautious and sensible. The choleric child may misunderstand the adult, perceiving this cautiousness and sensibleness as a lack of enthusiasm for his activities. A phlegmatic adult should make sure he expresses his enthusiasm and praise for the choleric child's work in a way that will be understood by the child. If the adult is not able to adapt to the choleric child's needs, he will need to explain to the child that he is very enthusiastic about the child's work, but that he simply expresses himself in a different way.

The phlegmatic adult enjoys frequent periods of solitude and introspection, which may leave the choleric child feeling rejected. The choleric child has a much greater need to connect than the phlegmatic adult. To balance the choleric child's need for intimacy with the phlegmatic adult's need for privacy, the phlegmatic adult can make an extra effort to give the choleric child additional hugs and express his love and appreciation more often when they are together. When the connections between the phlegmatic adult and the choleric child are consistently intense enough, the choleric child will not need the connections to be as frequent.

A phlegmatic adult is often cautious about what he reveals to other people. The choleric child may perceive this to be secretive, cold or distant and may feel shut out of the phlegmatic adult's life. This feeling can be exacerbated by the fact that the phlegmatic adult obviously feels self-sufficient in or out of a relationship and often chooses solitude over socialization. This misunderstanding can cause a divide between the adult and the child if it is not explained. A choleric child needs to be aware that his phlegmatic adult's mannerism is like this with everyone and has been like this since he was young. If the child is not made aware of this fact, he may take the behavior personally and think the phlegmatic adult does not like him.

- Discipline

Good discipline always stems from a sense of trust, love and harmony between the adult and child. The more the adult and child understand and respect each other, the more discipline happens naturally. To have a healthy discipline relationship with the choleric child the phlegmatic adult should first read the sections above on how to best understand the child and how to help the child understand the adult.

The biggest challenge in the discipline relationship between the phlegmatic adult and the choleric child is that the phlegmatic adult prefers to keep his thoughts to himself, but the choleric child needs these thoughts repeated frequently, firmly and regularly to maintain stability in his behavior.

As a choleric child grows and matures he will take on more and more responsibility. However, as the choleric child is learning to be more responsible and balanced he needs more guidance from the adults in his life. Because the choleric in this relationship is a child and the phlegmatic is the adult, it is the responsibility of the phlegmatic adult to learn to express his needs more clearly and regularly. As the phlegmatic adult is able to do this more often, the choleric child will have a less frequent need for direction and will grow to be a quiet self-sufficient teenager or young adult. When given proper guidance as a young child, choleric children often mature into self-sufficiency at a young age. For the phlegmatic adult this will take some effort and patience. However, knowing that the situation is temporary should make the task easier. In addition, learning to express oneself on a regular basis is one of the spiritual practices that help to balance the phlegmatic temperament, and this will result in better overall health for the phlegmatic adult.

A choleric child may have trouble taking the phlegmatic adult seriously if the adult does not speak firmly, often, or loudly enough. If the phlegmatic adult can find an effective way to convey these sensations to the choleric child, then discipline will be effective. If the choleric child does not feel a sense of authority, either through voice, firmness, action or repetition, he may not understand that the person who is making the request is serious and may not complete the tasks that are requested of him. To the phlegmatic adult, this may seem as if the choleric child is defying him and he may start to feel the stirrings of anger or frustration. However, this frustration can be avoided if the choleric child understands the seriousness of the requests being made. If the phlegmatic adult initially has trouble communicating with the choleric child in an effective way, the phlegmatic adult should consider asking for help from a spouse, friend or other adult who can help the choleric child to better understand the phlegmatic adult's way of communicating. This intermediary can also lend an air of authority to the phlegmatic adult if the child knows that they will be a consistent and regular supporter.

Two years ago I counseled a couple that were at wits end because of their vibrant and energetic choleric child, Maria. The father, Robert, was of the melancholic temperament and the mother, Rosa, was of the phlegmatic temperament. Rosa was frustrated that Maria always seemed to listen to Robert but not to her. When we explored the dynamics between the three of them, we discovered that Rosa had trouble being firm and expressive with Maria. Robert had no problem being firm and expressive, but he often scolded Rosa for not being firm enough with Maria thus undermining Rosa's already diminished authority. In addition, Robert was often unaware of the household rules or of Maria's responsibilities as he was at work most of the day.

Rosa and Robert were able to discuss and agree on some basic household rules and responsibilities for Maria, and Robert was able to understand that Maria's silence was not a sign of weakness. Subsequently, he was then able to support Rosa more effectively. It was not long before Maria realized that Robert and Rosa were a team. Although Rosa did not become the firm and regular disciplinarian that Maria needed, Maria still felt the authority in her requests by knowing that her father, Robert, was part of the team.

- ## Teaching Relationship

A choleric student is inspired by others when he learns. A phlegmatic adult, on the other hand, may lean towards more traditional methods of education and feel that it is important for students to work individually. The phlegmatic adult may not realize that the choleric student actually learns more effectively in groups, and may see his constant interaction with other students or siblings as disruptive to the educational process.

A choleric student learns by movement and may enjoy moving around the classroom or exploring different ways of sitting or studying. A phlegmatic adult may not realize that this is an effective way to study for the choleric student. Because a phlegmatic adult needs to have a regular place to study or work to be most effective, he may assume that this is the most effective way for all people to learn. However, in the case of the choleric student, sitting in one place or studying in the same location day after day may actually impede his desire to learn.

A choleric student learns most efficiently when he is excited and enthusiastic about the topic he is learning about. A phlegmatic adult does not share this same need so he may not realize his choleric student is lagging behind in his lessons. The phlegmatic adult must be diligent in observing the choleric student to ensure that he appears enthusiastic about the student's work. When the choleric student appears disinterested or stoic about the task at hand, the phlegmatic adult may wrongly assume that the student has simply turned inward to focus more effectively, as the adult would. Instead, this is a sign that the adult is losing the interest of the choleric student and must do something to help the student regain his motivation. Allowing the choleric student to change topics, change locations or change working partners can often help him to regain his enthusiasm.

A choleric student finds his imagination inspiring. A phlegmatic adult is inspired by the pursuit of knowledge and facts. This difference in inspirations may mean that the phlegmatic adult may not provide the choleric student with enough inventive lessons to capture his attention. The phlegmatic adult finds the information already contained in the lessons exciting. Conversely, the choleric student needs more visionary and creative lessons. However, the phlegmatic adult need not worry that he will need to work harder to create extra lessons for the choleric student. On the contrary, the choleric student may actually help teach the class. If the phlegmatic adult gives the choleric student permission to expand his lessons, the choleric student will thrive and may inspire other students in the process. On the other hand, telling the choleric student he must do the lessons in a certain manner or in the "right way" will generate conflicts.

Earlier this year I counseled a phlegmatic adult, Mr. Bask, who was having difficulty with one particular choleric student, Samantha. Samantha was always talking to other students during class and moving around the classroom quite frequently. She was eager to learn, but rarely the lessons that Mr. Bask was teaching. Fortunately Mr. Bask's classroom an open classroom model, so the children had freedom to move about the classroom and were encouraged to cooperate as long as they followed certain guidelines of respect for the other students. After counseling, Mr. Bask was able to understand how important the movement and cooperation in the classroom was to Samantha, and he was able to communicate with her using this as a common talking point. He explained to her that she was welcome to move about the classroom and partner with different students, but that she must do so within certain guidelines or she would be disrupting the class. Students who disrupted the classroom were traditionally asked to sit alone at a table and work until the class found its balance again. When Samantha understood that Mr. Bask was not trying to make her sit down all day and was actually encouraging her to do what she loved, she was happy to follow the simple guidelines he put forth. Previously, she had perceived that Mr. Bask was asking her not to walk around or interact with other students at all and this caused her a lot of frustration.

Additionally, Mr. Bask started rewarding Samantha with teaching responsibilities when she was able to complete the tasks assigned to her. Samantha was thrilled with the opportunity to create her own lessons and actually became a class favorite when it came time to teach composition. Her enthusiasm for writing and her original ideas inspired the entire classroom. At the end of the year, Mr. Bask commented that because of Samantha, the entire class was much more enthusiastic about writing than any other class he had ever taught.

- A Story to Share

The Phlegmatic Goose and the Choleric Sparrow

A Chinese Folktale

Confucius had a son-in-law, Kung Yeh Chang, who understood birds. He built a pavilion in his garden, which was rich in flowers, trees, shrubs, and ponds, so that the birds loved to gather there. Thus he was able to spend many delightful hours near them, watching.

One day while Kung Yeh Chang was resting in his pavilion, a small house sparrow lit in a tree near-by and started to sing and chatter. A little later a wild goose dropped down by the pond for a drink. Hardly had he taken a sip when the little sparrow called out, "Who are you? Where are you going?"

To this the goose did not reply and the sparrow became angry and asked again, "Why do you consider me beneath your notice?" and still the goose did not answer. Then the little sparrow became furious and said in a loud, shrill voice, "Again I ask, who are you? Tell me or I will fly at you," and he put his head up, and spread his wings, and tried to look very large and fierce.

By this time the goose had finished drinking, and looking up he said, "Don't you know that in a big tree with many branches and large leaves the cicadas love to gather and make a noise? I could not hear you distinctly. You also know the saying of the ancients, 'If you stand on a mountain and talk to the people in the valley they cannot hear you'," and the wild goose took another drink.

The little sparrow chattered and sputtered, shook his wings, and said, "What, for example, do you know of the great world? I for my part can go into people's houses, hide in the rafters under their windows, see their books and pictures, what they have to eat and what they do. I can hear all the family secrets. I know all that goes on in the family and state. I know who are happy and who are sad. I know all the quarrels and all the gossip, and I know just how to tell it to produce the best effect. So you see that I know much that you can never hope to know."

"It may be good to give others an equal chance with ourselves, or even to give them the first choice," said the goose. "We geese therefore fly in a flock in the shape of the letter V and take turns in flying first. No one takes advantage of the other. We have our unchanging customs of going north in the spring and south in the winter. People come to depend on us, and make ready for either their spring work or the cold of winter. Thus, we stay away from gossip and are a help to man.

"You sparrows, however, gossip and only thinking of your own good. Now, we geese are respected. Is there not a proverb that says, 'There are many people without the wisdom and virtues of the wild goose'? You sparrows, however, chatter about small affairs beneath my notice and I bid you good-day."

The sparrow now trembled with so much rage that she could not fly away nor keep her hold on the branch. Kung Yeh Chang exclaimed after he had looked on it all, "Sad, sad, there are those in mankind that are like the goose and those that are like the sparrow and yet neither see the benefit of the other."

When stories are told they speak to the child on a basic level. The reason one tells stories instead of explaining things to a child is because stories have the ability to adapt to the child's needs. When a person explains a situation to a child he is putting forth a concept that the child needs to grasp at or reach to understand. When one simply *tells* a story the child is given permission to understand the story in any way he wishes and to gain wisdom and knowledge from it in the way that best suits him at that moment. For that reason, it is not recommended that the story be explained to the child or that the child be provided with the ubiquitous "moral" at the end. Rather, it is best to give them a chance to enjoy the story for what it becomes to them and provide them with numerous chances to hear the story told. The stories in this book help the different temperaments understand each other. If the adult or adult would like to explore this understanding on a deeper level they can ask questions once the story is finished. However, one must be sure to ask open questions and allow the child to express his feelings.

Sanguine Adult - Sanguine Child

- ## General Relationship

In general, the sanguine adult and sanguine child will experience many joyous moments together. Both will enjoy having fun and exploring new things. Both are enthusiastic about many things in life, are easy to be with, and live in the moment. The sanguine adult may even find herself preferring to be with the sanguine child and wondering why every other child is not like the sanguine. This adult and child pair will likely admire each other and be amazed at what each can accomplish.

The sanguine temperament of the child will naturally be more extreme than that of the adult as the sanguine element is most prominent in childhood. Because of this the sanguine adult may find herself worrying about the child's tendency to do too many things and spread herself too thin. The adult has most likely mellowed and become more balanced as a sanguine adult, however, she may have some bad memories of days when she used to be the same way. This worry may interfere with the adult's ability to interact with the child in an authentic way. The sanguine adult may react out of fear instead of interacting with the child out of compassion and understanding.

If the sanguine adult is still struggling with extremes in the sanguine temperament, being with the child may create an explosive reaction. For example, if the sanguine adult is still struggling with finding ways to temper her desire to do everything and say "yes" to everything and the child is doing the same, the adult may find that both of them are often over-stressed and over-booked. Without a good example to follow, the sanguine child will not realize what she is doing. Without a child who complains about the fast pace the sanguine adult sets, the sanguine adult will not think to slow down.

- ## Helping the Sanguine Adult Understand the Sanguine Child

The sanguine adult will probably not have much trouble understanding the sanguine child unless she is avoiding an issue in herself. Sanguines love to understand other people and observe how and why they do things. For this reason, the adult will quickly see how similar the child is to herself and will enjoy, appreciate, and understand her. The sanguine child enjoys experiencing good things and may not feel comfortable with her depressed or angry moods. At the same time, a sanguine adult may not be looking for these different moods. The adult needs to understand that even if the child does not express these emotions, the child does have bad moods, depression, and other struggles. The child will not usually approach the adult about these because a sanguine is very independent and does not want to "be a bother" to others. The adult should take some time each week to connect with the child and ask her about her needs and moods. As mentioned earlier, as a sanguine adult, one is often not looking for these things, either. For the adult, life is flowing and beautiful unless someone says otherwise. If no one mentions an issue, it might not occur to the adult that there is a problem. One of the adult's favorite mottos may be, "if it is not broken, do not fix it."

The sanguine adult must be careful not to assume that just because she shares the same temperament with the child that the child enjoys the same things. For example, the sanguine adult may enjoy reading but not enjoy dancing. However, it is possible, even though the child is also sanguine that she may actually prefer dancing and not enjoy reading as much.

• Helping the Sanguine Child Understand the Sanguine Adult

The sanguine child will enjoy relating to her adult's child-like nature, however, he/she may also find it confusing. Show the child healthy examples of how adults can be both responsible and playful at the same time. Let the child know that an adult can enjoy being young at heart, and also reliable and responsible in life.
Because both the adult and child expresses her frustrations with anger and because this anger is quick to come and quick to fade, one will find that the sanguine child is rarely upset by the adult's expressions of frustration or what one may perceive to be her mistakes in relating to the child. Because the child's emotions also come and go so quickly, she assumes the adult is the same and so she doesn't spend a lot of time worrying about the adult's feelings or emotions, or if the adult is still angry at her for something that happened two days ago. The sanguine child will feel very comfortable with the way the adult expresses herself and will usually understand her quite well.

Because the child is young and has not had experience with different people outside the home, she may have a hard time understanding/recognizing some of the things the adult and child have in common. Although both adult and child have a strong sense of purpose, the sanguine child may experience the adult's as overwhelming, and may often feel like the adult is always telling her what to do and how to do it. The child also has the same trait. However, when the child sees it in the adult, all she sees is that this sense of purpose is very powerful and the child is not sure how to overcome the force of it. The child forgets that she also has a strong sense of purpose, but at the same time she is very open minded and willing to go with the flow if better ideas or purposes reveal themselves. Allowing the child to recognize this in herself and in the adult will help the child understand the adult more intimately. When sharing ideas or requests, the adult should try to do so in a way that leaves some space for the sanguine child's ideas too. Without realizing it, the adult's enthusiasm and sense of purpose may be shutting the child out. If the adult makes it clear to the child that she also have a voice and that the adult is open to dialogue about topics, then the child will understand the adult's intentions better instead of assuming that the adult expects everyone to agree with her.

Another trait both adult and child have in common is that they do not like to be confined. The adult enjoys action and learns through movement. However, combined with the adult's enthusiasm and sense of purpose, all this movement can make the sanguine child feel it is hard to connect with the adult. Because the child is constantly moving too, the adult needs to take time to sit with the child and connect with her on a daily basis in some way either through sharing a meal, reading together, or other peaceful activity. Without the opportunity to connect on a daily basis, the sanguine child could just assume the adult is too busy for her. Even though the child is also very busy, the adult needs to remember that the child does not understand the concept of temperaments. The child is not seeing the adult's similarities. The child sees that her adult is or is not meeting her needs. A sanguine needs to feel the comfort of a constant adult and may not understand that the adult is there for her if the adult is always active and seems out of reach.

In observing her adult the sanguine child will be learning to understand her and, without realizing it, start to understand herself. The adult can help balance the sanguine temperament by providing healthy examples of what a sanguine adult is like. Although the sanguine adult likes to stay busy and take risks, the adult needs to share with the child some of the thought processes that went into the decisions made and to show that she also knows how to rest and relax.

As a sanguine, one is a pioneer and is usually confident about one's actions. The adult may even border on being competitive, ambitious or both. As the child watches the adult's confidence and ambition, the adult should help the child to understand that these qualities are just part of who the adult is and that one balances this ambition with the wisdom to take some things in life slowly. The sanguine adult may openly discuss one's accomplishments with friends and family and even the sanguine child. However, be cautious that the child understands the difference between bragging and sharing.

Both adult and child are very compassionate, so the sanguine child may worry about her adult when the adult is under pressure or stressed. However, as a sanguine adult, one is more comfortable with pressure and stress than the other temperaments. The child needs reassurance that the adult has things under control and that the adult is able to manage the pressure she is under.

The sanguine adult may often make decisions based on intuition. The child will also have this skill. However, it is sometimes difficult for a sanguine to define when intuition is speaking or when fear or desire is taking over. Help the child understand how one makes decisions. Does the adult double check her intuition to make sure she are on the right path? Does one have a certain way of distinguishing between the feelings of intuition, fear and/or desire? Sharing these pieces of information with the child will help her development as a sanguine, as well as make adult's decisions seem less frightening and sudden to them.

- Discipline

Good discipline always stems from a sense of trust, love and harmony between the adult and child. The more the adult and child understand and respect each other, the more discipline happens naturally. To have a healthy discipline relationship with the sanguine child the sanguine adult should first read the sections above on how to best understand the child and how to help the child understand the adult.

Making sure the child gets her needs met will prevent a lot of problems from arising in the first place. Sanguine children usually need little discipline. Sanguine children learn from observing and are eager to please. They want to see the adult happy so she often does "the right thing". The most common place where discipline comes into play between the sanguine partner/adult and sanguine child is when the sanguine "blows up". This will happen because a sanguine child is very easygoing and does not like to ask for things or create trouble for the adult or adult. The sanguine adult will not realize anything is wrong, because in her worldview everything is also peaceful.

Over time the sanguine child will say "yes" so much that one day they will wake up and realize they need something desperately. Because the child lives in the present and is not yet fully aware of her temperament, she may feel this need is a simply a need, not realizing where the need has come from or why it is so strong, perhaps even painful. When this happens the sanguine will suddenly make demands. The sanguine adult may be shocked at the sudden behavior change and may not react well. The adult may wonder what happened to the sweet sanguine child and wonder why they are making "trouble" now, when they were happy to go along with life before.

Shanon tells the following story about her sanguine child, Tasha: "One day she was sitting playing with her toys and became distracted by another color or sound somewhere else. Meanwhile, her brother started playing with her toys. She glanced down a few times and it didn't seem to bother her. Then suddenly, after fifteen minutes, she let out a scream and started protesting about her brother's intrusion. I didn't know what to do. She had been fine for fifteen minutes, so how valid was her complaint now?"

The answer is – very valid. As an adult who grew up with the sanguine temperament, the adult has learned that it is much easier just to "let things go". Because the adult "lets things go" the majority of the time, when she does complain, she expects others to listen. Even though the adult can understand what the sanguine child is expecting, the adult may fall into the same trap as most other adults and assume that because the child has not consistently said "no" or because the request or complaint seems sudden that it does not need to be honored. The sanguine adult may even get angry with the sanguine child for interrupting the beautiful and peaceful flow of the day.

This can be avoided if the adult can teach the child to be more direct in her communication and to say "no" more often. This can also be avoided if the adult can practice being more intuitive to the child's needs instead of insisting that the child always ask. Take note of what the child's needs are and try to make sure those are filled without the child asking. This will reduce stress in the child's life helping the child to feel more at ease and more peaceful.

Be aware that these "rebellious outbursts" may increase as the child becomes older, depending on how much she has been holding back as a young child. At some point in every sanguine's life, the sanguine realizes how much potential she has and will start to realize how much she have been neglecting her own needs.

Keep this in mind when evaluating certain behaviors the child may have. For example, a young child who always shared her toys and bought gifts for people with her allowance may grow up and realize she has completely neglected herself. At this point she may compensate by purchasing more things for herself and by being less willing to compromise or share.

The adult may tend to be harder on the sanguine child when she do something "wrong" because the adult is expecting more out of her. In the adult's mind, this is the good child who is making life easier. When the child suddenly has an outburst, the suddenness and the surprise may upset the adult more than the outburst itself. Try to treat the sanguine child equally to her siblings and/or peers. The child will notice if the adult becomes less angry with another child for doing the same thing and then the sanguine child will become confused and upset. This will interfere with the discipline relationship.

• The Teaching Relationship

The sanguine child might be the adult's idea of a perfect student. The sanguine adult's teaching style and the sanguine student's way of learning usually mesh perfectly. The student is eager to learn when inspired and is interested and enthusiastic about many topics. The student is eager to please the adult and will work hard and show the adult their best. In fact, the adult may be so enchanted with the student's skills that the adult may not notice the two areas the student is weakest in – accuracy and consistency. Because these issues are not of the utmost importance to the sanguine adult, they may not stand out in the student's work. When the student doesn't finish an assignment because she is excited about another idea she just had, the adult will feel proud and admire the way the student follows her inspiration. When the student writes a brilliant paper but spells some words incorrectly, the adult may shrug her shoulders and say, 'But the paper was brilliant. I'm not going to penalize her that much for those few words she misspelled."

However, to get a balanced education a sanguine must learn discipline as well as skills.

The sanguine student needs a guide, not always another sanguine enjoying the learning process by their side. Because the sanguine student is a natural leader, the adult can fill this role for her provided the adult is aware that it needs to be filled. The adult needs to make sure there are times when the adult and student enjoy "going with the educational flow" while emphasizing the importance of accuracy and dependability at other times (no matter how silly it may seem at the time). Taking care of pets on a daily basis, eating breakfast or waking at the same time each day, are all good ways to teach dependability. Accuracy can be taught through math work and spelling work. However, it can also be taught by knitting, sewing, and music.

There is a risk that the sanguine adult and the sanguine student could both wear each other out. Because both adult and student are so enthusiastic about learning, the adult and student may pull each other in different directions so much that both become lost or over-committed. Be sure to focus on common interests and then allow the student to explore additional interests alone. If the adult follows the student onto every path she takes, the adult will become lost. If the student follows the adult down every path, the student will become overwhelmed. Every once in a while the sanguine student needs a break from the sanguine adult.

- ## A Story to Share

When stories are told they speak to the child on a basic level. The reason one tells stories instead of explaining things to a child is because stories have the ability to adapt to the child's needs. When a person explains a situation to a child she is putting forth a concept that the child needs to grasp at or reach to understand. When one simply *tells* a story the child is given permission to understand the story in any way she wishes and to gain wisdom and knowledge from it in the way that best suits her at that moment. For that reason, it is not recommended that the story be explained to the child or that the child be provided with the ubiquitous "moral" at the end. Rather, it is best to give them a chance to enjoy the story for what it becomes to them and provide them with numerous chances to hear the story told. The stories in this book help the different temperaments understand each other. If the adult or adult would like to explore this understanding on a deeper level they can ask questions once the story is finished. However, one must be sure to ask open questions and allow the child to express her feelings.

In the following story a sanguine musician appeals to the sanguine nature of the children in a town and leads them all away. What is symbolic about this story and how does it relate to one's relationship with the child? What does the child think of this story? Would she go with the musician or would she like to have the same powers as the musician?

The Children of Hameln: The Sanguine Musician and the Sanguine Children

Adapted from Grimm's Tales

In the year 1284, a mysterious man appeared in Hameln. He was wearing a coat of many colors, made of bright cloth, which is why he was called the Pied Piper. He claimed to be a rat catcher, and he promised that for a certain sum he would rid the city of all mice and rats. The citizens struck a deal, promising him a certain price. The rat catcher then took a small fife from his pocket and began to blow on it. Rats and mice at once came from every house and gathered around him. When he thought he had them all, he led them to the River Weser where he pulled up his clothes and walked into the water. The animals all followed him, fell in, and drowned.

Now that the citizens had been freed of their plague, they regretted having promised so much money and, using all kinds of excuses, they refused to pay him. Finally he went away, bitter and angry. He returned on June 26, Saint John's and Saint Paul's Day, early in the morning at seven o'clock (others say it was at noon), now dressed in a hunter's costume, with a dreadful look on his face and wearing a strange red hat. He sounded his fife in the streets, but this time it wasn't rats and mice that came to him, but rather children: a great number of boys and girls from their fourth year on. Among them was the mayor's grown daughter. The swarm followed him, and he led them into a mountain, where he disappeared with them.

All this was seen by a babysitter who had followed them from a distance, carrying a child in her arms, but had then turned around and carried the news back to the town.

The anxious adults ran in droves to the town gates seeking their children. The mothers cried out and sobbed pitifully. Within the hour messengers were sent everywhere by water and by land inquiring if the children -- or any of them -- had been seen, but it was all for nothing.

In total, one hundred and thirty were lost. Two, as some say, had lagged behind and came back. One of them was blind and the other mute. The blind one was not able to point out the place, but was able to tell how they had followed the piper. The mute one was able to point out the place, although he [or she] had heard nothing. One little boy in shirtsleeves had gone along with the others. He had turned back to fetch his jacket and thus escaped the tragedy, for when he returned, the others had already disappeared into a cave within a hill. The citizens of Hameln recorded this event in their town register, and the following lines were inscribed on the town hall:

In the year 1284 AD
From Hameln were led away
One hundred and thirty children, born at this place
Led away by a piper into a mountain.

Sanguine Adult - Melancholic Child

- ## General Relationship

The relationship between the sanguine adult and the melancholic child will be challenging for both the adult and child. However, it has the potential to be very enriching and provide an amazing opportunity of growth for both of them.

- ## Helping the Sanguine Adult Understand the Melancholic Child

The melancholic child is ruled by a sense of organization and order and the way things "should be". While the sanguine adult views the world as an endless ocean of possibilities. To be able to understand the melancholic child the sanguine adult must be able to overcome his fear of confinement, regulations, and boundaries and learn to appreciate the value of such principles. Without this essential understanding of what makes the melancholic child "tick", the sanguine adult will be continually frustrated with the narrowness of the melancholic style in comparison to his approach to life. This may result in the sanguine adult taking on a limited view of the melancholic child's qualities which will then cause the adult to focus most of his energy on trying to change the child instead of understanding him/her.

Once the sanguine adult can establish this basic understanding of the melancholic child, he can begin to explore what the boundaries and limits of the melancholic child include. A sanguine adult may initially view the melancholic child as narrow-minded and short-sighted. However, if there is a basic understanding of the melancholic core values, the sanguine adult will then be able to comprehend that each of the traits of the melancholic child is beautiful, useful, and unique. They will also come to realize that as a sanguine, one needs to learn from these traits to help balance one's own temperament.

The melancholic child is very comfortable with the feeling of sorrow and melancholy. The sanguine adult usually has trouble expressing any feelings of sorrow for more than a fleeting moment. To the sanguine, sorrow feels unnatural and painful and is not something one wishes to experience often. The sanguine adult needs to overcome this dread of the melancholic emotion, so he can understand the melancholic child. The melancholic child may appear depressed. However, the child has the ability to experience the emotion of despondency and contentment at the same time. The melancholic child is often at peace with his melancholy. The sanguine adult should resist the urge to cajole the melancholic child into expressing cheerfulness in the way the adult thinks it should be expressed. Instead, by supporting the melancholic child's unique way of expression, the adult can help the child become more self-confident in his temperament. Through watching the melancholic child's experience with this emotion, the sanguine adult can learn to experience his own occasional gloominess in a more positive and effective way.

The melancholic child develops a mature outlook on life from a very young age, whereas the sanguine adult experiences his entire life with childlike curiosity and excitement. The sanguine adult may be disturbed by the melancholic child's serious approach to life, yet the adult must realize that this view is part of who the melancholic is and does not represent a deficiency in his character.

The melancholic child experiences life and learns through touch. However, the sanguine adult can be very hard to touch as he rarely sits in one place for too long. Unless the sanguine adult makes an effort to find quiet moments to sit still with the melancholic child, the child may feel disconnected or distant from the adult. By making an effort to create moments of intimacy, the sanguine adult can nurture his relationship with the melancholic child and establish a greater bond of trust between them.

A melancholic child has a fear of crowding and being pushed. A sanguine adult can honor this fear by trying to rein in his own propensity to interact with people without limitation, and respect that boundaries are very real and very important to the melancholic child.

A melancholic child likes to maintain an organized personal life and live in an organized and predictable environment. The more relaxed style of the sanguine adult can be upsetting to the melancholic child who may make requests that the sanguine adult feels are finicky or demanding. If the sanguine adult can try to imagine the melancholic child's world and how deeply they feel about order, he can begin to move away from a feeling of resentment and more towards a feeling of compassion about the melancholic child's needs. This does not mean that the sanguine will need to fulfill all of the melancholic's needs. Since the sanguine adult is of a very flexible temperament, it may be easier for he to adapt to many of these needs and thus reduce stress in the environment.

This certainly worked with Autumn and her daughter Paige. When I consulted with Autumn and Paige, I gave Autumn the idea to try and fulfill some of the requests she was calling "picky". She shrugged her shoulders and said, "well, it's not really that big of a deal - I can try." Autumn's response, in itself was interesting because although she was quick to say "it's not as big a deal", Paige was visibly upset about many of the requests she had made that had not been fulfilled. Paige felt as if she was not being respected in the house and that nobody really cared about how she felt. Upon returning home, Autumn made a commitment to listen more carefully to Paige and not just "brush off" what she said under the heading of "picky". By labeling Paige's requests with a negative label in the past, it had been easy for her to ignore them. Now that she was asked to consider these requests as valid, new possibilities opened up.

During that first week, Autumn listened as Paige made requests that she had made before. Paige didn't want anyone to drink out of her special blue cup, she didn't want the cat to sleep on her bed, she wanted her eggs soft in the middle instead of firm, she wanted only half a glass of milk in the morning, and she wanted to make afternoon tea in the teapot that matched the tablecloth.

Previously, Autumn had chuckled at what she saw as silly requests. But this week, however, she listened and tried to do her best. After all, in Autumn's world these were small things and easy to accomplish. It was not difficult for her to take Paige's egg off the stove earlier than the others, to reach for the red teapot instead of the green one, or to pour half a glass of milk instead of a whole one. After only one week Autumn was surprised to see how much more relaxed and happy Paige seemed to be. Towards the end of the week, she was surprised to hear Paige say, 'It's okay mom, it's not a big deal" about a new request she made. Autumn learned that when she was able to honor some of Paige's requests and create a more comfortable environment for her, Paige's stress levels decreased and she became more flexible herself. A melancholic child will always become more rigid when their stress levels increase.

The sanguine adult should expect that the melancholic child will usually restrain himself when expressing opinions or emotions. It is important for the sanguine adult to be aware of this, because a sanguine person can often have a very fast paced and enthusiastic conversational style. This manner can sometimes cause the melancholic to be shut out of many dialogues and to feel he is not being listened to, or does not have a say in the conversation. The sanguine adult must be careful to pause frequently in his talks with the child, to ask leading questions, and to listen attentively so the melancholic feels safe in participating in the exchange.

The sanguine adult has the ability to see potential in every situation, person, and lesson. For the sanguine, these possibilities are endless. Thus, a sanguine adult has trouble choosing just one topic to focus on. The sanguine adult may feel they are depriving the child of a good educational experience if there is too much focus on one topic and not enough diversity. On the contrary, the melancholic child enjoys moderation in all things, and will feel more at ease when social situations, meals, lesson, chores, and other things in his life are done in a moderate, more focused manner.

- ### Helping the Melancholic Child Understand the Sanguine Adult

The most important tool one person can use in understanding another person, is communication. For this reason the most important thing a melancholic child must understand about the sanguine adult, is he has an extremely different conversational style. The melancholic child will carefully think through what he wants to say before presenting and discussing it, and prefers to focus on one subject at a time. The sanguine often uses conversation as part of the thinking process, will often explore many ideas at once, and will explore those ideas in a verbal manner rather than an introspective manner. The melancholic child needs to know that the sanguine adult does want to listen to him/her and that the quick tempo of the conversation is due to the sanguine temperament and not any lack of interest of the adult towards the child. Dialogue can be more effective between the adult and child if, the adult can practice tempering the pace of the conversation. The melancholic child can practice being more proactive and assertive in his conversational style. They can both understand their differences, so they don't take them personally.

The melancholic child also needs to understand that the sanguine adult often expresses himself in a raised voice or intense manner. This is sometimes anger, but more often it is purely the intensity of the sanguine temperament. Because the melancholic child is more tempered in their expression of emotion, even a hint of anger or raised voice can put him on the defensive. However, the more the melancholic child can understand that this is a method rather than something to take personally, the less apprehension he will feel towards interacting with the adult.

Another important thing for the melancholic child to understand, is the sanguine adult often displays a strong sense of purpose in his speech. However, this sense of purpose does not have the same meaning as when a melancholic would express it. For the sanguine adult, everything is said with a sense of purpose because he lives in the now and each word and idea lives quite vividly as he is expressing it. In the world of the melancholic, he would only express confidence and powerful intent after carefully considering a matter and coming to a decisive conclusion or decision. This can create confusion between the melancholic child and the sanguine adult. As the melancholic child wants to please the sanguine adult and enjoys following clear guidelines, he may become attached to every purposeful statement the sanguine adult makes, only to discover later that it was not really said with that much purpose or that there were twenty other purposeful statements to try to follow as well. The melancholic child can become very frustrated with this situation and feel like the sanguine adult is unclear, always changing his mind or does not even know what he wants in the first place. Over time, trust for the adult can erode. This can be prevented, if the melancholic child can be aware of the sanguine adult's temperament and mannerisms in speech.

Another important aspect of the sanguine temperament for the melancholic to understand, is that the sanguine adult experiences life through movement and thrives on action. This may be disconcerting for the melancholic child as he is careful with actions and words and indentifies action with purpose and meaning. The sanguine adult, may gesture while they are speaking, walk while they are teaching, or move while they are listening, simply because the sanguine body must be moving. Movement for the sanguine does not need to have purpose, but may simply occur for the sake of the movement itself. In fact, in some cases the sanguine's movements may even seem to contradict what they are doing. For example, a sanguine might meditate as they are walking, gesture while they are describing a peaceful event, or pace while they insist they are focusing only on what another person is saying. To better understand and relate to the sanguine adult, the melancholic child must learn to separate this action from what is being said or done and allow himself to listen without being influenced or confused by those actions that occasionally seem contradictory.

Along with this craving for movement, is also a desire to keep busy. The sanguine adult can often be seen in action and rarely sits down or is still. This can cause the melancholic child to stop communicating with the adult as they may be unsure as to the best time to approach them. A melancholic child will have a hard time adapting to the constant movement of the sanguine adult. It is most effective if the adult can set aside a certain block of time each day for the melancholic child and let them know that, during that block of time, the adult is available to talk to the child. The sanguine adult may feel uncomfortable with this and feel as if they are telling the child they are not available at other times of day. The adult may even feel like this statement shuts the child out, instead of inviting them in. However, a melancholic child does not experience this statement in the same way a sanguine would. If someone told a sanguine adult "I am free to talk to you at five o'clock every day" he would feel like they were unwelcome and unwanted the other hours of the day. The melancholic child, hearing the same phrase, feels welcomed and honored that he is being given his very own block of time with the adult.

Another important aspect of the sanguine adult, is that he relies strongly on intuition and this skill increases with age. A sanguine adult who relied on intuition for only twenty percent of his decisions as a child, may rely on intuition for eighty percent of his decisions as an adult. The melancholic child will most likely feel more confident with this than the melancholic adult would, because as a child there is an inherent trust of adults and adults that often goes unquestioned. However, if questions do arise, the melancholic child will need to be able to accept that there will not always be an answer and the sanguine adult may want to prepare short answers for the melancholic child to reassure them. Even if the answer the sanguine adult prepares does not describe the entire reason or the core reason behind the decision that was made, the melancholic child will feel more secure when a reason is given.

- ## Discipline

Good discipline always stems from a sense of trust, love and harmony between the adult and child. The more the adult and child understand and respect each other, the more discipline happens naturally. To have a healthy discipline relationship with the melancholic child the sanguine adult should first read the sections above on how to best understand the child and how to help the child understand the adult.

The melancholic child is naturally disciplined in his behavior, so the best approach for the sanguine adult is to support the child's inner discipline. For example, if the melancholic child requests a planner so he can plan lessons, then the adult could support the child by purchasing a planner. If the child announces that he has created a chart on the wall that lets the family know when it is time to change toothbrushes, then the adult could support that effort by purchasing toothbrushes in bulk so when it is time to change, the melancholic child will be able to find a new one. If the melancholic child decides that the dinner table must be set according to the standards of an English Tea Ceremony, then the

166

adult could support that by assigning the melancholic child the duty of setting the table each evening. This method of discipline will work well for the sanguine adult with a melancholic child because, sanguines enjoy being adaptable, flexible, and supportive of others and melancholic's enjoy creating order.

With such a system in place, it almost seems impossible for disharmony to occur. However, disharmony is a process of life and will, of course, occur with this pair, just as it would with any other adult-child relationship. One difficulty the sanguine adult and melancholic child may encounter, is misunderstandings about motivations. A sanguine adult may assume that a melancholic child is being stubborn and a melancholic child may think the adult is being insensitive when, in actuality, neither is trying to make the other upset at all. At times when the two reach a block in communication, it is best to take a step back, remembering the temperament of the other, and re-calculate the approach that is being taken in the situation.

Another point of contention between the sanguine adult and melancholic child, may be the basic fact of discipline. The melancholic child likes to think of himself as above reproach and as always following proper procedure, staying true to standards and morals. When the sanguine adult tells the melancholic child that he has made a mistake, the child may feel indignant and unwilling to listen to what the adult has to say. When approaching a melancholic about something they have made a mistake with or done wrong, it is best to make sure the conversation is private, the situation is explained in a gentle way, and the child is given a chance to correct the mistake so he may once again feel successful. Whereas a choleric child needs the steady reinforcement of strict boundaries and consequences, the melancholic would actually benefit more from being given more "second chances" and "reminders".

- ## The Teaching Relationship

The melancholic student tends to see situations as "black and white", while the sanguine adult sees situations in shades of grey. This can be a source of great frustration when the sanguine adult tries to explain something to the melancholic student. What may often happen is the student, seeking a "right" answer, may become confused at all the different possibilities. The sanguine adult, seeking to open the student's mind to different potentials, may become frustrated with the student's insistence that he be given a precise and defined answer. This will not present a problem during math or grammar lessons, but may be a challenge with other lessons. Despite the challenge, it is essential that the sanguine adult continue with one's efforts and persist in providing the melancholic student with examples of different ways in which there can be more than one "right" answer.

The sanguine adult is a vibrant instructor full of creativity, ideas, and energy. However, some of these positive traits may be lost on the melancholic student, who prefers to be in control of their own social environment and methods of learning. The melancholic student is most satisfied when lessons follow a standard structure and expectations are clearly defined either with charts or lists. A sanguine adult may simply follow a short list of goals for the week when he teaches. This is not detailed or planned enough for the melancholic student. The melancholic student demands a detailed schedule in which they are told not only that he will be "reading a book" but also which book that will be, how many pages he is expected to read, and what he will be doing after the reading is done. If a melancholic student is not provided with this structure, his mind can wander or he will lose interest in studies altogether. If the sanguine adult finds it difficult to create such a detailed schedule, the melancholic student is capable of creating his own schedule. This may even provide an added benefit for the melancholic student's education, as he enjoys being in control of the lessons.

A sanguine adult is usually free with praise and enthusiastic about any progress his students are making. However, to a melancholic, being praised can start to feel contrived if done too often or too casually. It is better to compliment a melancholic student in an accurate and exclusive manner less often, rather than a frequent, easy, and unbound manner.

One of the skills of the sanguine adult, lies in his ability to create lessons that are creative, hands-on, and outside of tradition. A sanguine adult may prefer to teach math through living examples and stories instead of through rote memorization or recitation, or may prefer to teach literature through theater and art, rather than through simple reading assignments. To a sanguine adult it seems inadequate and perhaps even boring to make students suffer through dry educational materials. To the melancholic student, however, it is these "dry" educational materials that help them feel secure, confident, and able in the learning process. Although the melancholic student will benefit greatly from inventive, hands-on lessons, he also needs a daily dose of conventional lessons to keep them on track.

The sanguine adult has the ability to see where ideas lead, to join ideas together, and to go with the flow of learning – even if it flows in a different direction than was originally intended. A melancholic student, however, enjoys being methodical and following a system. It may become confusing if the sanguine adult is eagerly following a train of thought. The melancholic student will focus more effectively if he is able to stay on one topic.

As long as the sanguine adult provides a solid structure, organized lesson plan, and a good percentage of traditional lessons, the melancholic student will be a content student. The melancholic student is always inspired by those adults that appear to have authority or competence on the subjects he teaches. The sanguine adult always exudes confidence in everything – even if he does not have all the information and expertise.

- A Story to Share

When stories are told they speak to the child on a basic level. The reason one tells stories instead of explaining things to a child is because stories have the ability to adapt to the child's needs. When a person explains a situation to a child he is putting forth a concept that the child needs to grasp at or reach to understand. When one simply *tells* a story the child is given permission to understand the story in any way he wishes and to gain wisdom and knowledge from it in the way that best suits him/her at that moment. For that reason, it is not recommended that the story be explained to the child or that the child be provided with the ubiquitous "moral" at the end. Rather, it is best to give them a chance to enjoy the story for what it becomes to them and provide them with numerous chances to hear the story told. The stories in this book help the different temperaments understand each other. If the adult or adult would like to explore this understanding on a deeper level they can ask questions once the story is finished. However, one must be sure to ask open questions and allow the child to express his feelings.

In the following story, a melancholic cobbler with a very good work ethic is helped by the generous and spontaneous sanguine elves. It is a beautiful story about how someone of the melancholic temperament, and someone of the sanguine temperament, can help each other so that both benefit and learn from the experience.

The Sanguine Elves and the Melancholic Cobbler
Grimm's Fairytale adapted by Kristie Burns

There once was a shoemaker who was very organized, industrious, and skilled. Every day, he woke at seven to sort his leather and his tools. Then he would cut the patterns for the day, eat lunch, and finish the shoes in the afternoon. Just before dinner, he would tidy up his shop, lock the door, and walk through the village to his little hut in the forest and eat with his lovely wife and children. However, although he was a hard worker and made wonderful shoes, business was not going very well. In the next village, a large shop opened that offered imported and exotic shoes from all around the world. The people in his village all wanted to try the new shoes, so they stopped ordering from him and he soon became poor. Finally, one morning, as the cobbler was sorting his leather and tools, he realized he only had enough leather left for one pair of shoes.

So, he cut out the shoes intending to make them in the afternoon as usual. But, he paused before he completed the pair and decided to wait until the next day to finish. He thought to himself, "Well, I will have no work tomorrow if I don't save some from today, so I will complete this task tomorrow."

In the morning, after he had sorted his tools (for he had no more leather), and was just going to sit down to work, the two shoes stood quite finished on his table. He was astounded, and knew not what to say to it. He took the shoes in his hands to observe them closer, and they were so neatly made that there was not one bad stitch in them--just as if they were intended as a masterpiece. They appeared even more exotic than the imported shoes of the next village. In fact, they almost looked as if they had come from another world.

Soon after, a buyer came in, and as the shoes pleased him so well, he paid more for them then what was customary. With the money, the shoemaker was able to purchase leather for two pairs of shoes. He cut them out at night, and next morning was about to set to work with fresh courage. However, he had no need to do so for, when he got up, they were already made. Soon after, buyers arrived who gave him money enough to buy leather for four pairs of shoes.

The following morning, he also found the four pairs made. So it went on constantly. What he cut out was always finished by the morning. Soon he had his honest independence again, and at last, became a wealthy man.

Now it befell that one evening not long before Christmas, when the man had been cutting out, he said to his wife, "What think you if we were to stay up tonight to see who it is that lends us this helping hand?" The woman liked the idea, and lit a candle. Then they hid themselves in a corner of the room behind some clothes which were hanging up there and watched. When it was midnight, two pretty little ragged men came, sat down by the shoemaker's table, took all the work which was cut out before them and began to stitch, and sew, and hammer so skillfully and so quickly with their little fingers that the shoemaker could not turn away his eyes for astonishment. They did not stop 'til all was done, and stood finished on the table, and they ran quickly away.

Next morning the woman said, "The little men have made us rich and we really must show that we are grateful for it. They run about so, and wear only rags, and must be cold. I'll tell you what I'll do: I will make them little shirts, and coats, and vests, and trousers, and knit both of them a pair of stockings, and do you too, make them two little pairs of shoes."

The man said, "I shall be very glad to do it." One night, when everything was ready, they laid their presents all together on the table instead of the cut-out work and then concealed themselves to see how the little men would behave. At midnight, they came bounding in wanting to get to work at once. But, they did not find any leather cut out, only the pretty little articles of clothing. They were at first astonished, and then they showed intense delight. They dressed themselves with the greatest rapidity, putting the pretty clothes on, and singing,

*"Now we are boys so fine to see,
Why should we longer cobblers be?"*

Then they danced and skipped and leapt over chairs and benches. At last they danced out the door. From that time forth, they came no more. But as long as the shoemaker lived, all went well with him and all his undertakings prospered.

Sanguine Adult - Phlegmatic Child

• General Relationship

A sanguine adult often finds great comfort in a phlegmatic child. Because the sanguine adult is always active and vibrant, the calm steadiness of the phlegmatic child is reassuring or balancing to the sanguine adult's colorful lifestyle. A sanguine adult finds calmness around this child and there is usually very little conflict between this pair, although, some do exist (see below). The sanguine adult may experience some frustration with the phlegmatic child because this temperament functions at a slower pace and the phlegmatic child is less interested in the same variety of things as the sanguine person. A sanguine adult may constantly be thinking that her phlegmatic child is not "doing enough" when, in reality, the phlegmatic child is doing plenty.

A phlegmatic child, while not as interested in the variety of things her adult does and are less interested in such a fast pace, may actually really enjoy watching a sanguine adult do the many things she is doing. The phlegmatic child may find this adult slightly "intense" and confusing at times but always entertaining! The phlegmatic child gets to experience things with the sanguine adult that she would never experience on her own and will often find these things interesting. However, a phlegmatic child would rarely have thought of the idea and though he may participate less than the sanguine adult, will find these exciting activities enjoyable.

• Helping the Sanguine Adult Understand the Phlegmatic Child

A sanguine adult marches in cycles like the seasons or a classical piece of in four or more movements. A sanguine adult is full of variety, and loves to experience things intensely. A phlegmatic child does not march – she flows like the river - and at times, so slowly that it may appear that she is not moving at all. But she is – even if below a relaxed and serene surface, she is moving! The best way to understand a phlegmatic child is to sit with her, slow down, and observe the subtle details of her life. A phlegmatic child is not loud or showy and does not waste words. A phlegmatic child's choice of words is concise, so adults need to listen closely as not to miss the child's thoughts, expressions or messages. If a sanguine adults tries to get the phlegmatic child to run around and keep a fast pace and a day full of excitement and variety – the phlegmatic child may still benefit. However, to really understand a phlegmatic child, a sanguine adult needs to take the time to sit still, walk slower, and listen intently to her.

Phlegmatic children also have a great affinity to nature, so walking slowly with them in nature is also a good way to get to know them. However, a phlegmatic child will not see every detail of every flower and become distracted at every pretty color or breeze that blows by like a sanguine adult. A phlegmatic child will enjoy the physical movement of her body, the great feeling of the air in the lungs, and muscles moving in her legs. A phlegmatic child may stop and comment about one or two things that catches her attention so it may seem like only a few things are of interest, but this is not true, as a phlegmatic child absorbs her entire surroundings, in somewhat in an effortless way. She will quickly file everything into a quiet place in her heart without needing to explore or exclaim it. Gentle observance is a pertinent characteristic of a phlegmatic child, rather than intense or interactive participation.

When a sanguine adult listens to a phlegmatic child, she will find a small variety of emotions and feelings. However, these emotions are serious and are expressed in a very accurate and basic way. A phlegmatic child may even try to sneak in emotions into other places in the conversation – but are less direct about them than the sanguine adult's way of communicating emotions. Therefore, a sanguine adult should not wait for a phlegmatic child to express her needs all the time, nor should they wait for a phlegmatic child to share feelings. On the contrary, a sanguine adult needs to observe the phlegmatic child more closely. The phlegmatic child is not "all about" the talking and chatting and sharing that sanguine adults love, expect and do naturally – a phlegmatic child is more about observing, keeping the peace and staying in balance.

• Helping the Phlegmatic Child Understand the Sanguine Adult

At times the sanguine adult may seem confusing and overwhelming. The phlegmatic child needs to know that it is OK to ask for some time alone if she needs some time to recover from the barrage of words and activities. The key to a sanguine is communications. As long as one lets the sanguine adult know exactly what is needed and *why*, then the sanguine is usually very happy to accommodate. If not, then the phlegmatic needs to make sure she gets some time to be alone. The child may even need to ask "to read a book" just so she has a peaceful activity to do. Once the child sits down to read the book, that time is for the child only and the phlegmatic can read or skim as slowly as she wants to. If siblings or adults do not listening to the child's needs to simplify and make things more peaceful, the phlegmatic child can let them know what she will be doing and the adults will be fine. Sanguines like to "do things," so if someone lets them know that she is going to do something else and lets them know what that is, the sanguine will most likely leave the phlegmatic alone in peace. Sanguines understand the word "do".

Sanguines also ask "why" frequently, however the phlegmatic child should not worry about this. The sanguine adult does not intend to put pressure on the child or accuse the child of anything bad. Sanguines are naturally curious and always want to know why something happens.

The phlegmatic child should be encouraged to ask questions if she feels overwhelmed. A sanguine adult will often use about ten sentences to ask or say what the phlegmatic child could have said in one sentence. Sanguines also use vibrant language and can be very direct, but may often use flowery or creative language. All of this may just seem really confusing. Sometimes when the sanguine adult talks, the phlegmatic child may just hear a lot of confusing words or may think she hears conflicting language. It is acceptable for the child to ask the sanguine to clarify if she feels confused. People of the sanguine temperament love questions. If they say a lot of things it is better to ask for a clarification or explanation, rather than ignore her or pretend one understands. This will only cause more conflict in the future.

Let's give an example...let's imagine the sanguine adult is asking the child to clean something. The adult may talk for five minutes about different chores and what one should do in general, thus confusing the phlegmatic child. The child could say something like, "I didn't quite understand what you wanted me to do. Could you tell me exactly what task you wanted me to do?" or she could say "I understand that you want me to clean my room. Is that right? Did I understand correctly?"

A sanguine may get upset from time to time that the phlegmatic doesn't understand her verbalization immediately but the phlegmatic child should remain calm and not become frightened. The child has a right to know and to be able to communicate in her own language and a sanguine is usually very intense about her own emotions but those emotions can also fade just as intensely. The phlegmatic may perceive a sanguine's frustration as anger and feel like retreating or getting away from her but an intense sanguine is just being herself. The choleric child needs to know that she is safe, and everything is going to be fine · sanguines are just naturally a bit louder, more vibrant and more expressive than people of the phlegmatic temperament.

The phlegmatic child must also realize that the sanguine adult moves at a fast pace and likes a lot of variety. She is not always going to intuitively know what the phlegmatic needs or wants. It may be obvious to the phlegmatic what her needs are but not to a sanguine adult. She may miss those feelings in the flurry. The more the child can express those needs to the sanguine adult, the better things will be. As much as the phlegmatic child is confused with a sanguine's colorful lifestyle, a sanguine can also be confused by the phlegmatic child and the best way to help out in the relationships to communicate feelings and emotions.

- Discipline

Good discipline always stems from a sense of trust, love and harmony between the adult and child. The more they understand and respect each other, the more naturally discipline happens. For a sanguine adult to have a healthy discipline relationship with a phlegmatic child, she needs to remember the sections above on how to best understand a phlegmatic child and how to help cultivate mutual understanding.

The discipline relationship of a sanguine adult and a phlegmatic child may be difficult to maintain and to understand. Because sanguine adults live in the moment and see the wisdom in each situation as it arises, sanguines may tend to create rules for different nuances of the same situation or change rules when the status quo does not seem to be working. A sanguine is well known to be in a constant state of creating a better world and this means that rules, consequences and even the way she reacts to things may change on a weekly or monthly basis.

This makes it very hard for the steady and traditional phlegmatic to understand the sanguine adult's needs and requests. A phlegmatic child is seeking a steady and clear set of rules and will have a hard time following the changing nature of a sanguine's. No matter how wise and fair these changes are, the phlegmatic child would rather have them to be steady and predictable.

One sanguine adult I worked with, Christy, had a son, Adam, who was causing her constant frustration. She felt like he was always ignoring her, forgetting the rules and completely disregarding what she said. He seemed to do fine with some tasks but others seemed to present great difficulty. Christy tried changing his chores at home but there was no improvement. She tried asking if there was something she could do to make it easier for him to complete his work and chores, but as a private phlegmatic child he didn't know or didn't want to share his thoughts on the matter. Christy tried creating consequences for rules that were broken and this seemed to work for some time but then it fell apart one day and never seemed to work again. As we explored her relationship with her son we discovered that she had been changing the rules and consequences too often for him to keep up. Becoming frustrated with the constant changes he had created his own set of rules based on what seemed most constant in her rule book combined with what he thought should be done.

When Christy decided to make things steadier and clear for Adam by writing them down on a list, their relationship improved. She also gained more insight and perspective on her own tendency to change the rules too often. When I originally suggested this idea to her she said, "I am very regular in what I request from my children." However, once she wrote down her expectations, the children's chores and schedules on a list, she was surprised at how often she wanted to change the list. After two weeks of Adam unloading the dishwasher she felt that he was getting bored of the task and was tempted to change it. When it seemed like her youngest son was having trouble taking out the trash she considered switching his task with Adam's easier chore. When she had to consider re-typing the list every time she had a new and improved idea, she realized that she was tempted to change it at least three times a week.

While this method worked well with her own life, it did not work well for her parenting relationship with her phlegmatic son. So she learned to continue being adaptive with her own "to do" and task lists but kept the expectations for her son more steady and predictable.

A sanguine adult lives in the "now". A sanguine makes requests of her children, friends and spouse when the thought appears in mind, or when there is a sudden need, rather than planning ahead. For the phlegmatic child, this will feel disruptive and uncomfortable. When making a request from the phlegmatic child, she needs some time to complete the request so a sanguine adult should not try to make requests for urgent or instant favors. For example, a phlegmatic child will be quite happy to help rake the lawn if is given sufficient time to consider helping, i.e., raking the lawn needs to be done in the near future. A sanguine adult can even ask the child when might be a good time for them to help. Or, for example, a sanguine adult could let the child know of plans to rake the lawn over the weekend so that the phlegmatic child can fit it into her weekend plans. However, if a phlegmatic child is approached in the middle of reading or writing or talking to friends or even just sitting with the request, "could you help me rake the lawn now," they will most likely say no, even if they are not doing anything else at the time.

A phlegmatic child is very concerned that things in life must be "fair." A sanguine adult may have a more relaxed view of what is fair and not fair. To a sanguine, fair means treating each person in the way that best suits them. To a phlegmatic child, fair means that the same rules apply for each person. It is very important for a phlegmatic child to see she is being treated the same as the other children in the home or in the classroom. If a phlegmatic child feels there are different rules for her (and there may be), these rules need to be followed with a logical explanation so the phlegmatic child becomes more comfortable and accepting of the situation. If a phlegmatic child feels that she is being treated unfairly, she may be uncooperative and difficult to communicate with.

• The Teaching Relationship

In some ways the phlegmatic child is an easy student. The phlegmatic student is undemanding and will not usually disrupt the harmony of classroom. The phlegmatic student has the ability to perform tasks on their own and work at a steady and peaceful pace. The order of the class and the lessons are comforting and dependable, much like the phlegmatic student's behavior. These traits, however, make a phlegmatic student a difficult student for the sanguine adult or adult. A sanguine adult or adult is usually occupied with items of priority and students that demand attention. Like a firefly drawn to the light of a lamp, a sanguine adult is drawn to the action and chaos of the classroom, seeking to maintain order and to take care of the most urgent issues that present themselves. However, among all this, the peaceful phlegmatic student may become lost and forgotten.

The phlegmatic student will not be able to verbalize this problem however, and instead will begin to feel bored or unchallenged. The phlegmatic student may then start to seek out challenges to gain her adult's attention in destructive ways rather than constructive ways. Because both the sanguine adult and phlegmatic student begin feeling dissatisfied in the adult-student relationship, the phlegmatic student may become unmanageable or withdrawn and become difficult to draw out of their inner world.

The sanguine adult may get frustrated with the phlegmatic student because, to a sanguine adult, this student may seem unmotivated or lazy. They may even feel worry or want to push the student. There is a tendency to frustration, a little anger and the nuance to assert a little authority. A sanguine adult may end up forcing a phlegmatic student to enroll in extra activities or do more than he or she is comfortable doing. This is not the best way to approach this relationship. Sanguine adults need to understand more about the phlegmatic gifts which do not usually involve the same vibrancy and speed as them.

A phlegmatic student enjoys a peaceful flow, mostly staying at home or in a familiar environment. Visiting the same place more than once is acceptable and even appreciated by a phlegmatic student. However, visiting a new place may cause a phlegmatic student to become nervous and experience anxiety or even fear. By pressuring a phlegmatic student too much or by forcing them out of their comfort zone too far, anxiety and resistance are bound to surface. A phlegmatic student can be very stubborn. Anxiety related disorders may also arise if pushed or pressured too much and too often.

The phlegmatic student will feel uncomfortable when the sanguine adult starts adding "exciting" tasks and field trips to their day, when pushed to "do more" or "do it faster" or to do anything out of the comfortable slow paced, traditional desires. The phlegmatic student can get confused by this. A phlegmatic student knows that she is doing well and feels their life is exciting enough. When a sanguine adult "requests" more, a phlegmatic student becomes confused. A phlegmatic student feels that what she is doing is already enough, thus, it does not make sense that the sanguine adult wants to visit so many places and do so many things.

Although the sanguine adult and phlegmatic student have many challenges to overcome, their adult-student relationship can be a wonderful and an enriching experience for them. Because the sanguine adult is often distracted or focused on the disharmony in the classroom, the phlegmatic student can provide an important cornerstone for her teaching experience. Because the sanguine adult is filled with vibrancy, a phlegmatic student who needs outside inspiration to complete her work is suddenly awakened. When given a steady supply of lessons on a regular basis – enough to curb boredom – but not to the extent of over-stimulation – the phlegmatic student will work at a steady pace and will not require a lot of instruction or maintenance in the classroom.

The phlegmatic student also has a great ability to learn while watching others. While a sanguine adult enjoys teaching a student who interacts dynamically, the phlegmatic student will enjoy watching the lesson. This will work out well for both adult and student – so it is important that adults remind themselves to have phlegmatic students participate through observation. The sanguine need for instant feedback and an energetic dynamic is fulfilled and the phlegmatic student will feel fulfilled through watching and staying in the background. However, both students (the dynamic sanguine and the observatory phlegmatic) will learn the lesson just as well.

A sanguine adult can teach a phlegmatic student many tasks through demonstrating lessons of interest. Because sanguines enjoy so many diverse activities and the phlegmatic student may not, sanguines can continue pursuing their interests and allow the phlegmatic student to be a spectator instead of always participating. This way, both adult and student can avoid the frustration of feeling like the suggestions of the sanguine is constantly being rejected by the phlegmatic. However, through spectatorship, phlegmatics may develop and discover skills for certain activities.

A good example of how this can happen is the story of Sandra and Joseph.

Sandra enjoyed crafting and handiwork but every time she suggested handiwork or crafting to her son he seemed to reject the idea. At first Sandra thought it was because he didn't like what she was suggesting so she started suggesting things she thought were more suitable to a boy. She introduced Joseph to woodworking, woodcarving and even building. However, each time she introduced something new, he didn't seem very enthusiastic so she became frustrated and decided to give up for some time and return to trying later. She felt guilty about not doing any handiwork with her son, but she noticed that he did keep busy with other activities and figured that perhaps he just didn't like handiwork as much as she did. A few months later she was surprised when Joseph asked her if he could knit something for a friend's birthday. She was at first reluctant, knowing how hard it had been to introduce handiwork in the past, but she didn't want to miss the opportunity to teach him when he was asking her directly, so she set down her own knitting and found a pair of needles and some yarn for Joseph. Sandra then proceeded to show him how to knit but was surprised when he stopped her and said, "I already know how to knit, mom. I've been watching you." Sandra found this hard to believe but Joseph then picked up the needles and knitted a lovely scarf for his friend without asking her for any assistance. He only stopped now and then to make sure he was doing it right and to seek praise for a job well done.

- ## A Story to Share

When stories are told they speak to the child on a basic level. The reason one tells stories instead of explaining things to a child is because stories have the ability to adapt to the child's needs. When a person explains a situation to a child she is putting forth a concept that the child needs to grasp at or reach to understand. When one simply *tells* a story the child is given permission to understand the story in any way she wishes and to gain wisdom and knowledge from it in the way that best suits her at that moment. For that reason, it is not recommended that the story be explained to the child or that the child be provided with the ubiquitous "moral" at the end. Rather, it is best to give them a chance to enjoy the story for what it becomes to them and provide them with numerous chances to hear the story told. The stories in this book help the different temperaments understand each other. If the adult or adult would like to explore this understanding on a deeper level they can ask questions once the story is finished. However, one must be sure to ask open questions and allow the child to express her feelings.

In the following story, the mother of the family is very sanguine, prone to following her intuition and has a hard time sitting in one place at a time. Her phlegmatic children are confused by her behavior and feel frightened. What does this story tell you about expectations of the adult in society? What are your child's expectations of you? What could the mother in the story have done differently and still maintained her curiosity and desire to speak to the fairy folk? Do you think her decision to never speak to the fairy folk again was a good one?

The Sanguine Mother and the Fairy Realm

Adapted from "Legendary Fictions of the Irish Celts," by Patrick Kennedy, 1891

There was once a little farmer and his wife living near Coolgarrow. They had three children, and my story happened while the youngest was a baby. The wife was a good wife enough, but her mind was all on the different activities she would do all day with her family and her farm, and she hardly ever went to dinners or to gatherings where she had to sit. She much preferred to be active. So, friends, one day she let her man and her two children go before her one day to a church gathering, while she called to consult a fairy man about a disorder one of her cows had. She was late at the chapel, and was sorry all the day after, for her husband was in grief about it, and she was very fond of him.

Late that night he was awakened by the cries of his children calling out "Mother! Mother!" When he sat up and rubbed his eyes, there was no wife by his side, and when he asked the little ones what had become of their mother, they said they saw the room full of nice little men and women, dressed in white and red and green, and their mother in the middle of them, going out by the door as if she were asleep and having the most delightful dream. Out he ran, and searched everywhere around the house but, neither tale nor tidings did he get of her for many a day.

Well, the poor man was miserable enough, for he was as fond of his woman as she was of him. It used to bring the salt tears down his cheeks to see his poor children neglected and dirty, as they often were, and they'd be bad enough only for a kind neighbor that used to look in whenever she could spare time. The infant was away with a nurse.

About six weeks after—just as he was going out to his work one morning—a neighbor, that used to mind women when they were ill, came up to him, and kept step by step with him to the field, and this is what she told him.

"Just as I was falling asleep last night, I heard a horse's tramp on the grass and a knock at the door, and there, when I came out, was a fine-looking dark man, mounted on a black horse, and he told me to get ready in all haste, for a lady was

in great want of me. As soon as I put on my cloak and things, he took me by the hand, and I was sitting behind him before I felt myself stirring. "Where are we going, sir?" says I. "You'll soon know," says he; and he drew his fingers across my eyes, and not a ray could I see. I kept a tight grip of him, and I little knew whether he was going backwards or forwards, or how long we were about it, till my hand was taken again, and I felt the ground under me. The fingers went the other way across my eyes, and there we were before a castle door, and in we went through a big hall and great rooms all painted in fine green colors, with red and gold bands and ornaments, and the finest carpets and chairs and tables and window curtains, and grand ladies and gentlemen walking about. At last we came to a bedroom, with a beautiful lady in bed, with a fine bouncing boy beside her. The lady clapped her hands, and in came the Dark Man and kissed her and the baby, and praised me, and gave me a bottle of green ointment to rub the child all over.

"Well, the child I rubbed, sure enough; but my right eye began to smart, and I put up my finger and gave it a rub, and then stared, for never in all my life was I so frightened. The beautiful room was a big, rough cave, with water oozing over the edges of the stones and through the clay; and the lady, and the lord, and the child were poverty-bitten creatures—nothing but skin and bone—and the rich dresses were old rags. I didn't let on that I found any difference, and after a bit says the Dark Man, "Go before me to the hall door, and I will be with you in a few moments, and see you safe home." Well, just as I turned into the outside cave, who should I see watching near the door but poor Molly. She looked round all terrified, and says she to me in a whisper, "I'm brought here to nurse the child of the king and queen of the fairies; but there is one chance of saving me. All the court will pass the cross near Templeshambo next Friday night, on a visit to the fairies of Old Ross. If John can catch me by the hand or cloak when I ride by, and has courage not to let go his grip, I'll be safe. Here's the king. Don't open your mouth to answer. I saw what happened with the ointment." Molly looked so miserable and I could understand why. She had always loved running through the meadows and being under the sun and now she was stuck in one large dark cave for days on end.

"The Dark Man didn't once cast his eye towards Molly, and he seemed to have no suspicion of me. When we came out I looked about me, and where do you think we were but in the dyke of the Rath of Cromogue. I was on the horse again, which was nothing but a big rag-weed, and I was in dread every minute I'd fall off; but nothing happened till I found myself in my own cabin. The king slipped five guineas into my hand as soon as I was on the ground, and thanked me, and bade me good night. I hope I'll never see his face again. I got into bed, and couldn't sleep for a long time; and when I examined my five guineas this morning, that I left in the table drawer the last thing, I found five withered leaves of oak—bad luck to the giver!"

Well, you may all think the fright, and the joy, and the grief the poor man was in when the woman finished her story. They talked and they talked, but we needn't

179

mind what they said till Friday night came, when both were standing where the mountain road crosses the one going to Ross.

There they stood, looking towards the bridge of Thuar, in the dead of the night, with a little moonlight shining from over Kilachdiarmid. At last she gave a start, and "By this and by that," says she, "here they come, bridles jingling and feathers tossing!" He looked, but could see nothing; and she stood trembling and her eyes wide open, looking down the way to the ford of Ballinacoola. "I see your wife," says she, "riding on the outside just so as to rub against us. We'll walk on quietly, as if we suspected nothing, and when we are passing I'll give you a shove. If you don't do YOUR duty then, woe be with you!"

Well, they walked on easy and the poor hearts beating in both their breasts; and though he could see nothing, he heard a faint jingle and trampling and rustling, and at last he got the push that she promised. He spread out his arms, and there was his wife's waist within them, and he could see her plain; but such a hullabaloo rose as if there was an earthquake, and he found himself surrounded by horrible-looking things, roaring at him and striving to pull his wife away. But he held firm and bid them begone, and held his wife as if it was iron his arms were made of. Then, in one moment everything was as silent as the grave, and the poor woman lying in a faint in the arms of her husband and her good neighbor. Well, all in good time she was minding her family and her business again; and I'll go bail, after the fright she got, she spent more time on sitting, and avoided fairy men all the days of the week, and particularly on Sunday.

Sanguine Adult - Choleric Child

- ## General Relationship

In general, the relationship between the sanguine adult and the choleric child will be one of energy, joy and fun. Both of these temperaments have a great capacity for emotion, enjoy trying new things and doing many things. The sanguine adult will enjoy many hours of fun with this child. They may see shows together, go on long walks, explore new places, learn things together or even take classes. At a young age the sanguine child will usually enjoy tagging along to most anything the adult wants to bring them to and will usually be an enthusiastic participant in most activities. When the adult wants to try something new he will find himself seeking this child out. When the adult has a new idea, he may share it with this child and when the adult needs new ideas he may find himself asking the sanguine child. The sanguine adult already relies on feedback from those around him, and the choleric will give the adult more than enough of that! The adult will always be able to depend on this choleric child to show love, appreciation and enthusiasm for the lessons and events the adult plans.

- ## Helping the Sanguine Adult Understand the Choleric Child

The sanguine adult will most likely be delighted with the energy of the choleric child, but also overwhelmed by it at times. However, as the sanguine has a great capacity for understanding and adapting to the other temperaments, the sanguine adult should be able to easily appreciate and adjust to the choleric child's energy.

The most important difference to take note of between the sanguine and the choleric is the rhythm and pace they follow. The sanguine follows a rhythm of seasons and experiences the summer-like need to be vibrant, outgoing and expansive just as much as they experience the winter-like need to be inward, introverted and reflective. The choleric, on the other hand, burns constantly like a fire – their energy alternating between a blaze that licks the sky and short sparks that play on the logs – but most always extroverted and full of fire. When the sanguine is in the state of summer he will be in complete synchronicity with the choleric child. It would be wise to take advantage of these places where the two overlap so that more opportunities to connect can be made available. For example, if the sanguine adult is suddenly in the mood to go for an exciting explorative hike in the woods, it would be a good idea to invite the choleric child as he would be the most suitable companion for such an adventure, and this would provide an easy framework in which the sanguine adult and choleric child can connect. During other times, the sanguine adult needs to understand that the choleric child is not being inconsiderate of the adult's needs. It is only that the child does not understand that the sanguine's fire seems to come and go. It usually takes a village to raise a choleric child.

Tara, a sanguine adult is a good example of how one can accomplish this. Tara has two children. Her choleric child, Rachel, is the youngest. Tara shared with me that Rachel had always been very "demanding" since she was a toddler and seemed to need constant interaction with other people. I helped Tara see that Rachel was not being demanding, she was simply being choleric – and she loved being with other people. Rachel's trait would have served he well if they had been living in an extended family situation, community or culture where social interactions are an important part of the culture. However, Tara and Rachel lived in a quiet suburb outside of Chicago. Once Tara was able to see that Rachel simply had different needs that she or her other child did, she was able to look for opportunities to have those needs met. Tara started to invite more of Rachel's friends over to the house and, in turn, Rachel was invited over to her friend's houses more often. Tara looked for opportunities for Rachel to interact with her cousins, grandmother and aunt. One of Tara's friends even declared herself Rachel's "adopted aunt" and started taking her out once a month. When Rachel asked to have two play dates in a row Tara stopped worrying that it was too much and said "yes". Rachel thrived with the constant social interaction. Although she did often spend time alone in her room reading or writing, she had a rich social life. Tara started joking that Rachel was the social committee for the family.

The choleric child will often express himself with joy or laughter. When the sanguine adult is in his more inner states of being he may not be consistently responsive to the choleric child's expressions. One day the sanguine adult may express great joy along with the choleric child and the next day the sanguine adult may be so preoccupied with a project he is working on that he may simply nod his head at the child and go back to work. This may confuse the choleric child, as he expects and thrives on consistency. The sanguine adult must be careful to take time to respond as consistently as he can to the choleric child so the child is able to remain full of joy and excitement and does not become deflated by confusion or a feeling of rejection. This may mean that the sanguine adult needs to teach the choleric child to always wait for a response, or it may mean that the sanguine adult needs to make an effort to respond on a consistent basis even when he may be occupied with other thoughts. The sanguine adult should also make an effort to explain to the choleric child that he sometimes need time to be alone and think and that he may not always be responsive during those times, but it does not mean that he is not interested in what the child has to share. The sanguine adult could create a consistent "secret phrase" for those times so the choleric child knows that when the sanguine adult says this phrase it means, "I really want to share your joy or enthusiasm, but I need some space and peace right now. Please wait for me and I will join you soon."

The choleric child experiences and learns through interactions with the space. The choleric may organize things in an external manner which can appear disorganized or messy to the sanguine, who desires the grounding sensation of organization in his life. When the sanguine adult can start to understand the external and spatial organizational style of the choleric child he will start to become less bothered by what was previously perceived as a "messy room" or by the choleric's tendency to leave things laying around the house. Instead, the sanguine adult can ensure that the choleric has some space of his own in which he is free to exercise his unique methods of organization and that he understands that other methods of organization may apply to other areas of the home. As long as the choleric has his own room in which to be creative and use space, the child will be more able to keep the exterior spaces in the rest of the house in an order more suitable for the whole family.

Another misunderstanding that can occur between the sanguine adult and the choleric child is also based on the concept of how the choleric child experiences space. A sanguine adult usually has issues with space. Because they live in the always changing and moving world of the air element, the sanguine feels great comfort when the spaces they occupy are solid, organized and steady. The sanguine adult also feels great comfort when the people they interact with are solid, organized and steady. Because the sanguine naturally creates movement and chaos in his life it can be disturbing to also have this movement and chaos coming from external sources as well. For this reason, the sanguine may feel threatened or pushed by the constant incursion of space that the choleric child seems to engage in. It can be helpful for the sanguine adult to understand that this assault on their space is not intentional and that the choleric child is simply communicating and experiencing life in the only way he knows how. Once a sanguine person understands something it becomes less intense and less threatening to him.

Because the sanguine and choleric both experience life as having no limits they can experience and create amazing things together when they are able to cooperate and interact in a positive way.

• Helping the Choleric Child Understand the Sanguine Adult

Although the choleric child functions through space and the sanguine adult experiences life through movement, these traits are similar enough that a common ground for understanding is usually easy to come by.

The choleric child will naturally understand all those traits that he has in common with the sanguine adult – the love of adventure, the limitless view of life, the creative mind, the sense of humor, and the love of imagination, joy and play. However, the choleric child may become bewildered when those traits are not always present. Since the choleric child is apt to blame situations on himself, the child may assume he has done something wrong if the sanguine adult is not responding to him in the way he usually does. When this happens on a consistent basis the choleric child can become insecure about their relationship with the sanguine adult and can become clingy and needy. The choleric child can learn more about the different temperaments through listening to stories with many varied characters and being allowed to explore and comment on those characters. Through this exploration of the different temperaments the choleric child can start to grasp that the reactions he gets from his sanguine adult is not his fault, but has more to do with who the sanguine adult is.

A sanguine adult may often express imbalance with anger. When the sanguine is feeling hungry, tired, imposed upon or even deprived he may lash out in anger. For the sanguine anger is his natural way to balance what seems to be out of equilibrium in life. The choleric child can be frightened by this sudden anger, even if it is expressed in a soft, firm and responsible manner. The sanguine adult should take the time to explain to the choleric child that his use of anger is not necessarily one of rage or fury but rather an action that is taken to rebalance an equation, much like a catalyst is used in a chemical formula. Of course, this concept can be difficult for the choleric child to understand and could best be illustrated through theater and storytelling. At the same time, the sanguine adult should be working on his spiritual practice of taking time outs and try to find more constructive ways to balance the universe other than anger.

The choleric child and the sanguine adult both thrive with action and a sense of purpose. The sanguine adult can thus provide inspiration to the choleric child and the child can also provide inspiration to the sanguine adult. This is one area in which they will connect on a deep level.

The choleric child needs to learn that his sanguine adult is uncomfortable with the feeling of confinement and may be easily sensitized to the choleric's need for constant connection with people. It will be easy for a choleric to understand that the sanguine adult does not like to be restricted – for they have the same mind-set – however, it will be harder for the child to understand how this fear of captivity can affect the sanguine adult's feelings and responses towards the child.

A sanguine person likes to stay busy. Because he experiences life through movement, he is happiest when accomplishing something, moving, working, consuming, thinking, knitting, eating, walking or performing any action. If a sanguine adult sits for five or ten minutes and nobody asks him to do anything he will find something to occupy himself. The choleric child, eager to connect with the adult, may see them as always being unavailable and may feel sad or rejected. However, if the adult can somehow convey to the child that he IS available to the child, then the choleric child will feel more secure and loved. The state of constant action the sanguine occupies will be easily understood by the choleric child. In fact, the child will consider this a completely normal sense of being. It will be the fact that the adult appears to be unavailable for long periods of time that will bother him. This makes helping the choleric child understand the sanguine adult an easier task as the adult does not need to explain why he is busy all the time, he simply needs to explain that he is available to be interrupted at certain times or is available to stop what he is doing and interact with the choleric child.

The sanguine adult will often act on intuition, which merges well with the choleric child's ability to see beneath the surface of life more clearly than others. While the sanguine adult can feel what is going on in many situations, the choleric child can see what is going on in many situations and this can create a deeper connection between the adult and child. In fact, they may share many private jokes and secrets between themselves that only they understand. Often, when the sanguine adult wants to teach or share an intuitive feeling or inventive idea with someone else, it will be the choleric child that can best understand the adult and who will support and help him elaborate on the thought.

- Discipline

Good discipline always stems from a sense of trust, love and harmony between the adult and child. The more the adult and child understand and respect each other, the more discipline happens naturally. To have a healthy discipline relationship with the choleric child the sanguine adult should first read the sections above on how to best understand the child and how to help the child understand the adult.

The main disconnect in the discipline relationship between the sanguine adult and the choleric child is with where each temperament sets their limits. For a sanguine, life does not have defined limits and one must always be in the now and deal with each unique situation as it presents itself. For a choleric child, life has no limits at all, either. However, this means that without limits being defined externally, they will have a tendency to get out of control, become confused, disorganized and perhaps even insecure or needy. As a sanguine adult you may not naturally put these limits into place. However, they are essential to the discipline relationship you have with this child. You may even feel uncomfortable about putting so many "rules" into place. You may feel silly stating that it is a "rule" to get up at eight every morning when you know very well that some mornings this may not work out because you all stayed up too late or somebody is sick or there may be an event to attend at an earlier time. You may even feel uncomfortable restricting yourself with these "rules". However, it is better to put some guidelines and limits into place for the sake of your relationship with your child and your own sanity and then "make exceptions" from time to time instead of not having these limits in place to begin with.

A choleric child feels more loved and secure with limits. Without these limits he can feel himself spiraling out of control and are not sure how to stop himself. Over time he will learn or someone will teach him. However, as a child, he has not yet developed this ability and he needs your help.

The reason this is essential to the discipline relationship is that one of the main conflicts you will have with your sanguine child is his tendency to incessantly ask, request, chatter or interrupt. Because a choleric child does not feel there are any limits in the world he does not understand why others may have him. Even though he needs them too, he simply does not understand why other people get angry when he asks a question one hundred times or knocks on a door more than once. To understand his point of view, think about how he reacts to you when you approach him. A choleric child usually accepts a hug, stops what he is doing to talk to you, is happy to come along at the "drop of a hat" and can endure long periods of fun and entertainment. If he is on the phone with a friend he is happy to say "excuse me" and answer any question you may have or even talk to both of you at once. He is so open and loving and without limits. This is a positive trait.

However, it is hard to see this as positive when he is turning this on you. You may not enjoy being interrupted on the phone. Especially as a sanguine, you need to be able to focus on one thing at a time and constant interruptions may upset you. You experience life in seasons, so one day you may feel very energetic and full of fire and another day you may just need some peace. Many choleric children are "punished" for interrupting on the phone, asking for too much, not respecting someone's space, or waking up a baby or adult who is trying to sleep. A lot of these punishments could be avoided if the choleric child is aware of what the limits are, he understands what the consequences of pushing those limits are (use natural consequences) and is constantly reminded of those limits in a loving and gentle way. When reminding a choleric child, the sanguine adult wants to be creative and seek to help the choleric understand. However, the choleric will not understand that there are limits if too many words and inconsistent phrases are introduced. The choleric child needs to simply hear the rule stated over and over in the exact same way in a gentle and loving tone of voice.

A typical conversation between a sanguine adult and choleric child could be:

Scene: Sanguine adult is on the phone and choleric child interrupts him. Or a sanguine adult is talking to another student and the choleric child interrupts him. Keep in mind that this is just an example. I am assuming that you have appropriate phone habits and you have a classroom arrangement that allows you to interact fairly with each student. An adult who is ignoring a student or an adult who spends all day on the phone is not part of the example below.

Sanguine Adult: "You need to wait until I am off the phone to talk to me."
Choleric Child: 'Why?"
Sanguine Adult: "Because I cannot concentrate when you are talking to me and I am also trying to listen to someone else."
Choleric Child: "But what I wanted to say was really important. Couldn't you just listen and then go back to talking?"
Sanguine Adult: "I could but that would be really hard for me to keep up because you often ask a lot of questions. I can't have every conversation I have interrupted."
Choleric Child: "Well, since you are already talking to me, just let me ask just this ONE question..."
Sanguine Adult *(sigh...)*

The following is much more effective way of speaking to the choleric child. To the creative and compassionate sanguine it may seem harsh and stiff. However, it is the most effective way to let the choleric know what the limits are so that the adult may be creative with the child at a more convenient time. Compassion does not always mean the same thing to each person. Compassion is best defined as the action one takes that makes the other person most comfortable. So even though the sanguine adult feels awkward, he can keep in mind that the choleric child is feeling happiest when the adult is firm, defined and gentle.

Sanguine Adult, "Please wait until I am off the phone to ask me your question."
Choleric Child: "Why?"
Sanguine Adult: *Gives the "sign language" for "wait".*
Choleric Child: "But I just have a short question and I am going to forget!"
Sanguine Adult: *Smiles and gives the "sign language" for "wait".*
Choleric Child: "It is really amazing. I really want to show you right now."
Sanguine Adult: *Smiles and gives the "sign language" for "wait".*
Choleric Child: *Finally realizes that they are getting the same response and decides to wait.*

- ## The Teaching Relationship

The teaching relationship between the sanguine adult and the choleric student has potential to be one of the most enriching and dynamic relationships between an adult and a student. This is because the sanguine adult has the ability to nurture the balancing needs of the choleric student as well as the student's expansive needs.

When the sanguine adult is in his winter disposition, the choleric can feel a sense of balance between them and will feel at peace with the adult's flowing receptiveness to their energies. These kinds of interactions can happen between the sanguine adult and choleric student when they read books together, take walks together or do handiwork such as knitting together.

When the sanguine adult is in his spring disposition the choleric can feel joy at the synchronicity of their moods and will enjoy exploring the world with them and learning new things together. These kinds of interactions can happen between the sanguine adult and the choleric student when they attend a class together, they draw or paint together or they dance or participate in other physical activities together.

When the sanguine adult is in his summer disposition the choleric will be able to express himself without limits or boundaries and can experience the pure joy of being choleric. These kinds of interactions can happen between the sanguine adult and the choleric student when they play together, sing together or dance together.

When the sanguine adult is in his autumn disposition the choleric can learn balance and organization from the adult and can participate in the rituals of grounding oneself and rebalancing the psyche. These kinds of interactions can happen between the sanguine adult and the choleric student when they clean the house together, they organize school papers together, or they edit a piece of writing together.

Because the choleric student can experience so many different moods with the sanguine adult the student has endless routes in which he can learn and grow and can often find all the balance he needs from one good adult.

Thankfully, both the sanguine and the choleric are comfortable in very stimulating environments, although for different reasons and not always at the same time. The choleric will embrace the activity and sensations in the environment and participate in them. The sanguine adult has most likely learned to focus so well on one sensation at a time that he has the ability to shut out most of the stimuli and enjoy one or two experiences in the environment. The sanguine adult will not always be in the mood for a lot of activity and noise, but he does have the ability to be comfortable in such situations quite often. As a student the sanguine most likely enjoyed stimulating surroundings for the entertainment provided. So, although the sanguine adult experiences these atmospheres differently as an adult, he has a history of being at ease in such environments. This is fortunate for the choleric as he learns more efficiently in an environment that provides ample stimulation for his curiosity and constant need for interaction and attention.

The choleric student lives in the here and now and does not spend a lot of time dwelling on the past or worrying about the future. For this reason, the sanguine adult will need to teach the choleric student in the now and focus on creating lessons that can be experienced in one complete piece, rather than in parts. It is good practice for the choleric student to also experience projects that build upon themselves over time and that involve multiple steps. However, it is more efficient for the choleric to be allowed to follow most of his lessons in focused self-contained blocks. Even if the choleric will be completing a task over a longer period of time, it is important that the student feels closure or a sense of accomplishment with each lesson. This can be accomplished by checking off the step that was completed on a chart, by completing a page in a main lesson book and decorating it with a border or by performing or sharing the accomplishments of the day with another person either verbally or visually. This method of learning also plays to one of the choleric student's other strengths – the ability to completely focus on an event or topic that is happening around him. Because the choleric student has an ability to focus so well, this skill should be used to his advantage and not shuttled to the side in favor of too many long-term projects.

The sanguine adult will find joy and satisfaction in teaching a student that is so responsive and intuitive. The adult will find that they often do not need to explain the entire lesson before the choleric jumps in and says, "Oh! I understand!" This quick understanding is a typical trait of the choleric and should be taken seriously. If the choleric grasps the lesson quickly he will find it painful to have to listen to more of the lesson. It may be more useful for them to expand on the lesson in other ways.

• A Story to Share

This Chinese Folktale about dreams embraces the passion of the choleric as well as the wandering curiosity of the sanguine. When stories are told they speak to the child on a basic level. The reason one tells stories instead of explaining things to a child is because stories have the ability to adapt to the child's needs. When a person explains a situation to a child he is putting forth a concept that the child needs to grasp at or reach to understand. When one simply *tells* a story the child is given permission to understand the story in any way he wishes and to gain wisdom and knowledge from it in the way that best suits him at that moment. For that reason, it is not recommended that the story be explained to the child or that the child be provided with the ubiquitous "moral" at the end. Rather, it is best to give them a chance to enjoy the story for what it becomes to them and provide them with numerous chances to hear the story told. The stories in this book help the different temperaments understand each other. If the adult or adult would like to explore this understanding on a deeper level they can ask questions once the story is finished. However, one must be sure to ask open questions and allow the child to express his feelings.

Dreams

A story from China by Yu Hsiung, a Taoist Sage

In the time of King Mu of Chou, there was a magician who came from a kingdom in the far west. He could pass through fire and water, penetrate metal and stone, overturn mountains and make rivers flow backwards, transplant whole towns and cities, ride on thin air without falling, encounter solid bodies without being obstructed. There was no end to the countless variety of changes and transformations which he could affect; and besides changing the external form, he could also spirit away men's internal cares.

King Mu revered him as a god and served him like a prince. He set aside for his use a spacious suite of apartments, regaled him with the daintiest of food, and selected a number of singing-girls for his express gratification. The magician, however, condemned the king's palace as mean, the cooking as rancid, and the concubines as too ugly to live with.

So king Mu had a new building erected to please him. It was built entirely of bricks and wood, and gorgeously decorated in red and white, no skill being spared in its construction. The five royal treasuries were empty by the time that the new pavilion was complete. It stood six thousand feet high, overtopping Mount Chung-nan, and it was called Touch-the-sky Pavilion. Then the king proceeded to fill it with maidens, selected from Cheng and Wie, of the most exquisite and delicate beauty. They were anointed with fragrant perfumes, provided with jeweled hairpins and earrings, and arrayed in the finest silks, with costly satin trains. Their faces were powdered, and their eyebrows penciled, their girdles were studded with precious stones, and sweet scents were wafted abroad wherever they went. Ravishing music was played to the honored guest by the Imperial bands; several times a month he was presented with fresh jeweled raiment; every day he had set before him some new and delicious food.

The magician could not well refuse to take up his abode in this palace of delight. But he had not dwelt there very long when he invited the king to accompany him on a jaunt. So the king clutched the magician's sleeve, and soared up with him higher and higher into the sky, until at last they stopped, and lo! they had reached the magician's own palace. This palace was built with beams of gold and silver, and incrusted with pearls and jade. It towered high above the region of clouds and rain, and the foundations whereon it rested were unknown. It appeared like a stupendous cloud-mass to the view. The sights and sounds it offered to eye and ear, the scents and flavors which abounded there, were such as exist not within mortal ken. The king verily believed that he was in the Halls of Paradise, tenanted by God himself, and that he was listening to the mighty music of the spheres. He gazed at his own palace on the earth below, and it seemed to him no better than a rude pile of clods and brushwood.

The king would gladly have stayed in this palace for decade after decade, without a thought for his own country. But the magician invited him to make another journey, and in the new region they came to, neither sun nor moon could be seen in the heavens above, nor any rivers or seas below. The king's eyes were dazed by the quality of the light, and he lost the power of vision; his ears were stunned by the sounds that assailed them, and he lost the faculty of hearing. The framework of his bones and his internal organs were thrown out of gear and refused to function. His thoughts were in a whirl, his intellect became clouded, and he begged the magician to take him back again. Thereupon, the magician gave him a shove, and the king experienced a sensation of falling through space.
. . .

When he awoke to consciousness, he found himself sitting on his throne just as before, with the selfsame attendants round him. He looked at the wine in front of him, and saw that it was still full of sediment; he looked at the viands, and found that they had not yet lost their freshness. He asked where he had come from, and his attendants told him that he had only been sitting quietly there.

This threw King Mu into a reverie, and it was three months before he was himself again. Then he made further inquiry, and asked the magician to explain what had happened.

"Your Majesty and I," answered the magician, "were only wandering about in the spirit, and our bodies never moved at all."

Choleric Adult - Choleric Child

- ## General Relationship

The relationship between the choleric adult and the choleric child can be best illustrated by the phrase "put another log on the fire." What happens when we put another log on the fire? The fire becomes warmer and more enjoyable, the people around the flames are happy, and the world becomes a brighter and livelier place. However, sometimes the flames can rise too high and burn the tops of the trees in the forest, or singe the eyebrows of the people around the blaze. The fire can burn itself out by consuming the fuel too quickly.

- ## Helping the Choleric Adult Understand the Choleric Child

A choleric adult is usually more balanced than the choleric child in temperament, and may even have rejected some aspects of the choleric temperament to the point where she believes those aspects are unhealthy. As the choleric parent observes the choleric child, she must once again confront these aspects of her own persona and be open to possible adjustments in her point of view. Having a choleric child is an opportunity for the choleric parent to repair some of the damage that may have been done to her during her childhood. If the choleric parent can view her interactions with the choleric child as an opportunity for growth she will not only understand the child better, but will also have an improved understanding of the choleric temperament.

The choleric adult can best understand the choleric child by realizing the child is like the adult in many ways but not in all ways. Additionally, just because the choleric parent has been through many trials and tribulations in life does not mean that the parent should try to prevent her own choleric child from experiencing these same trials and tribulations. In many cases trials are important rites of passage for the choleric child; the choleric adult would better serve both she and the child by using past experiences as a confidence builder, rather than a springboard for fear.

Certainly, little gems of wisdom are important to insert into the choleric's mind. Many of the experiences the child encounters cannot be avoided and must be worked through. The choleric adult must allow the choleric child to not only learn her own lessons, but also let the child know that the adult is there for the child to lean on, if needed. This is especially important, because the choleric child is very willful and can only truly learn something by repetition and practice. A choleric child does not learn by watching others like the phlegmatic child, or by listening to wise advice like the melancholic child. The choleric adult must also recognize that as the choleric child matures, she will naturally balance as the childhood years pass, so many problems and challenges will easily take care of themselves.

A choleric adult will usually understand the choleric child's need to be held, loved and adored. The choleric adult and child both enjoy giving and receiving affection, thus the relationship between them can be mutually nurturing. As the choleric parent recognizes the enormous significance of this aspect of their relationship, she will be able to enjoy those lovely moments of connection and nurturing, and should be able to provide the choleric child with something she greatly needs.

A choleric parent must also appreciate that the choleric child enjoys being a leader as much as the parent does. People of the choleric temperament naturally enjoy taking over and leading situations, because they are usually so enthusiastic about their ideas, they want to ensure these ideas are carried out accurately. Because of this trait, both the choleric parent and the choleric child may have difficulty deciding who will lead. Recognizing the desire to lead within, the choleric parent should be able to realize the importance of letting the child develop leadership skills.

A choleric parent often has trouble understanding the similar qualities in both parent and child. This situation occurs when the choleric parent is still struggling with some aspect of her own temperament and has not yet come to terms with it. One possible area of inner discord may be in the area of fulfillment and desire. Many people who do not understand the choleric's motivations for fulfillment will use words such as selfish, self-centered or greedy to describe the choleric.

If a choleric adult has frequently been around people who view her in that light, the adult may still be struggling with that aspect of the temperament and may be conflicted as to how she feels about that personality trait in the child. A choleric parent may understand the choleric child's need to be fulfilled, but at the same time experience too many voices from the past that say "stop being so greedy."

The choleric parent may then fluctuate between indulging and depriving the choleric child. It is healthier if the choleric parent is aware of this possible inner inconsistency to better guide the child in her own struggles with this topic. A person of the choleric temperament can choose to appreciate that she has a healthy sense of personal respect and a natural ability to nurture she instead of viewing she as greedy or selfish.

As the choleric adult learns to appreciate the gift of self-nurturing in general she will also be able to appreciate this gift within the child. One must only look around at the large numbers of people who do not cherish or love themselves to see what disharmony and pain this lack of self-nurturing has brought about. The gift of self-love is a gift the choleric person can teach to her friends, spouse and child or something that the choleric adult can relearn from the choleric child.

The choleric adult may recall back to her own childhood and relationship with food to better understand the eating habits of the choleric child. A choleric child has a very powerful sense of smell and since the taste of food is mostly experienced through one's sense of smell, the choleric child can be very particular about the food she eats. If the choleric parent can understand and expect this, there will be fewer conflicts at mealtimes.

The choleric child often experiences life through laughter and joy. If the choleric adult has lost some of this joy and laughter from her own childhood she may feel uncomfortable with the amount of levity in the choleric child's view of life. However, if the choleric parent still maintains the same levity herself parent and child will experience many joyful and light moments together. The more the choleric parent can connect with this joyful aspect of the choleric temperament, the more they will understand and enjoy the choleric child.

The choleric child can be very optimistic and hopeful in spite of what other may say or believe. If the adult is a happy, balanced choleric, this trait will be encouraged and fostered in the choleric child and will help the child develop into a more balanced adult. However, in a choleric adult who has many difficult experiences in life, this trait may be discouraged as dangerous or potentially hurtful. The choleric adult must remind she often that many things they find disturbing in the choleric child are actually reflections of issues the choleric adult needs to deal with in her own life. Encouraging this optimism in the choleric child is healthy for both the child and the adult.

The choleric child enjoys being attractive, magnetic and the center of attention. An adult choleric may have tried to temper this feature of hers to better please social groups she was part of in the past and, as a result, may have disconnected from this desire or not be aware of how it is exhibited in her as an adult. As the choleric adult watches other children and adults react to the choleric child she may hear others suggest that the choleric child boasts too much, shows off too frequently, or bosses other children around. This may be difficult for the choleric adult to hear as most parents want to hear only positive things said about their child. However, in this case, hearing such things is an opportunity to support the choleric child and, in turn, help spread understanding of the choleric temperament. Often, the very traits that parents try to subdue in their young children are the same traits they try to cultivate later. If the choleric parent realizes that boasting is an early form of self-awareness, showing off is an early form of social confidence and bossing other children around is an immature version of leadership skills, the parent can come to appreciate the future potential of the choleric child. The adult can help direct her towards that future potential and help others understand that these traits must be nurtured and guided rather than eradicated from the child.

- Helping the Choleric Child Understand the Choleric Adult

Choleric children easily intuit what people around them are thinking and feeling, so it is nearly impossible to hide emotions from a choleric child. It is best if the choleric parent is open and honest, so the choleric child can better understand her parent. If the choleric adult is not open, the child may become frustrated and confused, because her perceptions will not match what the parent is saying or doing.

The most valuable connection that a choleric parent can make with the choleric child is to teach the child about the positive aspects of the choleric temperament, and to engage in loving conversations about those personality traits. As the choleric parent teaches the child to appreciate these traits within her, the child will develop a stronger ability to recognize and appreciate those same traits within the choleric adult. Some of the positive traits that can be discussed with the child are those of enthusiasm, generosity, leadership, the ability to enjoy the senses, compassion, intuition, warmth, energy, vibrancy, creativity, the ability to share, the ability to live in the now, the ability to forgive, a sense of humor, affection, empathy, optimism, and hopefulness.

A wonderful form drawing exercise for a choleric adult to do with a choleric child is one of stacking triangles. To do this exercise the teacher should sit down at a table across from the choleric child and place some drawing paper and colored pencils or beeswax crayons in the middle of the table. The choleric child and adult should start by drawing one triangle at the bottom of the page and should continue the lesson by attaching another triangle to the first and then a third triangle to the first and/or second triangle and so on. The choleric temperament is represented by a triangle. This process of connecting and stacking triangles on the paper will help the choleric adult and child gain more insight into each other and they way they can/could work together.

- **The Teaching Relationship**

The choleric child is an eager student, and the choleric adult is an eager teacher. This eagerness can sometimes cause conflict as the choleric student fights to pursue only her interests, while and the choleric parent struggles to keep the student's interest in the lessons. There are many solutions to this problem. One solution is to let the choleric student "teach" the class. When given the responsibility of creating lessons instead of just following their passions, the choleric student will often come up with complex and challenging lessons beyond anything the teacher would have imagined. Another solution is to place the choleric in a more social situation. A choleric student is more likely to engage in a painting lesson if the teacher or another student is painting along with her. A third solution is to present lessons in creative and magical ways. Choleric students love fairytales from countries all over the world, as this not only appeals to their sense of fantasy, but their sense of adventure. Although fairytales are most appropriate for the first grade, a choleric student will benefit from and want to hear fairytales well into her sixth grade year. As the choleric student matures, fairytales from unusual locations, as well as ones with more complex themes, can be told.

As with all the temperaments, the choleric student needs to be guided into balance, but also encouraged to embrace the natural aspects of her temperament. For this reason, it is also beneficial to allow choleric students ample time to create their own lessons and follow their own passions in learning.

It is helpful for the choleric student to learn appreciation for the simple life. Karen and Katie are a good example of how this can work.

Karen came to me because she was concerned that she was not able to balance Katie's temperament. She felt they fought often and rarely agreed on anything. Katie's demands for attention, time and entertainment became more than she could manage. After a few sessions, Karen realized she was encouraging Katie's demands by fulfilling them all. As a choleric herself, Karen loved to give, and loved to enjoy the look on people's faces when they received a gift. She enjoyed the process of creating fantastic situations for Katie to enjoy. Karen made the decision to take more time focusing on the joy in the ordinary aspects of life, instead of creating events that were "larger than life" for her daughter.

The very next day after Karen made her decision, an opportunity presented itself. Katie asked her mother why her magical fairy did not visit her. Instead of creating a lavish response inspired by Katie's fairy, Karen decided to reply in a different way. She said, "Perhaps your fairy has been leaving you gifts every day but you have not been seeing them. Remember the flowers that bloomed by surprise in the garden yesterday? Remember the adorable slugs that you found in the fairy house under the pine tree? Perhaps these were gifts you forgot to thank her for." Katie was enchanted at the thought of these hidden treasures and could not wait to wake up the next morning and search for gifts from her fairy. Last time I spoke to Karen, she shared with me that Katie was still finding gifts from her fairy on a weekly basis. She also shared with me that while the incident with the fairy was small, it taught both her and her daughter a big lesson. By appreciating the everyday and routine things in life, a choleric can learn the discipline to follow through with those things that are not initially attractive.

Although the choleric benefits from appreciation of the simple aspects of life, the choleric student will never be completely satisfied without the excitement of the exotic things as well. A choleric's lessons should be a combination of routine and excitement. Routine will help cholerics balance their expansive predisposition and excitement will keep them engaged in lessons. A choleric enjoys lessons that are creative, unique, moving, colorful, visual and physical. Cholerics would much rather learn math from stories, real life examples, songs and art than from recitation and memorization of facts. A choleric prefers to be involved in the story, rather than always listening to the story, and will often be motivated to modify the stories she is told. A choleric learns by asking "what if...?"

A choleric learns and experiences life through space. When a choleric teacher works with a choleric student, this movement should come naturally, as both have the same need. However, if the choleric teacher is following an external system of education or a structure in a way that seems "unnatural," this harmony of space between the choleric teacher and student may be lost. As long as the choleric teacher follows her heart and true desires when teaching the choleric student, the lessons will captivate and engage the choleric student.

One useful tool to use when educating the choleric student is to realize how attached she is to their social environment and   surrounding events. The choleric student can become completely involved in events going on around them without having any previous interest in such events. The choleric is like a firefly to a lamp. When the choleric sees a bright light they will want to explore it. If the choleric teacher is having trouble reaching the choleric student she needs only to create an event and allow the choleric student to attend.

One of my clients, Miranda, used this method with her son, Darik, to resolve conflicts that arose between them. Miranda was not too concerned that Darik had his own path he wished to follow. Darik always seemed to keep busy with some project and was not usually interested in television or sitting around much. He was altogether an industrious boy. For this reason, Miranda was largely unschooling Darik and letting him create his own lessons. When she tried to introduce lessons in the past, Darik seemed resistant and it always took so much time to convince him to follow her lessons she finally gave up trying. She surmised that he was probably learning just as much on his own and that her role as support for his ideas was probably a more suitable one.

However, there were two problems with this situation – Miranda was not happy and was not enjoying teaching. Darik was not learning some essential facts. He did not like math, and therefore would go weeks without exploring math concepts and was rapidly falling behind his potential in that area.

Because Miranda was also of the choleric temperament, she had many ideas of her own and was initially eager to share them in the homeschooling environment. She admitted that she envisioned days filled with excitement and lessons filled with movement all inspired by her. Instead, she felt as if she was not a very useful part of the homeschooling process and that she failed Darik by not teaching him his math facts. As a choleric, Miranda was always ready to take blame for the situations that happened around her.

I explained to Miranda that Darik did need time to pursue his own interests, but he also needed someone he could respect and be inspired to teach him. When Miranda introduced the lessons and said, "What do you think about this?" or "Would you like to do this today?" Darik tuned out and lost interest.

Miranda learned to introduce the lessons in a creative and enthusiastic manner that was reflective of her own excitement for the topic. She allowed Darik to explore some topics he wanted to learn, and together, they both chose topics for their group lesson. Miranda introduced topics like sewing, fencing, sculpting, and sacred geometry. Since these were topics Miranda was interested in, her enthusiasm and vibrant ways she approached them were hard for Darik to resist, although she claims he did give her a "strange look" a few times.

Initially Miranda undertook this as an experiment to see if she could develop a better homeschooling relationship with Darik. They could then, move on to the lessons that "really mattered" like composition and math. What surprised Miranda, however, was that during the lessons she was already giving, the topic of composition and math came up naturally and Darik was happy to cooperate under those conditions. Miranda discovered that as a choleric parent teaching a choleric student, learning was more joyful and productive if they both did the things they loved.

- ## Discipline

Good discipline always stems from a sense of trust, love, and harmony between the parent and child. The more they understand and respect each other, the more naturally discipline happens. To establish and maintain a healthy relationship with the choleric child, including the art of discipline, the choleric parent should first read the sections above covering how to best understand the choleric child and how to help the child understand her.

One common conflict between the choleric adult and the choleric child is over who will lead the lesson, discussion, planning or outing. As they are both cholerics, both want to lead and plan. It is healthy for both the parent and the child to learn to share these privileges. The more the choleric parent and child learn to share leadership, the more skilled they will also become at listening and following instructions. This arrangement may initially be a struggle for both parent and child. However, with patience and time, both will learn to enjoy their lessons together. However, for this to work, the choleric adult has to be sincere about following the choleric child's lessons and must participate fully, so the choleric feels a sense of fairness in the arrangement. This does not mean, of course, that the choleric child and parent are attached every moment of the educational process. On the contrary, the choleric child is very self motivated and will also be able to perform many lessons on her own and without a lot of instruction or supervision.

Although both the choleric parent and the choleric child have no trouble expressing their desires, needs and emotions, the irony is that often neither one is listening to the other. When conflict arises, then, they can deteriorate into shouting matches.

As each realizes the other is not listening, they may speak louder and louder with the hope they will eventually become heard. However, the choleric parent should know that anger and shouting are very hot activities and only fan the fire of the choleric child. This will cause the child to become angry and the discussion to become even more difficult if not impossible. As a child learns from imitating the parent, the best way to solve this problem is for the parent to initiate a lesson in listening. Each time a conflict arises the parent should take five minutes to sit in front of the choleric child, give the child her complete attention and listen to everything the child has to say. Initially this may encourage the child to talk more and simply dissipate their anger, which is productive in itself. However, over time this lesson will also encourage the choleric child to develop a skill for listening as well.

In addition, listening tools can help the choleric child who has a vivid imagination and rich fantasy life. Choleric children are big fans of the concept of the Native American Talking Stick. In the Native American tradition there is a special stick, decorated with feathers, beads and perhaps fur or other objects from nature that is passed around a social circle. When the stick is held by each person in the circle, it is that person's turn to talk, and everyone else's turn to listen. The talking stick concept can be used at home, in small groups, and even between two people. Choleric children have a deep connection with anything sacred, so the talking stick appeals to the connection they have with anything magical. Choleric adults may have a great need to maintain control over most situations in the household or classroom, and the talking stick helps her feel as if control is maintained. In this way, the talking stick method of conversation works for bother the choleric parent and the choleric child.

Discipline must be in the here and now. This should not be difficult for the choleric parent as she is very responsive and will usually not wait to express their feelings and correct wrongdoings on the topic. If, for some reason, discipline is delayed for any reason, the choleric parent needs to realize that every minute that passes makes the discipline less effective. For this reason the choleric parent needs to make sure that friends, other family members and even other teachers are "on board" with what the choleric child needs so that when the parent is not around, the choleric child will still be responsible for their actions and the choices she makes.

Discipline must be compassionate, empathetic, responsive, and intuitive. If the choleric parent does not believe in what they are saying the choleric child will sense their uncertainty about the topic and will resist.

This concept is best illustrated by the Richard's family. The mother, Emily, was a choleric having trouble communicating and disciplining her nine year-old choleric girl, Amanda. Emily was confused as to why many of her "rules" were not being followed around the house and became increasingly frustrated at what she felt was her daughter's defiance. She created a schedule of what she expected Amanda to do each day including brushing her teeth before breakfast, feeding the family cat, and practicing some math facts after lunch. She did not feel the schedule was difficult to follow so was upset when Amanda did not seem to make any effort at all. I was surprised that this was how a choleric chose to run the house so I asked her about it. Emily admitted that it was actually her husband's schedule and that he expected her to teach Amanda to follow it because he felt Amanda needed more restraint and order in her life.

Since Emily had seen Amanda's moods get out of control frequently, she agreed with her husband on this point. However, she did not realize that by presenting Amanda with second-hand version of what she felt, that Amanda could not relate to the new rules of the house. Amanda needed to know that her mother really believed in what she was saying or she needed to hear her father say it to her personally.

- ## A Story to Share

When stories are told they speak to the child on a basic level. The reason one tells stories instead of explaining things to a child is because stories have the ability to adapt to the child's needs. When a person explains a situation to a child she is putting forth a concept that the child needs to grasp at or reach to understand. When one simply *tells* a story the child is given permission to understand the story in any way she wishes and to gain wisdom and knowledge from it in the way that best suits her at that moment. For that reason, it is not recommended that the story be explained to the child or that the child be provided with the ubiquitous "moral" at the end. Rather, it is best to give them a chance to enjoy the story for what it becomes to them and provide them with numerous chances to hear the story told. The stories in this book help the different temperaments understand each other. If the parent or teacher would like to explore this understanding on a deeper level they can ask questions once the story is finished. However, one must be sure to ask open questions and allow the child to express her feelings.

The following stories show interactions between two cholerics. Although they both have standard "morals" that usually follow I have deleted these lessons from the end of the story because each story has much more than can be learned from it.

The Peacock and the Crane

A peacock, spreading its gorgeous tail mocked a crane that passed by, ridiculing the ashen hue of its plumage and saying,

"I am robed, like a king, in gold and purple and all the colors of the rainbow; while you have not a bit of color on your wings."

"True," replied the crane; "but I soar to the heights of heaven and lift up my voice to the stars, while you walk below, like a cock, among the birds of the dunghill."

The Raven and the Swan

A raven saw a swan and desired to secure for himself the same beautiful feathers. Supposing that the swan's splendid white color arose from his washing in the water in which he swam, the raven left the neighborhood where he picked up his living and started to live in the lakes and pools. But cleansing his feathers as often as he would, he could not change their color, and in the end he perished through want of food.

Choleric Adult - Melancholic Child

- ## General Relationship

The relationship between the choleric adult and the melancholic child can be extremely beneficial for both of them, but risks becoming distant if frequent efforts are not made to connect and understand each other. This relationship is characterized by a rhythm of connection and detachment between the two temperaments as they both have such different needs that they cannot tolerate a steady connection. The relationship between the two is like the relationship between the honeybee and the apple tree. They both need each other and benefit from each other, they can experience moments of joy together, but will rarely occupy the same habitat on a continuous basis for one needs the roots of the earth and the other, the breeze and the sky. Great love and respect can grow between this honeybee and apple tree, if the relationship is cultivated and maintained on a regular basis and if both of the temperaments can learn to respect the other's unique views and contributions in the world and not focus on the limitations he may feel the other has.

- ## Helping the Choleric Adult Understand the Melancholic Child

The melancholic child is ruled by a sense of order and how things and people should be. For this reason, the melancholic child may choose friends depending on how well those friends fit into his world view. The choleric adult, on the other hand, is ruled by the desire to connect with people so may have a hard time understanding why their child does not make an effort to maintain friendships with a variety of people. The melancholic child is most comfortable with a few close friends, whereas the choleric adult is more comfortable with many friends and by being liked by many people. The melancholic child cares little what people think of him and more about what he thinks of other people. A choleric adult may try to encourage the choleric child to be more agreeable with friends or may be concerned at the way the child runs their social life and be tempted to interfere.

However, the best thing a choleric adult can do for his child is to appreciate that he has a different style of relating to people and that this style will develop and mature over time as they learn their own lessons and gain wisdom from the choleric adult's example. In fact, the melancholic child will benefit much from the influence of the choleric adult as the adult's social life will help the child to increase his circle of friends. It will help them practice interacting with people the child would not usually choose to interact with. As the choleric adult invites a variety of people to the home and visits a variety of people, the melancholic child is given the opportunity to increase their social acceptance of people who are not like him.

The melancholic child is most comfortable when there is order and everything is in its place. The melancholic child may enjoy schedules and plans and may spend

200

hours creating them. On the other hand, a choleric adult feels most comfortable when unbound by time or space and likes to imagine that life and the resources in it are limitless. To the choleric adult it may feel like the melancholic child is always bringing the adult into a box, when the choleric would actually rather be flying in the sky. The melancholic child may prefer staying at home to exploring new events and may insist on a plan for the weekend or the lesson when the choleric adult would much rather plan according to the inspiration of the day.

When the choleric adult can understand that the melancholic child is not trying to confine them, the adult can relax anxieties about the child and start to explore solutions to the differences between them instead of becoming frustrated with his feeling of confinement with the child. When the choleric adult realizes that the melancholic child is happy in the world of order and predictability, the adult can also let go of the fears he may have about the child's happiness and feel more confident in his abilities to be a good adult. The choleric adult may find himself leaving the child at home with another adult or sitter while the adult fulfills the desire he has for excitement and activity. The guilt associated with this can be discarded as the adult realizes the melancholic child is actually happier staying at home and is most likely grateful that he is not forced to attend every event with the adult.

On the other hand, the melancholic child does benefit from attending some events and going on some adventures with the adult and this should not be avoided – even if the melancholic child protests. The choleric adult can recognize that although the melancholic child may not be enthusiastic about exploring many new things, he will benefit from the experience and will grow to be a more balanced person as he is allowed more experiences outside the confines of the melancholic temperament.

A melancholic child may often express sorrow, disappointment or grief. They may even seem depressed quite frequently. This may concern the vibrant and positively focused choleric adult and he may worry that the melancholic child is ill or unhappy. In actuality, the melancholic child is merely expressing himself in the most natural way of the melancholic. The melancholic child can actually be completely content and at the same time be complaining or expressing dissatisfaction with something. This can be confusing for the choleric adult who is accustomed to sharing their emotions in a completely transparent and direct manner. The choleric adult may listen to a melancholic child's complaints and assume he needs to help the child or change the situation the child is in. This may occasionally be the right thing to do, however, more often than not, the choleric adult just needs to listen to what the child has to say, nod their head and allow the melancholic child to continue what he is doing.

The melancholic temperament is most prominent in old age. For this reason, a child of the melancholic temperament may seem to be an "old soul" with a wisdom that exceeds that of his adult. However, the choleric adult must not forget that this self confident and able melancholic is still a child and has the needs of a child. The choleric adult must also realize that this appearance of old age wisdom is also a bit of an illusion. There are many wise and responsible aspects of the melancholic child. However, the choleric adult should not always defer to this apparent wisdom and must recognize that the child is seeking a leader and a guide in life and is looking to the choleric adult to provide that.

The melancholic child learns about life through the sensory experience of touch. Because of this he may be inclined to touch things that don't belong to them, explore other people's belongings and initiate physical contact when the person they are with does not want to be touched. As a choleric adult who is concerned about his own image in society, he may be embarrassed at the child's behavior and attempt to curb it by asking the child to refrain from touching so many things and people. However, by preventing the melancholic from the sensual experience of touch, the adult is also limiting the child's ability to learn about the world around them. A better approach would be to encourage the child's inclination to touch things and people, but to give him guidelines for such behavior.

A melancholic child will want to maintain a neat and orderly personal life. However, this does not always mean that his room is clean. Each melancholic has his own sense of order. For one it may mean that the bedroom is in order, another may be attached to keeping papers in order, and yet another may be predisposed to create lists. Because a melancholic can often be judgmental of people who are not like him and has a strong need to control the environment around them, the child may also try to impose this order on siblings, adults and classmates by telling them what they should clean and how they should keep it in order. A choleric adult needs to realize that the melancholic child will feel most comfortable when the home is in order and when there is a regular schedule.

As a choleric adult, this may not be the most attractive situation. However, as most melancholic children are very independent, the choleric adult can easily give the melancholic child freedom to create his own environment by giving them chores and tasks around the home. A melancholic is usually happiest when their environment is organized and clean on a regular basis, so it may sometimes be advisable to let him perform this job. However, it may not always be easy to convince the melancholic. The melancholic child may already have an order of how things should be done in the world and this order could include someone else cleaning the house and his room. Because of this, it is best to start the melancholic child early with household chores and responsibilities before he can define other roles around the home.

A melancholic child will restrain themselves from expressing emotion and prefers to think about what they say carefully. If a melancholic child does express emotion or opinions, it usually means that these opinions have been well thought out or the emotions have been simmering for some time. When a melancholic child takes the time to express a feeling to the choleric adult, the adult should listen closely as this provides a rare insight into the needs and desires of the melancholic child. There is no guarantee that once feelings and needs are expressed, that they will be voiced again. The melancholic child will assume that the choleric adult has heard and understood them.

The melancholic child is usually tasteful and discerning in his choice of friends, clothing, hobbies, toys and entertainment. The melancholic child also enjoys moderation, so will not likely be prone to addictions or excess desires.

Although the choleric adult is much different from the melancholic child in his motivations and desires, the adult will always know where he stands with the child as a melancholic is quick to let another person know what he is feeling about him. A melancholic may be slow to share his inner thoughts about life in general but will not have a problem sharing opinions about relationships with friends and family members. This should make some levels of communication between the choleric adult and melancholic child easier as the choleric adult appreciates it when people are straightforward and direct with him.

Because of the carefulness of thought that goes into each action and word and because the melancholic is very sensitive to the order around them, he may maintain some emotional distance from adults and siblings. This may cause siblings to think that the melancholic child does not like them or adults or adults to think they are doing something wrong in their attempts to connect with the child. A choleric adult may even feel more distance from the melancholic child as he is accustomed to intimate and intense relationships. To a choleric adult, not only is the melancholic child distant – the child may sometimes seem extremely remote.

A choleric adult is very sensitive and intuitive but when it comes to the melancholic child, the adult can often become confused. Because the melancholic does not give the choleric a lot of emotional information to process he may take it personally and wonder what he has done wrong.

The choleric adult will be reassured when he realizes that the melancholic may be an enigma, but is also very dependable in his requirements and demands. Once the choleric adult figures out what those requirements are, the adult can rest assured that they will not change and can focus on deciding which requirements he can fulfill, which must be compromised, and which need more discussion. Sometimes, agreeing to follow some of the order a melancholic requests is all that it takes to make him feel comfortable, loved and content.

- ## Helping the Melancholic Child Understand the Choleric Adult

The choleric adult may often express himself through joy and laughter. To the serious and orderly melancholic this may seem irreverent and the child may feel as if the adult is not taking the child seriously. When a choleric adult laughs or sees the sense of humor in a situation, as they often do, the melancholic child may also feel that the adult is laughing at them. If the adult can be careful to demonstrate to the melancholic child that laughter can be a safe form of emotional expression, then this conflict will become less likely. This can be done by sharing jokes or humorous stories with the melancholic child on a regular basis.

The choleric adult expresses himself through space. However, the melancholic child is very particular about the space he occupies. It is usually best to allow the melancholic child a space that belongs only to him and to be careful that the choleric adult's space is also well defined. If the choleric adult takes over the environment by leaving possessions, knick-knacks and other personal items around, the melancholic can feel shut out and irritated without knowing why. The melancholic will be better able to understand the different way he experiences space if he is able to see clear examples of the choleric adult's space and the child's own space existing side by side.

The choleric adult easily knows what others are thinking and feeling. However, this may be the last thing in the world the melancholic child wants to experience. A melancholic child is very protective of his thoughts and feelings. If a choleric adult confronts a melancholic child with the reality of his own inner thoughts the melancholic child may feel he is being attacked or accused of something. The melancholic child is better able to understand these insights when left to discover them on his own.

The choleric adult lives in the here and now and does not dwell a lot on the past or worry a lot about the future. This may be hard for the melancholic child to understand as he often dwells on the past and enjoys spending time making plans for the future. When the child does not see the choleric adult engaged in these same activities, the child may feel lost or alone or feel that these things are not important to the choleric adult. The choleric adult can help the child comprehend their way of thinking more clearly if they share his philosophies about the past and future with the child. Stories like, The Golden Thread, are good to illustrate this point.

The Golden Thread

Unknown Author/Traditional Tale Retold by Kristie Burns

There once was a girl named Melody who was a good student, loved her cat and her adults and enjoyed playing with her friends. She lived in a neat little house at the top of the hill surrounded by beautiful flowers – her life was idyllic in many ways. However, Melody was always planning for the future and wishing it could come more quickly so the things she worried about could become resolved. Melody worried about what the weekend plans were, where she was going to go to college, what she would work as when she grew up and even what she was going to eat for dinner that evening. She would often ask her mother about such things,

"What will we be eating tonight? When will we eat? What are the exact plans for the weekend?"

Melody's mother lived more in the now and when asked such questions she would respond, "Ah dear! Why are you worried about such things? Isn't the sunset beautiful right now? Isn't the weather lovely today? There is plenty of time to worry about the future. Now you should enjoy being a child!"

But Melody found it hard to enjoy the sunset, the weather and sometimes, even her cat. During school, she would think about what snack she would eat after school. After her snack, she would dwell on dinner. Before the weekend, she would make elaborate plans about what she wanted to do and when the weekend came her thoughts would turn to summer vacation and the endless possibilities it presented.

One day Melody was so lost in her thoughts about the future, she walked past her house on the way from school without even noticing she had passed it. This was very unlike Melody who was usually very careful and precise about her actions, but something she could not explain seemed to pull her farther away from her house and closer to the woods that bordered the yard. Melody considered that if she went for a short walk perhaps the time until dinner would pass more quickly, so she gave into the feeling that pulled her and continued down the forest path.

Suddenly, a rabbit with a golden ball jumped out in front of Melody. Melody had never seen such a large rabbit and certainly never such a large golden ball.

Melody stopped in her tracks and approached very quietly, hoping the rabbit would not be frightened and hop away. Instead the rabbit approached her and held out the golden ball without a word.

"Oh, do you want to play ball?" said Melody.

"No," said the rabbit, "this is a gift."

Melody was shocked that the rabbit had spoken but she accepted the gift graciously and said, "May I ask, please, what it is?"

The rabbit answered in a very serious voice, "This is the thread of your life. If you take care of it well, you will live a long life and time will pass as it always does. However, if you would like time to pass more quickly you need only to pull the thread and time will pass more quickly. Remember, though, once the thread is pulled it cannot be put back in."

Melody was thrilled. This golden ball was the answer to all of her problems. She would no longer have to wait to know what was for dinner or what would happen on the weekend or even wait to know what college she would go to. She was eager to try it out, but she was a cautious person, so she decided she would wait until she had a good reason and then pull the thread only very carefully.

An opportunity presented itself the very next day at school. Melody was wondering what she was going to eat for dinner. Instead of planning the meal in her mind as she usually did, she unraveled a bit of the thread. Immediately, she was seated at the dinner table eating the most delicious chicken and rice with vegetables. Rice pudding was for dessert. She was delighted. Melody continued to pull the thread just a little bit each time she felt she just could not wait anymore to know what was going to happen. But then, being of a logical mind, Melody realized one day that it didn't make sense to just pull the thread a tiny bit each time for such small events like dinner and weekend parties. It would be *much more efficient and satisfying to give the thread one big pull and move on to the more important events in her life. Melody was certainly done with childhood. It was filled with unknown events, surprises, suspense and she often felt out of control. She longed to be an adult and be at college where she would be able to do what she pleased. So Melody gave the golden thread a hard tug and closed her eyes. When she opened them she was in her college dorm room studying for a science exam. She was quite pleased. Aha! I knew I would be a scientist, she thought.*

So, Melody enjoyed her studies for some days and her newfound freedom. She ate what she pleased and woke and slept according to her own schedule and was very content with her life - until the first exam approached. She was apprehensive and wondered if she would pass the exam. In addition, she wondered if she was going to pass other exams that would come after the first one. She wondered to herself if she would be able to graduate and find a good job.

The more she thought about it, the less she was able to concentrate on her studies and the more she could not stop thinking about it. So, Melody decided to pull the thread again. She gave it another big tug and found herself sitting in a lab working at a new job. She was wearing a white jacket and had her own area to work in and even a wooden name plate above her work area. She felt very important and very pleased. She enjoyed her new job and her workmates but after some time she did miss her mother and also started to wonder if she would ever have a family of her own.

And she wondered. She wondered so much that she could not sleep at night. She drew pictures of what her house would look like and wrote different names on paper to see which names would sound best with hers. She planned how many children she would have and where she would live with them. Finally, she could not stand the suspense any longer. She pulled the thread again. When she opened her eyes she was thrilled to find three lovely children playing in the yard and a handsome young gentleman sitting by her side on the porch. It was a weekend day and they were enjoying time together as a family. Melody was happy with her new family and husband and her new life and was content for some time. She started to feel a bit sad about some of the moments she had missed in her life – such as her graduation day and her wedding. She was now a middle aged woman and vowed never to pull the thread again.

However, one day her son fell ill and was taken to the hospital in an ambulance. Melody immediately went to the cupboard where she kept the golden ball and took it out. She had vowed never to use it again but surely this was a good reason. She had to know what was going to happen to her son. So Melody tugged the golden string to find out. However, she pulled it so hard that when she opened her eyes she found herself once again on the porch of her house with children playing in the yard again. For a moment she thought that perhaps the rabbit had been wrong and she had gone back in time. But then she realize that she had actually gone so far into the future that she was now an old woman with grandchildren and her own children had grown, finished school and all been married.

She sat on the porch swing and cried. She had missed all their graduations and weddings and even the birth of her grandchildren. Why, oh why, had she pulled the string so hard? Melody wanted with all her heart to take back the time she had lost, but she remembered the rabbit had said she could not go back once she unraveled the thread. Melody was distraught, so she walked to the clearing in the woods where she had first seen the rabbit and she waited.

The sun was so warm and the breeze was so gentle and she was so old and weak that she soon fell asleep. She woke up some time later with the soft whiskers of the rabbit tickling her cheek.

"So, have you been enjoying your life more?" asked the rabbit of Melody.

Melody immediately started to cry remembering all the events she had missed in her life. "I don't want to be ungrateful" she said to the rabbit, "I enjoyed not having to suffer or endure the waiting in life, but I am now so unhappy as I have missed so many wonderful things and now my mother is also gone and I miss her so much!"

The rabbit felt sorry for Melody and asked if she would like to return the ball. Melody sighed with relief, "yes," she said, "I am afraid I may touch it just once more and my own life may be over. I wish to live out the rest of my life and enjoy every moment." So Melody handed the ball to the rabbit with every intention to walk back through the woods afterwards and enjoy playing with her grandchildren. But, when Melody looked down at her hands and feet she noticed she was now young again and was back right where she had started so many years ago in the woods when she first met the rabbit.

Melody ran back home as quickly as she could and gave her mother a big hug and said to her "Please don't tell me what we are going to have for dinner tonight. I am going to go pet the cat now and watch the sunset!"

The melancholic child accepts people more easily when he senses confidence and authority. A choleric adult may not always exude this confidence but the confidence of the choleric temperament often comes through in fairytales, spiritual stories, or epic stories that feature choleric heroes, so the melancholic child will benefit from hearing such tales and will reach a greater understanding and respect of their adult in the process. One such story about a King with a choleric son is a good example:

The King's Son Who Feared Nothing

Traditional Fairytale

There was once a king's son, who was no longer content to stay at home in his father's house, and as he had no fear of anything, he thought, "I will go forth into the wide world, where the time will not seem long to me, and I shall see wonders enough."

So he took leave of his adults, and went forth, and on, and on from morning till night, and whichever way his path led it was the same to him. It came to pass that he got to the house of a giant, and as he was so tired he sat down by the door and rested. And as he let his eyes roam here and there, he saw the giant's playthings lying in the yard. These were a couple of enormous balls, and nine-pins as tall as a man. After a while he had a fancy to set the nine-pins up and then rolled the balls at them, and screamed and cried out when the nine-pins fell, and had a merry time of it. The giant heard the noise, stretched his head out of the window, and saw a man who was not taller than other men, and yet played with his nine-pins.

"Little worm," cried he, "why are you playing with my balls? Who gave you strength to do it?" The king's son looked up, saw the giant, and said, "Oh, you blockhead, you thinkest indeed that you only have strong arms, I can do everything I want to do."

The giant came down and watched the bowling with great admiration, and said, "Child of man, if you are one of that kind, go and bring me an apple of the tree of life."

"What do you want with it?" said the king's son.

"I do not want the apple for myself," answered the giant, "but I have a betrothed bride who wishes for it. I have travelled far about the world and cannot find the tree."

"I will soon find it," said the king's son, "and I do not know what is to prevent me from getting the apple down." The giant said, "You really believest it to be so easy! The garden in which the tree stands is surrounded by an iron railing, and in front of the railing lie wild beasts, each close to the other, and they keep watch and let no man go in."

"They will be sure to let me in," said the king's son.

"Yes, but even if you do get into the garden, and seest the apple hanging to the tree, it is still not yours; a ring hangs in front of it, through which anyone who wants to reach the apple and break it off, must put his hand, and no one has yet had the luck to do it."

"That luck will be mine," said the king's son.

Then he took leave of the giant, and went forth over mountain and valley, and through plains and forests, till at length he came to the wondrous garden.

The beasts lay round about it, but they had put their heads down and were asleep. Moreover, they did not awake when he went up to them, so he stepped over them, climbed the fence, and got safely into the garden. There, in the very middle of it, stood the tree of life, and the red apples were shining on the branches. He climbed up the trunk to the top, and as he was about to reach out for an apple, he saw a ring hanging before it; but he thrust his hand through that without any difficulty, and gathered the apple. The ring closed tightly on his arm, and all at once he felt a prodigious strength flowing through his veins. When he had come down again from the tree with the apple, he would not climb over the fence, but grasped the great gate, and had no need to shake it more than once before it sprang open with a loud crash. Then he went out, and the lion which had been lying down before, was awake and sprang after him, not in rage and fierceness, but following him humbly as its master.

The king's son took the giant the apple he had promised him, and said, "Seest you, I have brought it without difficulty."

The giant, glad that his desire had been so soon satisfied, hastened to his bride, and gave her the apple for which she had wished. She was a beautiful and wise maiden, and as she did not see the ring on his arm, she said, "I shall never believe that you have brought the apple, till I see the ring on your arm."

The giant said, "I have nothing to do but go home and fetch it," and thought it would be easy to take away by force from the weak man, what he would not give of his own free will. He, therefore, demanded the ring from him, but the king's son refused it.

"Where the apple is, the ring must be also," said the giant; "if you will not give it of your own accord, you must fight with me for it."

They wrestled with each other for a long time, but the giant could not get the better of the king's son, who was strengthened by the magical power of the ring. Then the giant thought for a bit, and said, "I have got warm with fighting, and so have you. We will bathe in the river, and cool ourselves before we begin again."

The king's son, who knew nothing of falsehood, went with him to the water, and pulled off with his clothes the ring also from his arm, and sprang into the river. The giant instantly snatched the ring, and ran away with it, but the lion, which had observed the theft, pursued the giant, tore the ring out of his hand, and brought it back to its master. Then the giant placed himself behind an oak-tree, and while the king's son was busy putting on his clothes again, surprised him, and put both his eyes out.

And now the unhappy King's son stood there, and was blind and knew not how to help himself. Then the giant came back to him, took him by the hand as if he were someone who wanted to guide him, and led him to the top of a high rock. There he left him standing, and thought, "Just two steps more, and he will fall down and kill himself, and I can take the ring from him."

But the faithful lion had not deserted its master; it held him fast by the clothes, and drew him gradually back again. When the giant came and wanted to rob the dead man, he saw that his cunning had been in vain.

"Is there no way, then, of destroying a weak child of man like that?" said he angrily to himself, and seized the king's son and led him back again to the precipice by another way, but the lion which saw his evil design, helped its master out of danger here, also. When they had got close to the edge, the giant let the blind man's hand drop, and was going to leave him behind alone, but the lion pushed the giant so that he was thrown down and fell, dashed to pieces, on the ground.

The faithful animal again drew its master back from the precipice, and guided him to a tree by which flowed a clear brook. The king's son sat down there, but the lion lay down, and sprinkled the water in his face with its paws. Scarcely had a couple of drops wetted the sockets of his eyes, than he was once more able to see something, and remarked a little bird flying quite close by, which wounded itself against the trunk of a tree. On this it went down to the water and bathed itself therein, and then it soared upwards and swept between the trees without touching them, as if it had recovered its sight again. Then the king's son recognized a sign from God and stooped down to the water, and washed and bathed his face in it. And when he arose he had his eyes once more, brighter and clearer than they had ever been.

The king's son thanked God for his great mercy, and travelled with his lion onwards through the world. And it came to pass, that he arrived before a castle which was enchanted. In the gateway, stood a maiden of beautiful form and fine face, but she was quite black. She spoke to him and said, "Ah, if you could but deliver me from the evil spell which is thrown over me."

"What shall I do?" said the king's son. The maiden answered, "You must pass three nights in the great hall of this enchanted castle, but you must let no fear enter your heart. When they are doing their worst to torment you, if you bearest it without letting a sound escape you, I shall be free. Your life they dare not take."

Then said the king's son, "I have no fear; with God's help I will try it."

So he went gaily into the castle, and when it grew dark he seated himself in the large hall and waited. Everything was quiet, however, till midnight, when all at once a great tumult began, and out of every hole and corner came little devils. They behaved as if they did not see him, seated themselves in the middle of the room, lighted a fire, and began to gamble. When one of them lost, he said, "It is not right; someone is here who does not belong to us; it is his fault that I am losing."

"Wait, you fellow behind the stove, I am coming," said another. The screaming became still louder, so that no one could have heard it without terror. The king's son stayed sitting quietly, and was not afraid; but at last the devils jumped up from the ground, and fell on him, and there were so many of them that he could not defend himself from them. They dragged him about on the floor, pinched him, pricked him, beat him, and tormented him, but no sound escaped from him. Towards morning, they disappeared, and he was so exhausted that he could scarcely move his limbs, but when day dawned, the black maiden came to him. She bore in her hand a little bottle wherein was the water of life wherewith she washed him, and he at once felt all pain depart and new strength flow through his veins. She said, "You have held out successfully for one night, but two more lie before you."

Then she went away again, and as she was going, he observed that her feet had become white. The next night the devils came and began their trouble-making anew. They fell on the king's son, and beat him much more severely than the night before, till his body was covered with wounds. But as he bore all quietly, they were forced to leave him, and when dawn appeared, the maiden came and healed him with the water of life. And when she went away, he saw with joy that she had already become white to the tips of her fingers. And now he had only one night more to go through, but it was the worst. The hob-goblins came again: "Are you there still?" cried they, "you shall be tormented till your breath stops."

They pricked him and beat him, and threw him here and there, and pulled him by the arms and legs as if they wanted to tear him to pieces, but he bore *everything, and never uttered a cry. At last the devils vanished, but he lay fainting there, and did not stir, nor could he raise his eyes to look at the maiden who came in, and sprinkled and bathed him with the water of life. But suddenly, he was freed from all pain, and felt fresh and healthy, as if he had awakened from sleep, and when he opened his eyes he saw the maiden standing by him, snow-white, and fair as day.*

"Rise," said she, "and swing your sword three times over the stairs, and then all will be delivered."

And when he had done that, the whole castle was released from enchantment, and the maiden was a rich King's daughter. The servants came and said that the table was already set in the great hall, and dinner served up. Then they sat down and ate and drank together, and in the evening the wedding was solemnized with great rejoicings.

- ## Discipline

Good discipline always stems from a sense of trust, love, and harmony between the adult and child. The more they understand and respect each other, the more naturally discipline happens. To establish and maintain a healthy relationship with the melancholic child, including the art of discipline, the choleric adult should first read the sections above covering how to best understand the melancholic child and how to help the child understand him.

The melancholic child appreciates being thought of as responsible and mature. Thus, when the choleric adult needs to give the melancholic instructions or discipline the child, it should be done in a careful and respectful manner. A melancholic child will not easily take instruction from a choleric adult, who is apt to toss instructions and criticisms at them in an open, direct and uninhibited manner. Rather, the melancholic requires that the adult explain the reasons behind the requests and perhaps even consider his own opinion before making demands.

When discussing topics, giving constructive criticism or disciplining a child of the melancholic temperament, the choleric adult must consider that the melancholic child will often consider himself above reproach and completely impeccable in his behavior. Conversations will usually go more smoothly if the choleric adult tries to understand why a melancholic did something before he imposes his own judgment upon it. As long as the melancholic child is given a chance to explain his motives, he may be more apt to admit fault, although melancholics are not usually inclined to admit fault and more likely to simply drop the subject.

If a choleric adult observes that the melancholic child has retreated into rigid adherence to rules and regulations, he needs to realize that the child is not being stubborn, but simply trying to regain balance and reassert control over some disturbing or fluctuating circumstance the child encountered. This may happen quite frequently if the melancholic child is exposed to the very choleric existence of the adult they live or spend time with. In an attempt to balance the choleric nature of the adult in the environment, the melancholic child may actually become more melancholic in nature and desperately fall back onto the familiarity of schedules or rules.

When others are satisfied with their roles and obligations, the melancholic child expects life to be agreeable and sensible. The child's patience endures only as long as people do their share and follow established procedure, insuring that events happen according to plan.

• The Teaching Relationship

The melancholic works well in situations where goals and guidelines are well established. This is of the utmost importance in the educational environment. A melancholic will not be able to learn properly if lessons are not regular and expectations are not fixed and defined. If the choleric adult is unable to maintain a structure that the melancholic requires because the adult finds it too confining, then it is sufficient to have the melancholic child create his own schedule apart from the home or classroom and to follow some of that schedule on his own. A melancholic child feels most secure and confident when everyone around him is also following what they feel to be proper procedure. However, as long as he is able to follow a well defined agenda the actions of others become less disturbing to the melancholic child.

The melancholic child eagerly accepts lessons from adults that display competence with the subject at hand. While children of other temperaments may be more forgiving of a hastily planned lesson or creative approach to a problem, the melancholic child will listen and learn more effectively if he observes that the adult is competent and confident and that the lesson is well planned out. The choleric adult is easily able to provide lessons that are innovative and exciting for students, however, he must be careful to make sure these lessons are also organized and clear for the melancholic student.

Additionally, the melancholic student may need some extra time to process the lesson as he is very careful and methodical in his work. With math lessons or lessons that have defined and quick answers, the melancholic child will finish quickly and easily. However, with lessons that have less definition the melancholic child may spend extra time checking over and/or reorganizing the lesson in a way that is more clear to him.

The melancholic child enjoys lessons that are systematic and require analytical thinking. The melancholic child also enjoys solving puzzles and problems. The melancholic child may enjoy story problems, math tasks, grammar, spelling and other lessons that focus on an ordered and predictable system. However, the melancholic child must also be exposed to the dynamic painting, storytelling and writing lessons that are so dear to the choleric adult.

The melancholic child is motivated by organization and accomplishments and by praise for those accomplishments. The choleric adult will find praise comes naturally to him as the choleric person is naturally enthusiastic. However, he must be careful to praise the child's accomplishments rather than the visual or emotional effect the lesson evokes. For example, a melancholic child will be encouraged when praised for his quick completion of a lesson, neatness of presentation or success in completing a task accurately. However, a melancholic child will not feel praised if the choleric adult is enthusiastic about the beauty of his painting, the emotion his story evoked or the creativity displayed in presentation.

- A Story to Share

When stories are told they speak to the child on a basic level. The reason one tells stories instead of explaining things to a child is because stories have the ability to adapt to the child's needs. When a person explains a situation to a child he is putting forth a concept that the child needs to grasp at or reach to understand. When one simply *tells* a story the child is given permission to understand the story in any way he wishes and to gain wisdom and knowledge from it in the way that best suits him at that moment. For that reason, it is not recommended that the story be explained to the child or that the child be provided with the ubiquitous "moral" at the end. Rather, it is best to give them a chance to enjoy the story for what it becomes to them and provide them with numerous chances to hear the story told. The stories in this book help the different temperaments understand each other. If the adult or adult would like to explore this understanding on a deeper level they can ask questions once the story is finished. However, one must be sure to ask open questions and allow the child to express his feelings.

In this story the choleric encounters a melancholic that challenges him.

The Hare and the Hedgehog

Grimm's Tales

This story, my dear young folks, seems to be false, but it really is true, for my grandfather, from whom I have it, used always, when relating it, to say complacently, "It must be true, my son, or else no one could tell it to you."

The story is as follows. One Sunday morning about harvest time, just as the buckwheat was in bloom, the sun was shining brightly in heaven, the east wind was blowing warmly over the stubble-fields, the larks were singing in the air, the bees buzzing among the buckwheat, the people were all going in their Sunday clothes to church, and all creatures were happy, and the hedgehog was happy too.

The hedgehog, however, was standing by his door with his arms akimbo, enjoying the morning breezes, and slowly trilling a little song to himself, which was neither better nor worse than the songs which hedgehogs are in the habit of singing on a blessed Sunday morning. While he was thus singing half aloud to himself, it suddenly occurred to him that, while his wife was washing and drying the children, he might very well take a walk into the field, and see how his

213

turnips were going on. The turnips were, in fact, close beside his house, and he and his family were accustomed to eating them, for which reason he looked on them as his own. No sooner said than done, the hedgehog shut the house-door behind him, and took the path to the field. He had not gone very far from home, and was just turning round the sloe-bush which stands there outside the field, to go up into the turnip-field, when he observed the hare who had gone out on business of the same kind, namely, to visit his cabbages. When the hedgehog caught sight of the hare, he bade him a friendly good morning. But the hare, who was in his own way a distinguished gentleman, and frightfully haughty, did not return the hedgehog's greeting, but said to him, assuming at the same time a very contemptuous manner, "How do you happen to be running about here in the field so early in the morning?"

"I am taking a walk," said the hedgehog.

"A walk!" said the hare, with a smile.

"It seems to me that you might use your legs for a better purpose."

This answer made the hedgehog furiously angry, for he can bear anything but an attack on his legs, just because they are crooked by nature. So now the hedgehog said to the hare, "You seem to imagine that you can do more with your legs than I with mine."

"That is just what I do think," said the hare.

"That can be put to the test," said the hedgehog.

"I wager that if we run a race, I will outstrip you."

"That is ridiculous! You with your short legs!" said the hare, "but for my part I am willing, if you have such a monstrous fancy for it. What shall we wager?"

"A golden louis-d'or and a bottle of brandy," said the hedgehog.

"Done," said the hare.

"Shake hands on it, and then we may as well come off at once."

"Nay," said the hedgehog, "there is no such great hurry! I am still fasting, I will go home first, and have a little breakfast. In half-an-hour I will be back again at this place."

Hereupon the hedgehog departed, for the hare was quite satisfied with this. On his way the hedgehog thought to himself, "The hare relies on his long legs, but I will contrive to get the better of him. He may be a great man, but he is a very silly fellow, and he shall pay for what he has said."

So when the hedgehog reached home, he said to his wife, "Wife, dress yourself quickly, you must go out to the field with me."

"What is going on, then?" said his wife.

"I have made a wager with the hare, for a gold louis-d'or and a bottle of brandy. I am to run a race with him, and you must be present."

"Good heavens, husband," the wife now cried, "are you not right in your mind, have you completely lost your wits? What can make you want to run a race with the hare?"

"Hold your tongue, woman," said the hedgehog, "that is my affair. Don't begin to discuss things which are matters for men. Be off, dress yourself, and come with me."

What could the hedgehog's wife do? She was forced to obey him, whether she liked it or not.

So when they had set out on their way together, the hedgehog said to his wife, "Now pay attention to what I am going to say. Look you, I will make the long field our race-course. The hare shall run in one furrow, and I in another, and we will begin to run from the top. Now all that you have to do is to place yourself here below in the furrow, and when the hare arrives at the end of the furrow, on the other side of you, you must cry out to him, 'I am here already!'"

Then they reached the field, and the hedgehog showed his wife her place, and they walked up the field. When he reached the top, the hare was already there.

"Shall we start?" said the hare.

"Certainly," said the hedgehog.

"Then both at once."

So saying, each placed himself in his own furrow. The hare counted, "Once, twice, thrice, and away!" and went off like a whirlwind down the field. The hedgehog, however, only ran about three paces, and then he stooped down in the furrow, and stayed quietly where he was. When the hare therefore arrived in full career at the lower end of the field, the hedgehog's wife met him with the cry, "I am here already!" The hare was shocked and wondered not a little, he thought no other than that it was the hedgehog himself who was calling to him, for the hedgehog's wife looked just like her husband. The hare, however, thought to himself, "That has not been done fairly," and cried, "It must be run again, let us have it again."

And once more he went off like the wind in a storm, so that he seemed to fly. But the hedgehog's wife stayed quietly in her place. So when the hare reached the top of the field, the hedgehog himself cried out to him, "I am here already."

The hare, however, quite beside himself with anger, cried, "It must be run again, we must have it again."

"All right," answered the hedgehog, "for my part we'll run as often as you choose."

So the hare ran seventy-three times more, and the hedgehog always held out against him, and every time the hare reached either the top or the bottom, either the hedgehog or his wife said, "I am here already."

At the seventy-fourth time, however, the hare could no longer reach the end. In the middle of the field he fell to the ground, blood streamed out of his mouth, and he lay dead on the spot. But the hedgehog took the louis-d'or which he had won and the bottle of brandy, called his wife out of the furrow, and both went home together in great delight, and if they are not dead, they are living there still.

This is how it happened that the hedgehog made the hare run races with him on the Buxtehuder heath till he died, and since that time no hare has ever had any fancy for running races with a Buxtehuder hedgehog.

The moral of this story, however, is, firstly, that no one, however great he may be, should permit himself to jest at anyone beneath him, even if he be only a hedgehog. And, secondly, it teaches, that when a man marries, he should take a wife in his own position, who looks just as he himself looks. So, whoever is a hedgehog, let him see to it that his wife is a hedgehog also, and so forth.

Choleric Adult - Phlegmatic Child

- ## General Relationship

In an ideal choleric adult – phlegmatic child relationship there will be a feeling of mutual respect and balance. The choleric adult will feel soothed and balanced by being in the presence of the phlegmatic child and will enjoy the child's peace and gentle ways. The phlegmatic child will be entertained by the excitement her choleric adult provides and be motivated by the activities and inspiration that comes from the choleric temperament. The child's life will be enriched to a great degree by this balance and inspiration and, in learning from the child the adult's life will be healthier and more balanced.

However, just like in any relationship there is always a lot of potential for frustration and misunderstanding. In Chinese medicine the choleric is also known as the "fire" type and the phlegmatic is known as the "water" type. From this visual it is easy to imagine the characteristics of a typical relationship between a phlegmatic and choleric. Just as water can put out fire, a phlegmatic person can dampen a choleric person. In some ways, this can be good. For example, a phlegmatic child can teach a choleric adult to slow down and experience life at a slower pace. A phlegmatic child can teach an adult to enjoy meditation and slow nature walks and quiet sitting. If one is open to balancing the fire element within then all will be peaceful and harmonious. However, this can also create chaos. Choleric adults can often find their fires of enthusiasm put out by a phlegmatic child much like in the following dialogue:

Choleric Adult: *"Hey! I just got tickets to this wonderful musical! We are going on Friday!"* or *"We just got new paints for the classroom and are going to do a new water-coloring activity today!"*
Phlegmatic child: *"Oh, OK. That sounds nice. What's for snack?"*

Another scenario might sound like this:

Choleric Adult: *"This lesson is all about the Ancient Egyptians. Let me tell you an amazing story about this king!"*
Phlegmatic child: *"I don't really want to listen to a story right now. Can we go for a walk?"*

Over time the choleric adult may start to hold back with the phlegmatic child or take a slower pace. This will help the child but may create feelings of boredom or frustration in the adult or adult who will intuitively feel held back but may not be able to pinpoint the origin of such feelings.

On the other hand, phlegmatic children can often feel bombarded by the fire of the choleric.

Their water may be able to put out the fire but enduring hours of fire may cause their water to boil or even evaporate. They can start to feel worn down, harassed and defeated. They may even retreat into their own world to avoid this feeling. The phlegmatic child may feel invaded by all the stimulation and may become harder and harder to communicate with.

• Helping the Choleric Adult Understand The Phlegmatic Child

A typical choleric adult could be described in the following way: They are always ready to do something new and have a great need to interact with others. They enjoy being with people and often find themselves motivated when someone else is willing to share tasks or challenges. It is generally more fun to do anything with someone else. The phlegmatic child, however, feels almost the opposite. From the perspective of a choleric adult, it may seem like the child is not able to work well with others. A choleric adult, for example, may act upon this worry by creating situations in which the child needs to work with other students on a regular basis. However, this will not be helpful to the child. The phlegmatic child has different social needs than the choleric adult. The choleric adult may be amazed at how little the phlegmatic child wants to be with other people, even to the point of feeling hurt and rejected when the child wants to play alone.

However, it is important to remember that their way of working and being is completely normal and healthy for them. The phlegmatic child is content to be on the edge of social events as an observer. When planning events to share with them it is important to balance any big events with an equal or increased amount of alone time or home time. Choleric adults who have only one phlegmatic child will need to ensure they get their social needs met outside of this relationship because this child will not be one to take everywhere and include in every activity.

A phlegmatic child actually has the ability to feel very independent and can remain very detached and dispassionate about her relationships – the exact opposite of how a choleric adult experiences relationships.

The sense of taste is very important to phlegmatic children. When cooking meals for them or preparing their lunch allow them permission to choose their own foods as long as those foods are healthy and balanced. If the child really enjoys carrots, but does not want to eat cucumbers or squash, that should be allowed. The phlegmatic child's comfort zone with new things is smaller than that of a choleric. A phlegmatic eats more like a person in a traditional culture. In traditional cultures around the world people consume the same ten foods in a rotation by creating different dishes out of those same foods and rotating them through the month. Western culture, especially American culture, is the only one that considers such a variety of foods to be essential to the diet regardless of the rules of location, season and cultural preference. When it comes to eating, phlegmatic children follow rules of tradition that have stood the test of time, just as they do with many other parts of their life.

Phlegmatic children work in the dimension of time whereas their choleric adults work in the dimension of space. However, one of the greatest fears of phlegmatic children is the invasion of their personal space. Because of this, choleric adults in their life need to be careful of their expansive tendencies. While a choleric adult is constantly expanding into a world with no limits, the phlegmatic child is constantly protecting the border of his peaceful world with its very defined limits.

In mathematical terms these children are like circles while their choleric adults are like triangles. One can imagine how those two shapes might interact in order to gain more insight into this unique relationship. For example, a circle can fit into a triangle and the triangle can also fit into the circle. However, to do so one must expand or contract and the other must remain stable. Circles and triangles of the same size cannot share the same space, nor can they "fit together". Sometimes a triangle has sharp edges and sometimes a circle feels like it closes people out who are not on the inside. During form drawing lessons an adult or adult could talk about these two shapes and how they make each individual feel. He could draw the two shapes together on a paper to see where the child places the triangles and where she places the circles. It can be fascinating to see what insights can be gained from this exercise.

Phlegmatic children use the world of the imagination in a different way than does their choleric adults. For them it is an exercise in knowledge and an exploration of their abilities. It also serves as a way for them to do "test flights" out of their comfort zone. For this reason a phlegmatic child may explore ideas a lot more than he actually brings those ideas to fruition. A choleric adult, on the other hand can easily bring ideas into action and may often push ideas into being at all hours of the day, even at inappropriate times. For a choleric, once an idea is there it just has to come out! Choleric adults may be tempted to help bring a phlegmatic child's ideas out into the open. They may think that the child needs help or is just lazy. However, when trying to understand phlegmatic children one needs to understand that their imagination serves a different purpose than that of a choleric. The latter's imagination is a springboard to action; a flight-testing ground for the future. With a phlegmatic child many of the flights may never make it off the ground outside their mind; however, because of the ability to consider situations without acting on them, this child has the potential to become a great visionary. For example, a phlegmatic would be well suited to the careers of engineer, doctor or architect.

- ## Helping the Phlegmatic Child Understand the Choleric Adult

One commonality shared between a choleric adult and a phlegmatic child is that both really enjoy indulging their imaginations. The difference is the phlegmatic child will enjoy imagining within the world she can see while the adult will often enjoy imagining outside the visible realm. For example, phlegmatic children enjoy imagining how they are going to win the next chess game or what might happen if they counted for a year without stopping. They might also enjoy imagining what it will be like when they turn thirteen or what the hotel room their family is going to stay in might look like. Because choleric individuals also enjoy the realm of the imagination adults can connect with these children in this realm, but only if they can understand the child's different way of using imagination. These children like to take what they can see and expand on it. On the other hand choleric adults like to take what cannot be seen and expand on that. Choleric adults should take some time to enter their child's world of imagination and in the process both adults and children will understand each other more deeply.

The phlegmatic pursues her interests no matter what others consider important. Choleric adults will be able to understand and admire this pursuit of interests because that is one thing they also do well. However, for those adults it is most always essential to take into account what others consider important to the point that they may make decisions based on what other deem is right. Because of this, a phlegmatic child may feel like the adult is just following what everyone else is doing. Consequently, the child may have a hard time seeing the adult for who she is. As the adult, it is essential to help the child to see how important the things the adult does are to the adult and that will help the child be able to connect with the adult and participate more in the adult's world. For a phlegmatic the importance of things lies in those objects passing the internal test of value. She may assume that a choleric does not have such an internal test. Therefore, it is important for a choleric adult to communicate with a phlegmatic child in a deeper way about her interests, motivations and desires. This will help the child to respect the adult more deeply and respect is a key element in connecting with a person of the phlegmatic temperament.

The main expressions that a choleric uses in life are joy and laughter. Sometimes this may be through joking and sometimes through dry humor. However, this light-hearted element is always there. For the phlegmatic child, however, things are much more serious. These children may interpret a playful attitude as meaning that a choleric adult doesn't take things seriously and they may find this distressing, especially when it comes to their own requests and needs. When trying to reach them in conversation or in conflict, it is best to be serious with them rather than use humor. They will understand more clearly and there is less chance that they will become hurt or offended and retreat.

A choleric child experiences life through her interactions with space. This may frighten a phlegmatic child who experiences life through time and enjoys the comfort of confined spaces. As long as a choleric adult is careful not to force a phlegmatic child into such expanding spaces the child will be able to sit back and admire certain traits that the adult may possess. For example, the child might greatly enjoy watching an adult dance, paint a large mural or play a basketball. By watching the joy and excitement created in doing these types of activities, the phlegmatic child starts to understand the adult more deeply. The child will feel joyful simply by watching her adult experience joy. However, if the child is forced to play the game or dance or paint with the adult then she may start to feel threatened by the adult's expansive personality. It is important to remember that the choleric type tends to seek excitement while the phlegmatic may try to avoid it. Allowing a phlegmatic child to watch, learn and admire without forcing participation ensures that the child feels safe and non-threatened. When a choleric adult allows a phlegmatic child to experience joy in her own way this enables the child to connect with her adult through the adult's activities.

The choleric type is always seeking fulfillment while the phlegmatic type spends more time feeling fulfilled and exploring that feeling. There is sometimes a danger then that the phlegmatic will perceive the choleric as being greedy. Even as children, they may ask their adults, "Why are you spending so much money on that"? These children may even try to run the household budget by only asking for those things that they feel are essential and only rarely asking for anything extra. However, if they watch others in the house or classroom purchasing or enjoying extra tools, gifts or food items they may start to feel resentful and feel like they are not valued as much as other members of the classroom or home. By sharing extras with them they will feel more included. If others demonstrate an appreciation of the things they have, then the phlegmatic child will respect them more.

One cannot deny that a main trait of cholerics lies in their charisma. This can often be intimidating to the quieter phlegmatic child. It can be helpful to make an effort to include the phlegmatic child as much as possible and when appropriate. For example, when a choleric adult is telling a story and is able to enchant all the other children with the narrative, the phlegmatic children may feel like they don't have a place in the story and may feel excluded. By allowing them a part in the story they will feel included and more connected with the storyteller. However, one must be careful not to force them into the spotlight if they don't feel comfortable. For example, when telling an audience-participation story phlegmatic children may feel most comfortable being the person who shakes the gourd rather than the person who is assigned to beat on the drum or dress up in the cape and hat. Although when they are in familiar surroundings they can often be quite a clown and quite charming themselves.

- Discipline

Good discipline always stems from a sense of trust, love, and harmony between the adult and child. The more they understand and respect each other, the more naturally discipline happens. To establish and maintain a healthy relationship with the phlegmatic child, including the art of discipline, the choleric adult should first read the sections above covering how to best understand the phlegmatic child and how to help the child understand her/him.

The key element in a disciplinary situation with phlegmatic children is to remember that they are very fair, honest, dependable and protective. If one can respect those boundaries when speaking to them the conversations will most likely be smooth and any requests made by the adult or adult will most likely be honored.

The choleric also has a great sense of justice and fairness and is able to relate to this need in the phlegmatic child. However, it is important to keep in mind that ideas of what are just and fair may be slightly different. Adults should take the time to discuss with phlegmatic children what they feel is fair in different situations and be open to accepting some new parameters if they fit. In the absence of such a discussion the phlegmatic will need the choleric adult to take some time to explain why what is being proposed seems fair. The phlegmatic needs to understand new things to be able to accept them and will be happier and more likely to cooperate and learn from her mistakes if she understands the parameters and their reasoning.

Phlegmatic children are very honest. As previously mentioned, their idea of imagination is much more limiting than that of a choleric. If it seems as though they are making something up then take a good look at what they are saying. Does it fit into an already existing system in some way? If so, then it is possible they may be making something up. If not, then it is unlikely that they have gone so beyond an existing system to tell an untruth. Because of this one can usually depend on a phlegmatic to tell the truth.

Although the phlegmatic is very dependable that does not always mean she is responsible. However, a well-balanced phlegmatic child can grow into a very responsible adult. Phlegmatic children are dependable and one can always depend on them to be who they are. Unlike the choleric who can expand and grow and change within the short span of a day or a week, the phlegmatic child will remain steady. This can be frustrating when trying to teach a phlegmatic a new skill or when adding to a chore list at home or assignments at school. As a choleric, one would immediately take on the new tasks and responsibilities with gusto. However, a phlegmatic child needs some time to adjust. By understanding this many potential conflicts can be avoided.

Last, but not least, phlegmatic children are very protective. If the need to discipline them arises this should be done in complete privacy. If they are disciplined in public they will automatically turn on their protection mode and turn off their reception mode and may not even understand what they did wrong. They will be so concerned with protecting themselves that they will not be able to focus on the matter at hand. For the discipline to be effective it must be done in private. If it is not, it will have little chance of being effective as a phlegmatic has a very strong and quiet will that, once engaged, cannot be moved by any power. Once they do engage the will and begin to close off or push back then the adult will need to go back to the essential learning tool of the phlegmatic – time. If one simply allows the matter drop saying, "Okay, we will talk about this in another hour" or if the child is allowed to sleep with the adult and push the discussion to the morning, the conversation will improve greatly. With time, the phlegmatic child will recognize the consequences of her actions, come up with suitable disciplinary ideas, apologize and even change the behavior. Time is the best form of discipline for a phlegmatic child. The ideal discipline is to have a short but pleasant discussion, allow them time to think, and then revisit the issue at a later time.

- **The Teaching Relationship**

Phlegmatic students are always on a path of knowledge. They do not have a passion for learning as the choleric does; however, they do find learning is an essential part of their life. For the choleric learning is a sensual experience and is usually pursued for the joy or sensory pleasure it brings. For the phlegmatic, however, learning is a natural process that happens like the flow of the river. It is essential and always present, but is not extravagant or pushing forward. To be happy in school a phlegmatic must always be learning. However, they may not always keep the same pace as other students and will most likely not ask as many questions as the choleric adult would expect them too. They were certainly not exhibit the enthusiasm that the choleric adult would expect. To a choleric learning is more of a social, sensual and vibrant experience; therefore, one may assume that the phlegmatic student just does not enjoy learning or is bored by a particular lesson. It may seem as though the phlegmatic student is simply being disagreeable. In reality the phlegmatic is very enthusiastic about learning, they just express it in a different way.

Phlegmatic students express themselves with the voice of fear and not with joy or laughter as the choleric does. Because of this one may interpret their fear as an impairment or as something excessive that needs to be cured. One may have the desire to encourage them to laugh more and may even try teasing them as a method to bring out their humorous side. A phlegmatic, however, does not always understand teasing – even if it is done in a good natured way.

The way a phlegmatic uses her imagination, as mentioned before, is to expand on those things that can be seen or easily imagined. They may imagine what they will look like when they are the same age as their father or mother. They may imagine what a new game may look like. They may spend time imagining how many jelly beans you could fit into a jar or how fast the car would have to go to reach its destination. This realm of the imagination is the one place where the phlegmatic feels completely at ease going out of their comfort zone and this is a safe way for them to practice doing so.

Phlegmatic students should be encouraged to use their imagination through story problems, writing and drawing. When doing form drawing they can be encouraged to finish shapes started by the adult. These exercises will increase their ability to expand and enlarge their comfort zone area. Because choleric adults have a natural tendency to expand this will come naturally as a teaching tool. However, it is important to remember not to push phlegmatic students too quickly. They enjoy exploring the world of the imagination but at a slow and careful pace.

- A Story to Share

A classic story between the choleric temperament and the phlegmatic temperament is that of the *Tortoise and the Hare*.

The Phlegmatic Tortoise and the Choleric Hare

Aesop's Fable

There once was a speedy hare that was very proud about how fast he could run. One day, Tortoise challenged him to a race. All the animals in the forest gathered to watch. Hare ran down the road for a while and then and paused to rest. He looked back at Tortoise and cried out, "How do you expect to win this race when you are walking along at your slow, slow pace?" Hare stretched himself out alongside the road and fell asleep thinking, "There is plenty of time to relax." Tortoise walked and walked. He never, ever stopped until he came to the finish line. The animals who were watching cheered so loudly for Tortoise that they woke up Hare. Hare stretched and yawned and began to run again but it was too late. Tortoise was over the line.

When stories are told they speak to the child on a basic level. The reason one tells stories instead of explaining things to a child is because stories have the ability to adapt to the child's needs. When a person explains a situation to a child she is putting forth a concept that the child needs to grasp at or reach to understand. When one simply *tells* a story the child is given permission to understand the story in any way she wishes and to gain wisdom and knowledge from it in the way that best suits him/her at that moment. For that reason, it is not recommended that the story be explained to the child or that the child be provided with the ubiquitous "moral" at the end. Rather, it is best to give them a chance to enjoy the story for what it becomes to them and provide them with numerous chances to hear the story told. The stories in this book help the different temperaments understand each other. If the adult or adult would like to explore this understanding on a deeper level they can ask questions once the story is finished. However, one must be sure to ask open questions and allow the child to express her feelings.

Certain stories, such as the one above, help the different temperaments to understand each other. It is possible to explore this understanding on a deeper level by asking questions once the story is finished. However, it is important to ask open-ended questions and allow the children to express their feelings. For example, in the story of the Tortoise and the Hare one could ask they typical leading questions like, "Why do you think the tortoise won?" and then expectantly wait for the answer. Most children, when approached in this way, sense what the "right" answer is and will answer accordingly. But consider what would happen if they were simply asked what the story means to them? A phlegmatic child might be able to offer insights into the feelings and motivations of the tortoise that may not have been apparent from the story. And the choleric adult could explain what she thinks the hare was motivated by and why. This is another good opportunity for two temperaments to learn from each other and further understand one another.

Choleric Adult - Sanguine Child

- ## General Relationship

The general relationship between the choleric adult and the sanguine child will be vibrant, energetic and joyous. People of both temperaments enjoy adventure, action, learning new things and indulging their senses. The sanguine child may feel overwhelmed with the choleric adult's energy and a choleric adult may sometimes be disappointed that the sanguine child is not always up to every adventure he initiates. However, the energy balance between a choleric adult and sanguine child is more harmonious. Children naturally have more energy and older children have an excess of choleric temperament, which helps them to keep up with the boundless energy of the choleric temperament in general. At the same time the choleric adult may have tempered his temperament and thus the two will have more in common.

- ## Helping the Choleric Adult Understand the Sanguine Child

The sanguine child is sometimes described as a butterfly and to the choleric adult this may even appear exaggerated. This is because the sanguine child actually experiences different seasons of emotions and energy levels but the choleric adult will only easily connect to two of the four seasons the sanguine experiences. However, because this connection is so easy during the "spring" and "summer" seasons of the sanguine, the choleric can become confused on days when it is more challenging to connect with the child. Instead of considering that there are other ways to connect, the choleric adult continues to seek the easy and most vibrant connection. This is natural as cholerics are attracted to the brightest and smoothest pathways in life.

Because the choleric adult lives in a steady season of "summer" he will start to feel like the sanguine child is connecting and disconnecting at random times just like a butterfly does when it is sucking nectar from a flower. This can become frustrating for the choleric adult who will tend to plan activities and lessons based on the connections he has with the sanguine child, only to discover that one day these plans are met with enthusiasm and other days with disinterest.

A more effective way to understand the sanguine child would be for the choleric adult to realize that at some times he will have deep and intense connections with the child. At other times when the connection is not happening with ease there needs to be an alternate plan in place. When the choleric adult can start to appreciate the different seasons of the sanguine (see *Introduction: Sanguine* at the beginning of the book) rather than always expect spring or summer, the adult can become more adaptive to those rhythms. One example of disconnecting rhythms may be with the expression of joy and humor. The choleric adult often sees the sense of humor even in the worst situations and usually experiences life in a joyful way. The choleric adult is also apt to remember good events better than unpleasant events. The choleric adult will find that during the time when the sanguine child is in his spring or summer mood season the child will understand the adult's humor, will laugh with them and share joy more frequently. The choleric adult, enjoying this ease of interaction and opportunity to share his favorite emotions with the child will seek to connect like this on a regular basis. The choleric adult may become accustomed to joking with the child or laughing at situations together. This usually works well until the choleric adult runs into an autumn or winter mood with the sanguine child. Then this child may take some of the jokes personally and feel that all the laughing is inappropriate or irreverent.

The choleric adult naturally assumes the choleric point of view is the customary way to view the world. Since the sanguine child has displayed this ability to be "normal" the choleric adult may assume something is wrong with the sanguine child on that day. The choleric adult may think that as soon as the problem is gone the sanguine child will be back to "normal" laughing and interacting with the choleric adult. This belief appears to be confirmed when the sanguine child once again enters the state of spring or summer and resumes the lighthearted, easy connection he shares with the adult.

Over time this can create a feeling of insecurity in the sanguine child as they struggle to understand why the adult is more receptive on some days than others. The choleric adult needs to be careful to honor all the seasons of the sanguine child and find ways to maintain that wonderful connection even in the mood season of winter.

The choleric adult and sanguine child both tend to express emotions very intensely. This will make it easier for the choleric adult to understand the intense emotions of the sanguine child. The only emotion the choleric adult may have trouble completely understanding is the sanguine child's emotion of anger. A sanguine child may express anger for many reasons and not all of them are because the child is really angry. Sometimes the child is frustrated, sick, confused, sad, hurt or something else. However, the most natural emotion for the sanguine to express is one of anger so this is what may come out. The choleric adult, on the other hand, is usually very accurate in expression of emotion. The choleric adult knows what he wants and knows exactly how to express it. If a choleric is upset he will express anger. If a choleric is sad he will express agony. Emotions of the choleric adult may seem slightly exaggerated because of their intensity but they are most always accurate. The choleric adult needs to understand that not all expressions of anger by the sanguine child indicate that the child is angry. This will enable the adult/child to avoid unnecessary conflict and spend more time trying to find out the real problem.

Both the choleric adult and the sanguine child have a strong sense of purpose. However, the choleric adult may be motivated by an inward passion and the sanguine child more motivated by the praise of others and other people seeing the results of his work. The choleric adult must understand that this sense of purpose is very important for the sanguine child and that if it is removed the sanguine child will lose his motivation.

I worked with a Choleric mother, Sonya and her sanguine daughter, Petra, a year ago and helped them work through this issue in their homeschooling. Sonya and Petra worked well together because they both had wonderful energy and were both very interested in learning more and exploring things together. Overall they enjoyed the homeschooling experience. It helped that they also had similar interests. Sonya and Petra both enjoyed animals, gardening and writing. Sonya sometimes wrote articles for online websites or her own BLOG and Petra enjoyed writing books and poems. The problem Sonya was worried about was that Petra would seem to lose interest in some of her projects and not complete them. Petra had started at least five books in the past year and not finished any of them. Petra had a few research papers that were half done. Sonya would become frustrated with Petra and ask her to finish these assignments but Petra would complain and say she didn't want to.

As we explored Petra's experience together, Sonya and I realized that Petra had lost interest in the projects because she had lost her sense of purpose. Unless Petra had an end goal in mind or was encouraged in some way or given a specific deadline, she simply lost interest and went on to the next topic. When Sonya realized this she started to find ways in which she could motivate Petra. She offered to publish Petra's poems on her BLOG. She let Petra know that when she finished her book they could send it to an online publishing company and get it published. Sonya also took time to look over Petra's work on a regular basis and give her feedback and praise for the tasks she had completed. Within a week, Petra was more motivated than ever and retained this motivation on a more regular basis. Additionally, when she started to lose the motivation Sonya now knew what to do and was able to keep Petra engaged more actively in her work.

The sanguine child does not like to be confined and learns well when they are moving. The choleric adult also loves to move and experiences life without limits. This can be an amazing combination if the choleric adult can stay confident in his ability to educate and raise the sanguine child. Because this combination may bring about a number of creative learning approaches and parenting styles, the choleric adult may be criticized or questioned about the unique style they use with the sanguine child. The choleric adult should not be deterred by these questions or doubts. The adult can take comfort in knowing the unique energy they create together is simply something that does not fit into a traditional system of parenting or education. Therefore, some people may not comprehend it.

A sanguine child has many things in common with the choleric adult. They both enjoy staying busy and feel comfortable with intense emotions and experiences. They enjoy being unique and tend to be extroverted most of the time. They exude confidence and enjoy discussing achievements and accomplishments with others. The motivations behind some of these commonalities may be different but the result is usually the same – there is a great understanding between the two on such matters. The choleric adult rarely tells the sanguine child to "calm down" and the sanguine child rarely tells the choleric adult to "wait up for me".

However, the motivations and slight differences do offer some insight into the sanguine child. Although the sanguine child enjoys being busy, he is usually busy with purposeful work. The choleric adult, on the other hand, may simply like to stay busy even if that involves social interactions or entertainment. The sanguine child is comfortable being unique and even outlandish. However, the choleric adult enjoys being only "just unique enough" as long as he can still please the norms of the society he lives in. The choleric adult shares his accomplishments because of the enjoyment that sharing brings. The sanguine child, on the other hand, shares news of his accomplishments with hope that the other person will recognize them and encourage him. Knowing about these subtle differences can help the choleric adult offer the appropriate responses and support.

- ## Helping the Sanguine Child Understand the Choleric Adult

The sanguine child has a great capacity for understanding those of different temperaments. Combined with the natural insight children have into their adults, the sanguine child should have little trouble understanding, accepting and enjoying his choleric adult.

As a sanguine child learns by real life experience and by doing things, the best way for him to get to know his choleric adult is to spend more time with the adult. This may seem obvious, but this is actually not the case with all the temperament combinations. In some cases the amount of time does not matter as much as the quality of time or the kind of time spent together. In other cases too much time could actually interfere in the developing relationship. However, in the case of the sanguine child and choleric adult more time spent together equals more opportunity for the sanguine child to understand the adult. That being said, this time should not overwhelm the sanguine child's equal need for time alone.

A sanguine child also learns through stories and has a profound connection with storytelling. Of course all the temperaments benefit from storytelling, however, the sanguine child is most deeply touched by information relayed via legend, anecdote, fairy-tale or narrative. To help the sanguine child better understand the choleric adult the adult can share stories of choleric people including stories from his own youth or young adulthood.

Some characteristics that can be highlighted in these stories include the animation and enthusiasm of the choleric: the compassion, sincere intention, ability to enjoy life, enjoyment of physical contact, transparency of emotion, sense of humor, attachment to people, enjoyment of society, empathy, responsiveness, intuition, optimism, openness, sincerity, and charisma. Not every story chosen needs to have a sanguine character as well as a choleric character, however, in the story I have chosen, both are involved.

There are many stories and fairytales that involve choleric adults and sanguine children. Each one has a lesson to share and some insight to learn about the choleric adult. In the following story, adapted from the classical Greek myth, the choleric father tries to live out a dream with his sanguine son, only to see that dream shattered when the son cannot keep his focus and loses faith in the guidance of the father.

The Choleric Daedelus and Sanguine Icarus

Adapted by Kristie Burns

Among all those mortals who grew so wise that they learned the secrets of the gods, none was more cunning than Daedalus. He once built, for King Minos of Crete, a wonderful Labyrinth of winding ways so cunningly tangled up and twisted around that, once inside, you could never find your way out again without a magic clue. But the King's favor veered with the wind, and one day he had his master architect imprisoned in a tower. Daedalus managed to escape from his cell; but it seemed impossible to leave the island, since every ship that came or went was well guarded by order of the King. At length, watching the sea gulls in the air, the only creatures that were sure of liberty, he thought of a plan for himself and his young son Icarus, who was captive with him.

Little by little, he gathered a store of feathers great and small. He fastened these together with thread, molded them in with wax, and so fashioned two great wings like those of a bird. When they were done, Daedalus fitted them to his own shoulders, and after one or two efforts, he found that by waving his arms he could winnow the air and cleave it, as a swimmer does the sea. He held himself aloft, wavered this way and that with the wind, and at last, like a great fledgling, he learned to fly.

Without delay, he fell to work on a pair of wings for the boy Icarus and taught him carefully how to use them, bidding him beware of rash adventures among the stars. "Remember," said the father, "Never to fly very low or very high, for the fogs about the earth would weigh you down, and the blaze of the sun will surely melt your feathers apart if you go too near."

For Icarus, these cautions went in at one ear and out by the other. Who could remember to be careful when he was to fly for the first time? Are birds careful? Not they! And not an idea remained in the boy's head but the one joy of escape.

The day came that the fair wind that was to set them free. The father-bird put on his wings, and, while the light urged them to be gone, he waited to see that all was well with Icarus, for the two could not fly hand in hand. Up they rose, the boy after his father. The hateful ground of Crete sank beneath them; and the country folk, who caught a glimpse of them when they were high above the treetops, took it for a vision of the gods-Apollo, perhaps, with Cupid after him.

At first there was a terror in the joy. The wide vacancy of the air dazed them-a glance downward made their brains reel. But when a great wind filled their wings, and Icarus felt himself sustained, like a halcyon bird in the hollow of a wave, like a child uplifted by his mother, he forgot everything in the world but joy. He forgot Crete and the other islands that he had passed over. He saw but vaguely that winged thing in the distance before him that was his father Daedalus. He longed for one draft of flight to quench the thirst of his captivity. He stretched out his arms to the sky and made toward the highest heavens.

Alas for him! Warmer and warmer grew the air. Those arms that had seemed to uphold him, relaxed. His wings wavered, dropped. He fluttered his young hands vainly-he was falling-and in that terror he remembered. The heat of the sun had melted the wax from his wings; the feathers were falling, one by one, like snowflakes and there was none to help.

He fell like a leaf tossed down by the wind, down, down, with one cry that overtook Daedalus far away. When he returned and sought high and low for the poor boy, he saw nothing but the birdlike feathers afloat on the water, and he knew that Icarus was drowned.

The nearest island he named Icaria, in memory of the child; but he, in heavy grief, went to the temple of Apollo in Sicily and there hung up his wings as an offering. Never again did he attempt to fly.

- Discipline

Good discipline always stems from a sense of trust, love and harmony between the adult and child. The more the adult and child understand and respect each other, the more discipline happens naturally. To have a healthy discipline relationship with the sanguine child the choleric adult should first read the sections above on how to best understand the child and how to help the child understand the adult.

Some things the choleric adult and child have in common may cause conflict. Both enjoy leading and directing others and both can act suddenly and decisively before a careful plan is in place. This desire to lead others is a positive trait in both the choleric adult and sanguine child. However, conflict can arise when they both want to take leadership over the same project. The choleric adult must make sure to share leadership time equally with the sanguine child, as he needs to learn skills of being in both positions. The choleric adult should also look into programs, games and lessons that will encourage them to work together in a cooperative effort. The choleric adult is usually better than the sanguine child in cooperative situations; however, the exercises would benefit them both.

The choleric adult's style of discipline may be assertive and matter-of-fact. Whereas the sanguine child feels more comfortable through verbal interaction and prefers to discuss most topics even if they are topics the adult and child agree on. Although the choleric adult is easily and convincingly able to express what they would like the sanguine child to do, it is usually more effective to allow the sanguine child to discuss the requests with the adult. Usually these discussions do not indicate that the sanguine child is disagreeable to the request. On the contrary – the sanguine child loves to make people happy and adapt to other's needs. However, the child also has a need to be a part of the process and explore the ideas and requests first.

For example, a choleric adult may want the sanguine child to wash the dishes. In typical choleric style the adult would simply say, "Josh, could you wash the dishes after dinner?" Josh, being a sanguine, would be happy to do the dishes after dinner but first he wants to talk about it and may reply, "Why can't Nancy do it tonight? I did it last night?" or "Do you want me to do all of them – even the large pans?" or "Do you want me to dry them too?" The best way for the choleric adult to answer all these questions is simply to answer them in a calm, direct manner without blame or irritation. The choleric adult will initially react by wondering "Why can't Josh just do what I said – just ONCE?" However, the choleric adult needs to realize that this need to have people listen without argument is part of the choleric temperament and that the sanguine child has different needs.

A sanguine needs a regular schedule and dependable people around him to be able to feel stable and balanced, and be able to perform chores and finish lessons. If life becomes too chaotic the sanguine will need more time to finish lessons or chores around the house. The choleric adult is less affected by his environment so may not understand why the sanguine child has suddenly become less efficient and cooperative. The choleric adult can help the child by leading them through exercises to help earth him so chores and lessons can once again be focused on. One exercise the choleric adult can do with the sanguine child is called "The Roots". To do this exercise the adult and child must stand together facing each other with their feet on the ground and hands to their sides. The adult then leads the child through a visualization where they are a tree and are reaching their roots deep into the ground for nutrition and water. The child should be asked to close his eyes and visualize himself as this tree and to feel the roots stretching down as far as they can go into the earth. Ask the child to feel the branches and leaves and to feel how those branches and leaves are part of the sky but can still feel a connection with the trunk and the roots.

- ## The Teaching Relationship

The choleric adult and sanguine student will have a dynamic and distinctive teaching relationship. The choleric adult will have an eager student that he can guide through learning with adventures, unique experiences and inventive learning methods.

The choleric adult has a natural skill at teaching in creative ways and the sanguine has a thirst for creativity in education. The choleric adult can plan lessons with confidence knowing that the sanguine will always be up for a challenge and usually be willing to try anything new.

The sanguine student is especially motivated by lessons that have an immediate result or a purpose. A choleric adult must be aware of this, as often this purpose needs to be more defined for the sanguine than it does for the choleric. A choleric adult may open a painting lesson with enthusiasm and excitement – completely captured by the sensual experience of the brush on the paper and the bright colors of the paint. The sanguine, however, may not be as enthusiastic. Although he also loves sensual and creative experiences, he also needs just a little bit more. The choleric adult can help motivate the sanguine student by mentioning that the paintings will be used to decorate the wall, will be used as greeting cards, or will be used as a book cover for a poetry book. When knitting the sanguine will be most motivated by projects that can be used or given as gifts and when learning math the sanguine will be most motivated by real life experiences such as doubling recipes, calculating tax during a shopping trip or organizing his own business plan.

Although the choleric adult and sanguine student will have an energetic learning experience together they must be cautious to also find balance in their lessons. When a choleric and sanguine work together they may be inclined to focus on the creative, the unusual, the entertaining, the immediate and the active forms of learning. However, both the choleric and the sanguine need balance with lessons that include logical and orderly processes, long-term project goals, and familiarity with traditional systems. This can be accomplished by setting aside some lesson time each day for these tasks, by having the student attend lessons with a second adult or by enrolling in additional lessons as a pair.

Gwen, a choleric adult and Jacee, her sanguine daughter are an example of how this can work. Gwen was homeschooling Jacee along with one older melancholic child, Sam. Gwen and Jacee learned much through stories, art, reading, field trips and games. However, once in the morning and once in the evening Gwen would have Sam plan the lessons and they would all work on them together. Sam's lessons were always traditional, defined and usually included math, logic or puzzles. This helped both Gwen and Jacee maintain a balance in the day and also fostered a more cooperative and respectful relationship between the siblings.

Another adult, Tamara, consulted with me about her daughter who attended a private school. She had chosen the school because of their creative educational methods. However, she was concerned that in one of her daughter Sofi's classes the combination of adult and methodology was too unstructured for her sanguine daughter. After consulting Tamara decided to balance Sofi's school experience with some more structured activities outside of school. Tamara and Sofi joined a chess club together on the week-ends, and Tamara enrolled Sofi in a Tai Kwando class after school. After a few weeks Tamara noticed that Sofi seemed more balanced in general and was even able to focus better at school.

- ## A Story to Share

When stories are told they speak to the child on a basic level. The reason one tells stories instead of explaining things to a child is because stories have the ability to adapt to the child's needs. When a person explains a situation to a child he is putting forth a concept that the child needs to grasp at or reach to understand. When one simply *tells* a story the child is given permission to understand the story in any way he wishes and to gain wisdom and knowledge from it in the way that best suits him at that moment. For that reason, it is not recommended that the story be explained to the child or that the child be provided with the ubiquitous "moral" at the end. Rather, it is best to give them a chance to enjoy the story for what it becomes to them and provide them with numerous chances to hear the story told. The stories in this book help the different temperaments understand each other. If the adult or adult would like to explore this understanding on a deeper level they can ask questions once the story is finished. However, one must be sure to ask open questions and allow the child to express his feelings.

In the following story the sanguine tailor outwits the choleric giant. In most stories the giant is portrayed as fierce and ugly, but in this story the enthusiasm and choleric personality of the giant come through and in the end you almost feel sorry for his plight.

The Giant and the Tailor

Grimm's Fairytales

A certain tailor who was great at dreaming up wonderful plans but not so good at following through with them, took it into his head to go abroad for a while, and look about the world. As soon as he could manage it, he left his workshop, and wandered on his way, over hill and dale, sometimes here, sometimes there, but ever on and on. Once when he was out he perceived in the blue distance a steep hill, and behind it a tower reaching to the clouds, which rose up out of a wild dark forest.

"Thunder and lightning," cried the tailor, "What is that?" and as he was strongly goaded by curiosity, he went boldly towards it. But what made the tailor open his eyes and mouth when he came near it, was to see that the tower had legs, and leapt in one bound over the steep hill, and was now standing as an all powerful giant before him.

"What do you want here, you tiny fly's leg?" cried the giant, with a voice as if it were thundering on every side. The tailor whimpered, "I want just to look about and see if I can earn a bit of bread for myself in this forest."

"If that is what you are after," said the giant, "You may have a place with me."

"If it must be - why not? What wages shall I receive?"

"I shall tell you what wages you shall have – ha ha - every year three hundred and sixty-five days, and when it is leap-year, one more into the bargain. Does that suit you?"

"All right," answered the tailor, and thought, in his own mind, "A man must cut his coat according to his cloth; I will try to get away as fast as I can."

On this the giant said to him, "Go, little ragamuffin, and fetch me a jug of water."

"Had I not better bring the well itself at once, and the spring too?" asked the boaster, and went with the pitcher to the water.

"What? The well and the spring too," growled the giant in his beard, for he was rather clownish and stupid, and began to be afraid. "That knave is not a fool, he has a wizard in his body. Be on your guard, old Hans, this is no serving-man for you."

When the tailor had brought the water, the giant bade him go into the forest, and cut a couple of blocks of wood and bring them back.

"Why not the whole forest, at once, with one stroke. The whole forest, young and old, with all that is there, both rough and smooth?" asked the little tailor, and went to cut the wood.

"What? The whole forest, young and old, with all that is there, both rough and smooth, and the well and its spring too," growled the credulous giant in his beard, and was still more terrified.

"The knave can do much more than bake apples, and has a wizard in his body. Be on your guard, old Hans, this is no serving-man for you!" When the tailor had brought the wood, the giant commanded him to shoot two or three wild boars for supper.

"Why not rather a thousand at one shot, and bring them all here?" inquired the ostentatious tailor.

"What?" cried the timid giant in great terror. "Let well alone tonight, and lie down to rest."

The giant was so terribly alarmed that he could not close an eye all night long for thinking what would be the best way to get rid of this accursed sorcerer of a servant.

Time brings counsel. Next morning the giant and the tailor went to a marsh, round which stood a number of willow-trees. Then said the giant, "Hark you, tailor, seat yourself on one of the willow-branches, I long of all things to see if you are big enough to bend it down."

All at once the tailor was sitting on it, holding his breath, and making himself so heavy that the bough bent down. When, however, he was compelled to draw breath, it hurried him so high into the air that he never was seen again, and this to the great delight of the giant. If the tailor has not fallen down again, he must be hovering about in the air.

Closing

About The Author

Kristie Karima Burns, MH, ND is an artist, healer and teacher and owner of www.Earthschooling.com, www.TheAvicennaInstitute.com, www.TheWaldorfChannel.com and www.Herbnhome.com

Ms. Burns lived in the Middle East for 16 years and first studied the temperaments as they were used by Avicenna. She received a certificate in homeopathic first aid from the British Institute of Homeopathy in 1993 and studied temperament theory through her studies with the Institute. In 1996 Ms. Burns studied temperament theory as part of a Master Herbalist program with Trinity College. In 1999 Ms. Burns studied temperament theory as part of her training to work as a Waldorf early childhood teacher.

Ms. Burns teaches an online course in temperament and typology and has been lecturing on the topic since 1994. She has been offering temperament consulting since 1996 for couples, teachers, children and individuals who want to improve their health, harmony and relationships at www.Herbnhome.com. She offers a number of videos and classes on the topic through www.TheWaldorfChannel.com.

After traveling the world for 24 years Ms. Burns settled in Iowa in 2005 and now resides in Des Moines with her three children, 2 chickens, 4 cats, 3 birds, 2 rabbits, 2 rats, 1 tarantula and a dog.

Thank You

I would like to thank my editors for their generosity, skills, insights and dependability. It was an amazing experience to work with all these people and to feel the energy and bond that we all shared during the process.

Kelley Auld
Jacinthe Beaudin
Terrabeth Bivens
Cat *Bohemi-mom* Carter
Jennifer DiMonte
Alicia Garberoglio
Debbie Gattegno
Marisa Harder-Chapman
Grietje Laga
Cindy Law
Tania Leeds
Sharon McClesky
Robin McCloud McDonald
Michelle Moe
Elissa M. Ryan Morris
Natasha Oliarnyk
Denise Ridgway
Jennifer Rothwell
Sandy Smith
Elizabeth Thompson
Rebecca Thornton
Maria Zain

Donna Ashtond, founder of www.TheWaldorfConnection.com

Jeannine Bowes, owner or www.pixiedustandmoonbeams.com
A Waldorf inspired online toy store.

Mellisa Dormoy, founder and creator of www.KidsMeditationCds.com
Helping elevate the spiritual & emotional well-being of children everywhere.

Tara Felicio, Wife to a Darling Husband and Mama to 5 Loves who runs a homeschool enrichment program from their home in NJ and Holistic Moms *Network Chapter Co-leader www.holisticmoms.org*

Linda Johnson of Heart of Sailing www.HeartOfSailing.org
A nautical adventure for children with special needs;

Tamrha Richardson CD (CBI), Better Birth New York Representative
www.tamrhasdoulasupport.com

Made in the USA
Lexington, KY
16 February 2011